Hiding Behind the Keyboard

Hiding Behind the Keyboard

Uncovering Covert Communication Methods with Forensic Analysis

Brett Shavers

John Bair

Larry Leibrock, Technical Editor

ELSEVIER

AMSTERDAM • BOSTON • HEIDELBERG • LONDON
NEW YORK • OXFORD • PARIS • SAN DIEGO
SAN FRANCISCO • SINGAPORE • SYDNEY • TOKYO

Syngress is an imprint of Elsevier

SYNGRESS.

Syngress is an imprint of Elsevier
50 Hampshire Street, 5th Floor, Cambridge, MA 02139, USA

British Library Cataloguing in Publication Data
A catalogue record for this book is available from the British Library

Library of Congress Cataloging-in-Publication Data
A catalog record for this book is available from the Library of Congress

ISBN: 978-0-12-803340-1

For information on all Syngress publications
visit our website at https://www.elsevier.com/

Working together
to grow libraries in
developing countries

www.elsevier.com • www.bookaid.org

Publisher: Todd Green
Acquisition Editor: Chris Katsaropoulos
Editorial Project Manager: Anna Valutkevich
Production Project Manager: Punithavathy Govindaradjane
Designer: Matthew Limbert

Typeset by TNQ Books and Journals

Contents

Foreword

In the Introduction to *Hiding Behind the Keyboard*, Brett Shavers is far too modest in saying if you get one nugget of useful information from it, then his writing the book will have been worthwhile. Instead, you will surely find, as I did, an impressive cornucopia of golden nuggets throughout these pages.

A broad landscape of technical topics is thoroughly presented here, including encryption schemes and methods; steganography; the Tor browser; the TAILs operating system; password cracking; decoy storage devices; time stamp modification; file signature manipulation; bootable operating systems; using media address control (MAC) to identify source; portable apps; hidden and decoy operating systems; virtual machines; key loggers; antiforensic methods; electronic intercepts; trap and trace/pen registers; determining digital identity; navigating the Dark Web; and much more—Phew! Equally impressive are the numerous practical tips and examples in the book that come from Brett Shavers' many years spent in law enforcement and cutting-edge computer forensics.

Also valuable on the subject of smartphones and other portable devices are two exquisitely detailed chapters contributed by Tacoma Police Detective and University of Washington Lecturer, John Bair.

It would be selling this book short if one thought its sole focus was on how cops, robbers, and terrorists play hide-and-seek on the increasingly critical battlefield of computers, smartphones, transmitted electronic files, networks, and so on. It is also about making sure anyone who has to deal with vital digital information, whether on storage media or "live," is fully aware of all the tools out there to find and analyze not only what the bad guys are doing, but also what you can do to counter them. In other words, the book shines a bright light on "knowing what you don't know" so you don't pass up opportunities to find information so important and sensitive that a multitude of sophisticated ways have been employed to hide it.

Besides those who serve in frontline law enforcement, lawyers who practice in both criminal prosecutions and civil litigation need to read this book—not necessarily for a complete understanding of the technical content, but rather to understand what *can* happen with electronically stored information, and what options exist to detect it when purposely hidden. I am not ashamed to admit, even after practicing law for 40 years, first as a prosecutor and then as a civil litigator, with the last 20 of those years working primarily as an e-discovery expert witness and forensic examiner, that much of Brett's book offered me one fact or methodology after another that was new to me, and where I thought I knew something about a topic but in fact didn't.

This book also has several useful tips on what to do next if you think the digital evidence or lack thereof is taking you nowhere. Many practice tips throughout the book are alone worth the price of admission.

And when it comes to computer forensics, there is *nobody anywhere* I know who can match Brett's breadth and depth of knowledge, and I have had the good fortune to know some of the best. Is there some new forensic utility that does this or that? He is all over it. Is there a need to develop a self-executing set of programs on a CD or USB drive to render a target device read-only and shut down all other data ports for the examination? Well, OK, he writes the code for that and gets access to what he needs. He's fully versed in EnCase Forensics and like many experts happy with how it works; but then X-Ways Forensics comes along, and he wonders could that maybe do more? So Brett totally immerses himself in it for hours and days, he likes the tool, and then coauthors a book about it (*X-Ways Forensics Practitioner's Guide*)!

It is no wonder, then, that he has served as an adjunct instructor at the University of Washington's Digital Forensics Program; as an expert witness and digital forensics consultant; as a speaker at numerous conferences; and as a blogger on digital forensics.

And yet for such a gung ho guy, whenever we meet up at Starbucks to solve the problems of life and the world, he looks and softly talks like a Buddhist monk.

So congratulations to you on buying this book, because with it you get so many fruits from Brett's genius and remarkable life along with it.

Larry G. Johnson
Attorney and Forensic Technologist
Electronic Data Evidence, Newcastle, Washington

Introduction

INTRODUCTION

A person interacts with another for many reasons as a part of social connections. For the majority of contacts, human communications are productive and meaningful for personal and professional relationships. Other types of communications may be beneficial to a person but also carry negative consequences for others. One example of a negative benefit is the communication required between criminals that results in other persons being victimized. Terrorism also falls into this area.

WHAT THIS BOOK IS AND IS NOT

Hiding Behind the Keyboard describes the various means to identify covert communications using forensic analysis and traditional investigative methods. Along with identifying covert communications, the book intends to illustrate methods to identify the persons behind the communications, their mind-set, and technology used. This book intends to be a guide in your investigations with methods to intercept communications and find the persons behind them. Although the title of this book might be provocative, this is simply due to the frustrations investigators endure in cases where suspects are simply using computers and mobile devices anonymously. In no sense is this book intended to be anything other than geared toward the investigator.

A previously published book, *Placing the Suspect Behind the Keyboard*, focuses on overall case development and general investigative methods and techniques and briefly touches on the electronic aspects of placing a person at a keyboard. *Hiding Behind the Keyboard* goes beyond general aspects and delves more into the technical aspects of covert communication methods as well as the forensic analysis of electronic communications. In many cases, placing a suspect behind a keyboard may not be the obstacle as much as identifying the actual words and methods of communication used between suspects. In that aspect,

Hiding Behind the Keyboard supplements *Placing the Suspect Behind the Keyboard* to build and resolve an investigation.

This book is not a "how to" guide on subverting laws or communicating anonymously to commit crimes. The covert communications described are for the intended purpose of discussing how to identify and subsequently analyze the communications. Much like a driving course teaches someone how to drive but does not teach how to drive a "getaway car," this book shows methods of covert communication for the purpose of understanding how to use techniques to uncover the communication but not in committing a crime.

Also much like learning how to drive a car, this book shows the investigator how to use covert means of communication for their safety and the safety of information being exchanged with others such as with confidential sources or undercover assets. As with any tool, the use determines whether or not it is being used for good purposes.

Describing methods to uncover anonymous communication channels would be incomplete without describing the actual methods. In effect, throughout the book, there are discussions on the "how to" communicate covertly to understand how to discover the covert communications. After knowing the "how," you can more effectively find the communication methods and content.

THE INTENDED AUDIENCE

Law enforcement officers, criminal investigators, and civil investigators are the intended audience simply because they usually confront covert communications in their positions. In actuality, many of these professionals may not even be aware of the covert communications that are already occurring in their investigations. When you do not know what you do not know, you will almost always miss critical evidence and information.

Throughout this book, both these terms "suspects" and "targets" are used for the persons involved in covert communications you wish to investigate. The term target is used not as a political or tactical point other than a "target" being the subject of your investigation. A target can be a terrorist, criminal, or corporate spy for whom you want to uncover covert communications.

As a practical matter, every person fitting within this intended audience should be well-versed in technology as it relates to communication. The criminals and terrorists of today exploit every means to communicate covertly and anonymously, and most involve technology. To delay learning the methods being used is to delay effectively investigating your targets.

NOTE

Hiding Behind the Keyboard

Just because your targets use complex methods of covert communication does not mean you cannot use the same methods! Witnesses, informants, agents, undercover officers, and other persons should use secure communications to protect their identities and the information exchanged.

Duration of Relevance for This Guide

Similar to *Placing the Suspect Behind the Keyboard*, this book has been written as a guide to outlast technology advances. Although technology changes constantly by employing the principles in this guide, you should be able to transfer what becomes old technology to the latest technology. It is mastering concepts and principles that are most important in becoming a great investigator.

As for the technical information in the book, similar to other technologies, what is possible today may not be possible tomorrow and conversely, what is impossible today may be possible in the future. Simply some things get harder, and other things get easier. Either way, you are reading a book with tools to deal with both situations.

SUMMARY

Technology makes covert communications easier, faster, and more secure than ever before. However, most methods can be discovered, analyzed, and broken with the use of technology and investigative methods. This book will introduce and reinforce an investigative mind-set that you can use in any investigation, with any type of target, using any type of covert communication method. It is not easy or quick, but persistence and tenacity in your efforts can produce worthwhile outcomes in finding out what your targets are saying to each other.

The single and most important goal of this book is to give at least one nugget of information that can make a case, save time, identify suspects, and give justice to victims. If an investigator can find that one piece of guidance then the book will have accomplished its goal. After all, solving cases is the goal for the sake of victims. Let's start and find the nuggets!

About the Authors

BRETT SHAVERS

Brett Shavers is a veteran of the US Marines and former law enforcement officer of a municipal police department. He has worked just about every type of law enforcement specialty from mountain bicycle patrol, SWAT (Special Weapons and Tactics), detective, and undercover narcotics officer in state and federal task forces. After working undercover assignments inside and outside the United States, Brett created the first digital forensic lab at his police department as the first digital forensic examiner. Brett attended over 2000 hours of digital forensic training courses across the country, collected more than a few certifications along the way, and taught digital forensic analysis and investigative methods to hundreds of law enforcement officers.

Brett has been an adjunct instructor at the University of Washington's Digital Forensics Program, an expert witness and digital forensic consultant, a professional speaker at conferences, a blogger on digital forensics, and an honorary member of the Computer Technology Investigators Network. He has worked forensic cases ranging from child pornography investigations as a law enforcement investigator to a wide range of civil litigation and class action lawsuits as a digital forensic expert consultant, expert, and evidence special master. Brett's previous books include *Placing the Suspect Behind the Keyboard* and the *X-Ways Forensics Practitioner's Guide*.

JOHN BAIR

John Bair is currently employed as a detective with the Tacoma Police Department. He began his law enforcement career with the El Paso Police Department in 1989 after leaving the military. John created a mobile forensic lab in 2006 and also began collateral duties as a mobile forensic instructor with various vendors throughout the United States.

Fox Valley Technical College hired John as a contract instructor to assist in training in the Department of Justice—Amber Alert Program. His expertise with mobile forensics is being utilized to teach a segment within the digital evidence module. This targets investigators responding to scenes where children have been abducted. In Pierce County, Washington, he began a mobile forensic training program which is currently in its fourth year for Superior Court prosecutors and Judical Officers. The program stresses the technical origins of the warrant language, what to check for, validation of evidence, and how to present this dynamic content in court.

John recently created a mobile forensic program at the University of Washington, Tacoma (UWT). His lecture materials are covered in three different courses, which range from logical fundamentals, physical decoding, and advanced destructive techniques. All courses utilize manuals that he has authored and involve current and past case techniques.

As a contract instructor, he has instructed at various federal labs within the United States (Secret Service, Immigrations and Customs Enforcement). He has presented on mobile evidence as a guest speaker at Paraben's Innovative Conference, Washington State Association of Prosecuting Attorneys' (WAPA) Summit, and the Computer Technology Investigations Network Digital Forensics Conference. Recently he spoke at the 16th Annual Conference on Information Technology Education and at the 4th Annual Research in IT Conference in Chicago, Illinois. These conferences are sponsored by the ACM Special Interest Group for Information Technology Education (SIGITE). John and two other professors from the UWT recently coauthored a paper regarding the current mobile forensic program.

John has 31 certifications related to digital evidence. The following reflect the most significant related to mobile forensics: *Cellebrite Certified Mobile Examiner (CCME), Mobile Forensics Certified Examiner (MFCE), Cellebrite Certified Logical Operator (CCLO), Cellebrite Certified Physical Analyst (CCPA), AccessData Certified Examiner (ACE), Cellebrite Mobile Forensics Fundamentals (CMFF), AccessData Mobile Examiner (AME), and Cellebrite Certified Task Instructor (CCTI).*

Acknowledgments

I would like to thank John Bair for his work as a coauthor. John's expertise in mobile device forensics is beyond comparison, and this book benefited greatly from his experience. I was fortunate to have Larry Leibrock as the book's tech editor. Larry's extensive experience across a wide range of positions in digital forensics and his willingness to provide technical edits for content was invaluable.

I am humbled by Larry Johnson's foreword who wears many hats in my life as my attorney, advisor, confidant, and friend. I also want to give appreciation to other experts in the industry for taking the time to review, give input, and make sure that the book is relevant in topic and material—Chris McNulty of the Seattle Police Department, Tim Carver of Trine University, and Steve Beltz of T-Mobile. Every suggestion, recommendation, and comment was taken to heart and appreciated. And if not for Anna Valutkevich of Syngress, this book would have taken twice as long to finish and been half as good as it is.

Certainly not a day goes by that I do not thank my wife Chikae for her support. Although she may think I am her supporter, my strength comes from her to get things done right, no matter the obstacles. Of all my luck and timing, she has always been, and will always be, my precious treasure.

Brett Shavers

Brett Shavers was introduced to me while working on a project at the University of Washington. Many months later, Brett approached me and requested that I help write a few words regarding mobile forensics. I was quite humbled and agreed. Because of Brett, I have had to try and articulate a couple of things that may in turn help others. It is for that reason that Brett deserves nearly all of my thanks.

The remainder of my gratitude goes to my family. My late father, who spent 44 years with Bell and Mountain Bell Telephone—he gave me my passion for electronics. Today I have my current team which consists of Alexa, Zack, Hannah, Daisy, and Dexter (the last two on the list being of the K-9 persuasion).

Of course I can't forget the team captain Char. She binds my life together with companionship, laughter, much needed advice, and never-ending love. Without her I would not be who I am today. She has been and continues to be an endless blooming flower that I can't stop admiring.

John Bair

CHAPTER 1

Laying the Foundation of Covert Communications

INTRODUCTION

You have probably taken communication courses in either high school or college and been taught how to effectively communicate in business and personal relationships. These types of communication courses are valuable in many aspects, but do not relate to the investigative methods you will see in this book. I intend to give you sufficient and necessary principles, concepts, and practical methods to not only uncover covert communications but also determine the content of the conversations using both forensic analysis and interpretation of data.

You will notice that much of the information in this book details "how to communicate anonymously and covertly" alongside with "how to find anonymous and covert communications." Unlike driving a car where you do not need to know engines or transmissions work, as an investigator, you do need to understand how these types of communications take place in order to understand the methods to uncover and analyze them. The technical explanations may be beyond the scope of a nonforensic investigator, but do not be discouraged as you read the descriptions and methods. Investigators need to know how certain methods are used in order to look for them during investigations.

Fair warning, there will be communications that you will not be able to find or decipher if found in the course of your examination. Even the communications you uncover and decipher may not be directly attributed to your targets technology and good old-fashioned spy tradecraft works well to hide communications from the sets of prying eyes. We are going after the covert communications that can be found with gumshoe detective work to be analyzed and deciphered with effective uses of both technology and brain power. We are also hoping to find communication mistakes made by your targets. Given a 100 communication efforts using a dozen different types of methods, there is a risk of failure by your targets in one or more of their communication deliveries. These mistakes are more than freebies for your investigation; their contents are potentially a goldmine of information. As will be shown, having found one key bit of evidence can unlock an entire chain of communications.

Discussing covert communications sometimes involves breaking codes. However, the focus of this book is not code breaking as much as it is to first find the communications and then break the anonymity by identifying your targets. Much of the code-breaking topics in this book will be for illustrative purposes and not for mastering the cracking of ciphers since that is a topic already covered in many published books.

A BRIEF HISTORY OF COVERT COMMUNICATION

History is interesting, but understandably for some, history is in the past and therefore, not particularly important. In the manner of how history applies to your reading of this book, I refer to a few historical events where intercepting and deciphering communications were instrumental in outcomes and relevant to the present.

At a minimum, by understanding covert and anonymous communications has been in existence for thousands of years and is still being used, makes a strong point to consider the importance of the history of covert communication. In order for any nation to have security from enemies, covert communication is used to exchange information for national security. A nation that has access to its enemy's communications is at a tactical, strategic, and economical advantage.

During World War II, Germany employed the use of the "Enigma" enciphering machine, seen in Fig. 1.1. The Enigma "had the potential to create immense numbers of electrically generated alphabets" (Singh, 1999). Communications created with the Enigma were extremely secure, and the German war effort was substantially successful because of their security of communications. A nation at war that can safely and securely communicate is a nation with a distinct advantage. As Germany relied more upon the Enigma, the reliance became part of Germany's downfall once the Enigma code was broken. Once the Enigma code was broken, the Enigma was used against Germany as the Allies would know their most secretive plans. (German encoding machine—Enigma. World War II. Skanderborg Bunker Museum, Denmark—2004.)

The Enigma story directly relates to covert communications today, whether it is nation states fighting each other or between drug dealers conspiring to commit crimes. Once the communication methods are intercepted and decoded, your targets are operating in the clear, yet at the same time, they are blissfully unaware that their secret plans are no longer secret. When your investigation reaches a point where communications are being intercepted, it takes a concerted effort not to disclose or cause any suspicion the communication method has been compromised.

FIGURE 1.1
Enigma machine used during World War II.

Such is the case for wiretaps. The amount of time, effort, and energy to gain legal authority for a wiretap typically is immense. In fact, in most cases, all other methods are typically exhausted leaving a wiretap as the only option in the investigation. Being legally approved to conduct a wiretap is only the beginning as the telephone numbers must be identified along with the targets. Again, this is a very difficult process, especially since cell phones are constantly being replaced with new phones and new features.

To enable gaining the most intelligence from a wiretap, investigations are generally prolonged without disclosing the existence of a wiretap. During this time, investigators act upon some of the information obtained in the wiretap without disclosing the fact there is a wiretap in hopes the criminal organization will continue to use the telephones to communicate (or e-mail, etc.). As with many wiretap investigations, as soon as the targets feel law enforcement is closing in, phones are discarded ("dumped"), just in case they are compromised, to be replaced by entirely different phones and phone numbers. It is a careful balance to act upon information gained from a compromised communication channel and tipping off the targets.

There are few greater threats today than the war against terrorism and uncovering covert communication that facilitates terrorist attacks is a priority in every country. A well-known covert communication method used by not only terrorists but also anyone wanting to avoid sending e-mails that may be discovered is that of using web-based e-mail draft folders. With this method, two or more persons have the login credentials to an e-mail account. To communicate, any person with the credentials simply creates an e-mail and rather than send it, stores it in a draft folder which physically resides on an e-mail server of the e-mail provider. The other users of the account can access the drafts, and the e-mail is never sent outside the service provider's network.

As an analogy, this method is akin to having a safe-deposit box in a bank vault with more than one person having access to the box. Messages can be left in the box for another to read, yet the message never leaves the vault. E-mail drafts are an extremely simple, yet effective means of communication using a third-party service provider as long as the e-mail account is unknown to investigators.

An important point to make about this older method using a draft e-mail folder is that even as the disclosure of this technique is now common knowledge, it is still employed today. Even those who can be considered experts in covert communication use this method with the knowledge that the security is only in concealment of the e-mail account. A recent example of this draft e-mail method in 2012 was an extramarital affair discovered through a Federal Bureau of Investigation (FBI) investigation between the Central Intelligence Agency (CIA) Director General David Petraeus and author Paula Broadwell (Beary et al., 2013). The FBI, investigating a cybercrime allegation, discovered that Petraeus and Broadwell communicated secretly using a draft e-mail folder, which effectively ended their careers by uncovering their extramarital affair. By not sending e-mails to each other, the risk of discovery was very low.

Communicating through e-mail drafts, as seen in Fig. 1.2 is effective for covert communications until the account is discovered. Once discovered, potentially only a single e-mail may be left in the e-mail account since it most likely being used for a single draft e-mail communication. Potentially, once the message has been read by the intended party, the e-mail is deleted. In the case of this type of communication, the best method of investigation is monitoring the account draft folder in real time in order to capture the communications and not rely upon an empty folder as an indication of nonuse. Chapter "Anti-Forensics" details e-mail investigations as well as other means of online anonymous and covert communications.

The draft e-mail folder is easily defeated with search warrants, but only after the e-mail account has been identified. Throughout your investigations, you will find that nearly all communications between your targets involve an innocent third party, such as an e-mail provider or cell phone service provider. The reliance on third parties to communicate is a double-edged sword for your targets. For security, a third-party provider helps maintain anonymity if they do not require users to disclose personal information. Third-party providers also reduce research and development costs for communication methods since using commercially available tools are available worldwide and many times are free.

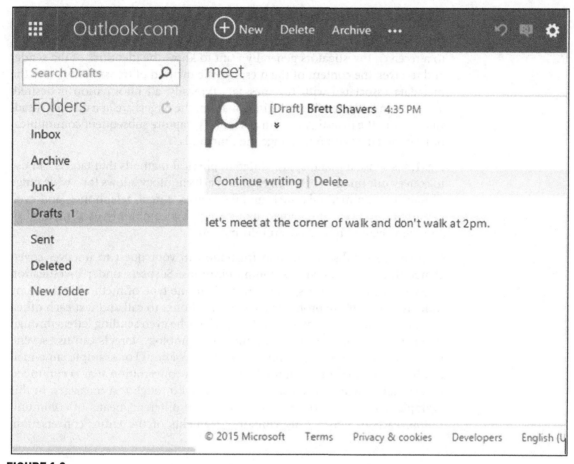

FIGURE 1.2
Draft e-mail stored but not sent.

Conversely, because of the reliance of third-party providers, your efforts as an investigator should also focus on obtaining assistance from these providers to identify your targets. Although some third-party providers may either refuse to cooperate with law enforcement or intentionally discard user information as part of their service, the vast majority of companies wish not to be part of the facilitation of crime or terrorist acts. Tips on gauging the cooperation of a third party before asking for their help is covered throughout this book as it is also not uncommon that a third party will warn a user of a pending civil or government investigation.

If a country can lose a war and a general lose a career by having their covert communications compromised, you can succeed in your investigations using the same methods that have been in use for thousands of years to uncover and break covert communications. The key is first finding the communications.

COVERT COMMUNICATION OVERLOAD

In its basic form, communication consists of a source sending information to a receiver. Investigators generally want to know the identities of the sender and receiver, the content of the message, the method of transmission, and the metadata associated with the message. Typically, all information is desired, and once investigators have the information, the targets are at a distinct disadvantage and the investigators can most likely, capture subsequent communications if the targets do not change their methods.

Fig. 1.3 is a visual that displays different physical methods that targets can use to convey information between each other. Technology allows for a wide range of transmission methods, such mobile devices, e-mail, telephones, and even fax machines. Even the regular mail system is a commonly used method of conveying clandestine of covert information.

Be prepared for discomfort and frustration in your quest to uncover covert clandestine and anonymous communications. Suspects under investigation are typically, if not always, using more than one type of method at the same time. Your targets are probably using smartphones to call and text each other, using computers to e-mail each other, and maybe even sending letters through the mail. To compound the multitude of technology, targets can use several modes of transmission to continue one conversation. For example, an e-mail can be sent to a coconspirator which begins a conversation that is continued on a social networking website and concluded through text messages. In this example, an investigator contends with three different means of communication, each of which only contains fragments of the entire conversation.

FIGURE 1.3
Physical methods of conveying information.

In chapter "The Tor Browser", the types of devices used for covert communications along with guidance on gaining access are discussed in more detail.

Note that one fragment of a conversation may be meaningless without the content of the remaining fragments. If the targets use methods to hide or encrypt the information in addition to using several different methods of transmission, it is easy to feel overwhelmed in searching for these conversations only to find that the content is incomplete, encrypted, or inaccessible. The more targets involved using different communication methods, the more complex your task becomes. As an investigator, accept the fact that you will attempt and may not find everything, but continue to uncover all that you can, and interpret the totality of all communications in every case. In a perfect world, you will gain access to all means of communication and be able to decrypt all messages. This is not a perfect world, so we will do with what we have.

The key concept is that communications exist in all of your cases unless you have a single individual acting solely on his own with no need to communicate with anyone. This is a very rare case, if it exists at all. The most important advice is not to give up searching for communications, nor feel as if you have uncovered everything because you do not know what you do not know. Even as the National Security Agency, with its virtually unlimited resources, tries to uncover covert communications, only to find, some communications are practically inaccessible, at least for today.

Investigative Goals
Hollywood spy and forensics science movies aside, investigators rarely solve a case in less than 2 hours. Investigators know that every case requires hard work, intuitive decision-making, reasonable interpretation of information, and sometimes chance. Most investigations are not difficult because the target attempts to make it difficult, but because finding information to develop intelligence and evidence is difficult and requires good tradecraft. When targets add to the complexity of an investigation by using covert communications, investigators have that much more work to do and have that much more risk of missing evidence.

Most investigators do not have the luxury of a turn-key surveillance system where e-mails and telephone calls can be monitored with a flip of a switch. Even in countries where massive government surveillance is widespread, the analysis of mass data can be overwhelming. Gaining access to communications is only the beginning because the content, context, and target identification is necessary to determine which communications are both available and relevant. Investigators and analysts reading this book are the ones who do the legwork, paperwork, and use effective investigative tradecraft in dealing with the investigation.

The spoken (or written) words of your investigative target are invaluable. Words spoken by your targets can give you evidence of behavior, values, past crimes, current crimes, and future planned crimes. Coconspirators and potential victims may be identified. An entire criminal organization can be mapped out through conversations that have been captured. As the easiest case is one where the suspect freely admits guilt, the easiest investigation is one where you have access to covert communications without this being disclosed to your target.

Nearly all of the investigative methods in this book require necessary legal support in your jurisdiction to legally employ. Citizens enjoy liberties and freedoms to be protected and not intruded upon in the course of your investigation. I write this book as a guide of creating the necessary stepping-stones to gain the sufficient legal authority to conduct your investigations. For example, finding one small piece of information may lead to another larger piece of information, which may be the tipping point of gaining legal authority to use additional methods, such as an oral intercept (wiretap). The methods you choose are based on your legal standing as an investigator. One thing to keep in mind regarding legal authority is that it is always best, and expected, that investigators stay well within the proscribed legal limits and avoid becoming a lawbreaker.

COVERT COMMUNICATION GOALS

Suspects, like most people, desire to communicate covertly. An e-mail intended for one person to read will only send to that one particular person. Personal phone calls are generally made away from earshot of others. Letters are expected to be opened only by the recipient. Personal conversations involve only those persons for which the conversation is intended. These normal covert communications are hardly worth any other person's interest, nor illegal. They are simply private communications with steps taken to ensure privacy (covertness).

The steps to keep a private conversation private can be simply speaking softly away from others or encrypting an electronic message and sending it through the Internet to the recipient. The goal is to keep the communications private and away from prying eyes. Businesses, governments, and individuals have always had covert communications. For reasons of business operations, national security, or personal privacy, the goal of keeping the communications private is the same. For a business, confidential and proprietary information that a competitor steals can be disastrous, potentially causing a business to close due to unfair competition and theft of trade secrets. A government has much to lose if its communications are intercepted by an enemy of the state. Individuals whose private messages are disclosed may face embarrassment or worse depending on the content of the messages. In practice, nothing is wrong or illegal by having private communications for legitimate purposes.

Your target's goals are the same as a government, business, or individual in that they want their communications kept secret among their coconspirators. The most important difference is that their communications consist of planning, executing, and discussing criminal activity. On the surface, an encrypted e-mail between two friends can appear just as guilty as an encrypted e-mail between two terrorists, yet they are not. The point being that the mere fact a communication method intended to keep communications secret is being used does not prove that the contents are illegal or critical to any investigation. Actually, it is quite the opposite. Private conversations should be kept private; examples are those between attorney and client, doctor and patient, husband and wife, and so forth.

Another aspect of covert communications is the language used. Not that of a foreign language, but that of coded terms or language. Coded language can be very clearly understood or impossible without more information. As an example, a suspected drug dealer stating on a phone call that "a full one is 25" would appear to be a price quote for a measurement of some drug is $25 or $25,000. Conversations where only words are exchanged, such as exchanging the word "kilo" with the word "king" not only is not covert communications, but gives clear intention of trying to hide the illegality of the conversation with coded words.

Covert communications also do not need to convey anything other than a connection to the recipient to relay a message. As an example, if the targets have preplanned actions based upon a specific preplanned communication, then the content of the communication can be very minimal or nothing at all. A phone call from one target to another can signal intentions without even answering the phone to deliver a message. If there is a preplanned method that "one ring" indicates a certain message and "three rings" indicate a different message, the phone does not even have to be answered for the message to be delivered, and the recipient can act upon the message as delivered.

No one knows how many successful covert communications occur daily, since if anyone knew, the communications would not be covert. Uncovering covert communications require the tradecraft of a spy, the mindset of a detective, the curiosity of a child, and the tenacity of a bulldog to keep trying after many failed attempts. In terms of labor, expect to spend days, weeks, and months to find the one break, or key, that allows you to work your investigation backward to decipher communications that were previously captured.

Detectives can spend weeks following a single person around in hopes of catching a break to find methods of communication being used in order to identify coconspirators. There is not a day of surveillance that most detectives want to give up since 99% of the time results in nothing gained in terms of information or intelligence. However, in every case of this sort, investigators come across some bit of information that makes it all worthwhile and allows the ability to connect the dots. Observing a suspect discard a phone into a public trash container may give a single piece of information that can piece together the entire case, from the phone number, phone records, and subsequent investigation into each call made with that phone. Weeks of surveillance can pay off in minutes.

SUMMARY

Even the best intelligence analyst will be overwhelmed at the start of an investigation. The sheer amount of information to collect, not to mention the analysis of information, to find relevant data can be overwhelming. Determining the methods of communication is a constantly changing effort in every investigation as targets change methods due to security or convenience, and each minor change in their methods requires a major effort to keep up.

REFERENCES

Beary, B., Clouting, A., Ewing, H., Fecteau, L., Feinberg, M., Heffner, J., … Smith, R. K. (2013). *Historic documents of 2012*. Thousand Oaks: CQ Press.

Singh, S. (1999). *The Code book: The science of secrecy from ancient Egypt to quantum cryptography*. London: First Anchor Book Edition. September 2000.

CHAPTER 2

The Tor Browser

INTRODUCTION

Few Internet technologies have had more of an impact on anonymous Internet use than The Onion Router browser, commonly known as "Tor," Tor is simply an Internet browser modified from the popular Firefox Internet browser. The browser modifications hide the user's originating Internet Protocol (IP) address when surfing websites or sending e-mail. By hiding the true IP address of the user, attempts to trace or identify the user are nearly impossible without the use of extraordinary methods.

Tor combines ease of use with effective anonymity in which practically anyone can use without technical instructions. The sheer ingenuity of the Tor browser combines ease of use without any requirement of how the software operates to operate effectively. Although there are other means of browsing the Internet anonymously, the Tor browser is by far one of the simplest to use and is freely downloaded. In theory, anyone with an Internet connection and the Tor browser can anonymously surf the Internet and communicate without being identified.

HISTORY AND INTENDED USE OF THE ONION ROUTER

Tor's intention is to allow unfettered and anonymous communication over the Internet. Tor allows anyone to connect to websites that may be blocked by oppressive governments, allows whistleblowers to communicate with officials anonymously, and gives a means for legitimate communication between businesses and persons who desire to keep their private conversations private. However, much like a car that is used to take your kids to school can also be used as a bank robbery getaway car, the Tor browser can be used to either facilitate crimes or commit crimes.

Although Tor was initially developed by the US government in 2002, it is not presently controlled by the US government. In fact, Tor is practically not controlled by any one entity but rather open for improvements by virtually anyone with the technical ability to test and improve it. For that reason alone, Tor receives worldwide input from privacy motivated experts to ensure it remains relevant and effective. As a point of irony, the US government not only created Tor but is also researching methods to deanonymize users of it.

Two Ways of Looking at The Onion Router

Before you finish reading this chapter, you will invariably think back to every forensic analysis you have conducted and wonder if you missed a golden nugget of evidence. The Tor browser is not typical of any other Internet browser in purpose or design. The mere existence or Tor on electronic evidence should give you concern on the evidence you can easily overlook along with the evidence you know will not be found because of Tor use.

One perspective of looking at Tor is that of forensically examining devices that may have had Tor installed. From this perspective, the examination of the device for Tor artifacts is your target and not so much an ongoing use of Tor. The forensic analysis of Tor is detailed later in this chapter, but at this point, keep in mind that a forensic analysis of Tor artifacts is one way we will be looking at Tor. Tor can run on Windows, Linux, and Mac. In the section of forensic analysis, the focus will be on the Windows operating system as it is the most commonly used operating system.

The other perspective of looking at Tor is that of it being currently used by your suspect. Without having the actual devices to examine, your investigation will have to depend solely on defeating Tor to either capture communications or identify your suspects who are using Tor. There are some aspects of Tor use that currently are unbreakable, at least to the nonintelligence agency investigator, and even then, Tor remains one of the most difficult systems to beat. Even with that, the last thing you should do is throw up your arms in defeat without trying. There are some methods that may work in your investigation now and others that may work later.

HOW THE ONION ROUTER WORKS

In the most basic explanation, Tor directs the route of a user's Internet traffic through random relays on the Internet. The data is first layered with elliptic curve cryptography, which is currently unbreakable with brute-force. As the encrypted data enters the first relay ("entry"), one layer of encryption is stripped and sent to the next relay ("middle"). The middle relay strips another layer of encryption and sends the encrypted data to the last relay ("exit"). The exit relay now connects to the user's desired target with an unencrypted connection.

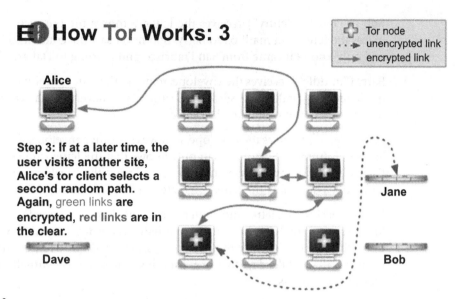

FIGURE 2.1
How Tor Works https://www.torproject.org/about/overview.HTML.en.

The exit relay does not know anything of the traffic route other than the single previous relay. Making Tor traffic even more difficult, if not impossible, to track is that this random route chooses a different entry, middle, and exit relay every 10 minutes or so. Fig. 2.1 shows a graphic from Tor Project (n.d.) visualizing this concept of Tor.

An analogy of Tor would be mailing a letter that is received and forwarded by different people. Let's say Mary wants to mail Johnny a letter, but does not want Johnny to know where the letter originated. The steps Mary needs to take to remain anonymous would be as follows:

1. Mary writes a letter and places it into an envelope addressed to Johnny in Boston.
2. Mary places that envelope into another and addresses it to Susan in Seattle.
3. Mary places that envelope into another and addresses it to Barry in Dallas.
4. Mary places that envelope into another and addresses it to Bob in Denver.
5. Mary places the letter in a mailbox from her home in San Francisco.

In this analogy, an envelope represents a layer of encryption. Using the rule that each person in this analogy can only unwrap the first envelope, the contents remain hidden (encrypted) in the most inner envelope.

Bob in Denver ("entry") receives the letter, removes the outer envelope, and places the letter in a mailbox to Barry. Bob never saw the contents of the letter and only knows it came from San Francisco and is going to Dallas.

Barry ("middle") receives the envelope, removes the outer envelope, and places the letter in a mailbox to Susan in Seattle. Barry never saw the contents and only knows that it originated in Denver.

Susan ("exit") receives the envelope, removes the outer envelope, and mails the letter to Johnny in Boston. Susan only knows that the letter came to her from Dallas. At this point, the contents can be read since the envelopes are removed. Susan does not know the letter originated in San Francisco.

Johnny receives the letter and contents, but only knows it came from Seattle. If Mary wants to mail another anonymous letter to Johnny, she will send through three different people with the same process. The main difference is that where regular mail will take days to arrive, Tor is instantaneous, yet virtually and completely anonymous.

As to the name "The Onion Router", you can see that sending data over Tor is like an onion, where a layer of encryption is peeled off as it goes through the Tor nodes to its final destination.

I'M JUST AN EXIT NODE! I'M JUST AN EXIT NODE!
Sometimes the IP address you get is not the IP address you need.
In 2011, Immigration and Customs Enforcement (ICE) executed a search warrant on Nolan King's home and seized his computers because an ICE investigation found that child pornography was being distributed from his home IP address (Hoffman, 2011). No child porn was found because King was simply operating a Tor exit node

A Few Important Points About Tor
Before continuing, a few more explanations are needed to describe how Tor works along with the terminology used with Tor. As we continue, you will begin to understand why breaking Tor is practically impossible without extraordinary resources, but there are some aspects of Tor that may be compromised.

The Tor network of relays is run by volunteers. Anyone, including you, can configure a server to be one of the thousands of relays used by hundreds of thousands of Tor users. Being a volunteer means your server would simply "remove the outer envelope and forward the inner envelope" to the next destination. Keep this in mind when investigating IP addresses with any investigation

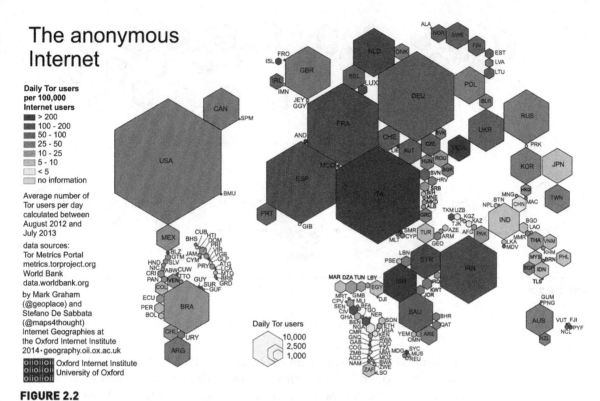

The anonymous Internet

Daily Tor users per 100,000 Internet users
- > 200
- 100 - 200
- 50 - 100
- 25 - 50
- 10 - 25
- 5 - 10
- < 5
- no information

Average number of Tor users per day calculated between August 2012 and July 2013

data sources:
Tor Metrics Portal
metrics.torproject.org
World Bank
data.worldbank.org

by Mark Graham (@geoplace) and Stefano De Sabbata (@maps4thought)
Internet Geographies at the Oxford Internet Institute
2014 · geography.oii.ox.ac.uk

Oxford Internet Institute
University of Oxford

Daily Tor users
10,000
2,500
1,000

FIGURE 2.2

Number of daily Tor users compared to Internet users http://geography.oii.ox.ac.uk/.

where Tor is involved. The IP address you believe may be your target just may be an innocent volunteer running a Tor relay.

Perhaps the most enlightening aspect of Tor is the amount of users since anonymity is strengthened with more users making it difficult to find one user among many. Fig. 2.2 is a graph of the number of worldwide, daily Tor users. According to the Tor Metric Portal (Tor Metrics, n.d.), there are over 750,000 users of Tor using over 6000 relays worldwide.

From Fig. 2.2, you can see where tracing Internet traffic on a Tor network can literally take you around the world, through the relays of innocent volunteers, and still not be closer to reaching the originating target. Additionally, even if the Tor circuit could be broken, gaining cooperation in foreign countries adds another layer of legal and diplomatic issues to identify the Tor users. In short, if a victim receives a harassing e-mail that appears to have originated in Italy do not assume that the suspect was physically in Italy.

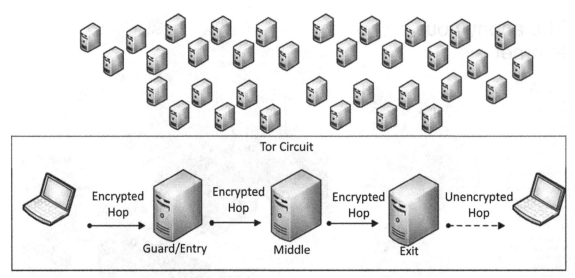

FIGURE 2.3
The Tor Circuit.

A simple visual of a Tor circuit can be seen in Fig. 2.3. The entry relay, or node, is also the "guard." The Tor client chooses entry guards at random to be used only for the first encrypted hop. If an entry guard is suspected of being compromised, it is no longer used. A random middle node is chosen for the encrypted middle hop which then sends the encrypted data to the exit node. The exit node then sends unencrypted data to the target. Keep in mind that not only are there over 6000 nodes from which the Tor client will choose from but that after 10 minutes or so, the Tor circuit changes the nodes among the thousands to choose.

The middle node does not know the origin or the data nor the final destination, and by the same token, neither the origin nor destination will know the middle relay. This makes it safe as a volunteer of a middle node to avoid being wrongly suspected of criminal activity based on IP addresses.

Each of these relays is publicly posted on the Internet for use by Tor clients. However, there are "bridges" which are typically not posted publicly. Since Tor relays are public, Internet Service Providers, or governments, can block them. But bridges are not normally listed publicly which makes blocking bridge relays nearly impossible. In countries where Internet blocking occurs, Tor bridges are used more commonly. Tor directory servers maintain Tor router information that is publicly listed.

TOR NODES
Fig. 2.4 Where is this list of Tor nodes?

There are several websites that provide lists of Tor nodes and allow to search for specific IP addresses to confirm if it had been, or is currently, used as a Tor node. Fig. 2.5 is one example of a website providing this information.

ExoneraTor

Enter an IP address and date to find out whether that address was used by a Tor relay:

IP address 86.59.21.38   **Date** mm/dd/yyyy   Search

About Tor

Tor is an international software project to anonymize Internet traffic by encrypting packets and sending them through a series of hops before they reach their destination. Therefore, if you see traffic from a Tor relay, this traffic usually originates from someone using Tor, rather than from the relay operator. The Tor Project and Tor relay operators have no records of the traffic that passes over the network ant therefore cannot provide any information about its origin. Be sure to learn more about Tor, and don't hesitate to contact The Tor Project, Inc. for more information.

About ExoneraTor

The ExoneraTor service maintains a database of IP addresses that have been part of the Tor network. It answers the question whether there was a Tor relay running on a given IP address on a given date. ExoneraTor may store more than one IP address per relay if relays use a different IP address for exiting to the Internet than for registering in the Tor network, and it stores whether a relay permitted transit of Tor traffic to the open Internet at that time.

"Tor" and the "Onion Logo" are registered trademarks of The Tor Project, Inc.

FIGURE 2.4

Where is this list of Tor nodes? (ExoneraTor, n.d.)

From a Tor User's Perspective

As mentioned, the Tor browser is simply a modified Firefox browser. Besides downloading the Tor browser, the only user technical skill required is that of entering URLs in the browser or entering terms in a search engine. Even the skill of installing a Tor is less than installing most programs. The Tor browser bundle is a portable application and only needs to be extracted, not installed, to run. The Tor browser file is self-executable to make the process even simpler for anyone to use. As the Tor browser is a portable application, it can be installed (extracted) to any location on a computer or external media device without any default paths.

From downloading to using the most anonymous browser in the world only requires about 10 mouse clicks and 10 minutes to download, extract, and configure. When accepting default settings, which fits the needs of most users, the Tor browser configuration step is completed in one click as seen in Figs. 2.5–2.7.

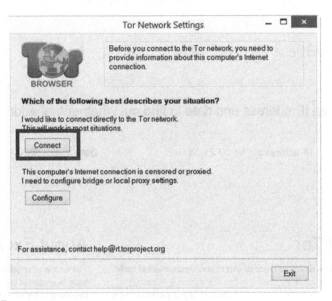

FIGURE 2.5
Step 1 of Tor setup.

Most users do not need to configure Tor to use with a bridge or local proxy settings. However, if this is necessary, it only adds a few minutes of setup time and is not terribly difficult for most computer users. Generally, Tor is just as effective with or without bridges, except in countries where Internet censoring will require bridges for Tor to work with the Tor network.

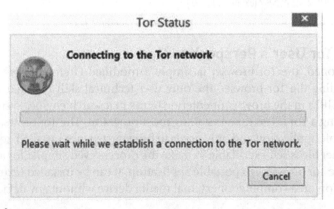

FIGURE 2.6
Step 2 of Tor setup, just have to wait.

FIGURE 2.7
Tor setup is complete.

At this point, Tor is ready to use similar to any web browser. As you can see, the simplicity of Tor coupled with the strong anonymity makes it a great choice for legitimate purposes as well as a prime choice for illicit use. It's free, fast to set up, easy to use, portable, and provides near breakable anonymity.

So What's the Big Deal?

Using Tor as an anonymous Internet browser is more than just surfing the web anonymously. Tor allows criminals and terrorists to communicate, share files, target, and attack with near absolute anonymity. For example, information transmitted using a webmail provider without Tor for criminal activity is easily discovered by law enforcement through search warrants and subpoenas once the e-mail address is known. The user's true IP address is also captured in e-mails and web browsing. Everything the user does online is potentially able to be captured, intercepted, and recovered down to the physical address of the computer system.

However, with Tor, this is not completely possible. Using a webmail service with Tor provides that service provider with the random exit node IP addresses and not the true IP address. Even by knowing the e-mail address, obtaining the originating IP address is practically impossible. Servers logging visitors will also only be able to log the random exit node IP addresses as well. This allows criminals to communicate openly without being identified. By using encryption methods with the communications, not only are they anonymous online, but the contents may also be encrypted end-to-end. Tor works to protect innocent communications but also provides that same level of protection to criminal and terrorist communications.

From Your Perspective

Generally, as an investigator, you will be looking at Tor either through the device on which it was used or the Internet traffic that is using Tor. As a forensic analyst, you may see more use of examining the Tor artifacts rather than the use of Tor, but as an investigator, you may be tasked with harassing or threatening e-mails being sent anonymously through Tor. Either way, your task to unmask Tor is more than difficult, it is overwhelming.

One thing to keep in mind is that it is the manner of use that determines whether or not Tor is a tool for legitimate use or illicit use. Businesses use Tor to browse a competitor's website to avoid the competitor logging the traffic. Whistleblowers, government agents and informants, and tourists use the Tor browser to protect their communications from being disclosed for legitimate communications. Law enforcement should encourage the use of Tor in their investigations to avoid suspects being aware of government IP addresses looking at websites being investigated.

FORENSIC ANALYSIS OF THE ONION ROUTER

First things first, you have to look for the Tor browser to find it. If you have not made it a routine part of a forensic analysis to look for the Tor browser, particularly when Internet and e-mail use is part of the investigation, you may be missing a vital piece of information. Since the Tor browser is a portable application, the Tor browser folder can be anywhere on a device. Users trying to hide Tor use may even change the name of the executable while placing the folder in a path inconsistent with where you'd expect a browser to be, such as under a system folder. Obviously, the fastest and most accurate method is to search for matching hash values for Tor in addition to searching for "Tor."

As the Tor browser is constantly updated, your device may have various versions of Tor in various states of active files and deleted files. Creating your

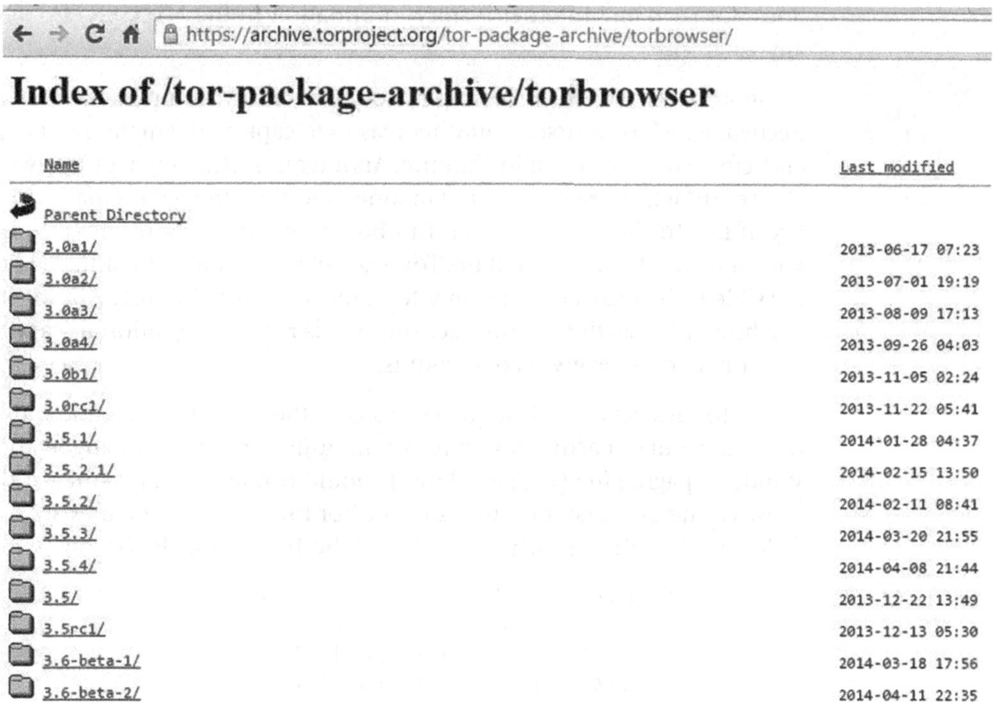

FIGURE 2.8

The Tor browser archives.

own hash set of Tor versions is as easy as downloading current and past versions to create a hash set unique to Tor browsers. The Tor Project archives all previous versions at Index of /tor-package-archive/torbrowser (n.d.) as can be seen in Fig. 2.8.

One of the purposes of searching for older versions of Tor that may have been used is that as an investigator, you can get a sense of how long your suspect has been using Tor as an anonymous communication and Internet surfing tool. If nothing else but to bolster your knowledge for an interview with a suspect, you may be able to determine by days, months, or years of use contrary to what a suspect may admit to using. A regular user of Tor will update their Tor browser as soon as notified that an update is available to avoid being compromised by an older browser weakness.

Internet history forensics can be one of the most enlightening aspects of a forensic analysis as it is a window to the soul of intention. Internet searches, bookmarks, visited websites give a clear description of a user's likes, intentions, wishes, and desires. Unfortunately, with the Tor browser, you most likely find no remnants of Internet use, specifically, the Internet history. The Tor browser does not keep any Internet history information in the NTUSER.DAT file, nor anywhere else.

In order to recover Tor browsing history, a memory dump of the machine is needed, which of course, is another reason to capture the memory of computers before shutting down for capture. Another unfortunate investigative aspect of Tor artifacts in memory is the manner and time the data remains in memory. If the Tor browser has been run but closed, the data in memory is gone almost instantly. However, if the Tor browser is running, remnants of URLs are possible to be recovered but only for a few minutes after use. Approaching a machine that has the Tor browser running is a clear indication to capture the memory because every second counts.

Other Tor artifacts exist but are few. Mostly, the artifacts give some indication of Tor use, but not actual contents of communications or browsing history. The Windows paging file (C:\pagefile.sys) should contain the filename for the Tor browser and you may find traces of the Tor browser in cache files such as the following. The thumbcache should hold the Tor browser logo icon.

```
C:\Users\suspect\AppData\Local\Microsoft\Windows\Caches\
cversions.1.db
C:\Windows\AppCompat\Programs\RecentFileCache.bcf
C:\Users\Suspect\AppData\Local\Microsoft\Windows\Explorer\
thumbcache_32.db
C:\Users\Suspect\AppData\Local\Microsoft\Windows\Explorer\
thumbcache_32.db
C:\Users\Suspect\AppData\Local\Microsoft\Windows\Explorer\
thumbcache_96.db
C:\Users\Suspect\AppData\Local\Microsoft\Windows\Explorer\
thumbcache_256.db
C:\Users\Suspect\AppData\Local\Microsoft\Windows\Explorer\
thumbcache_ thumbcache_1024.db
C:\Users\Suspect\AppData\Local\Microsoft\Windows\Explorer\
thumbcache_sr.db
C:\Users\Suspect\AppData\Local\Microsoft\Windows\Explorer\
thumbcache_idx.db
C:\Users\Suspect\AppData\Local\Microsoft\Windows\Explorer\
IconCache.db
```

Conducting a keyword search for HTTP-memory-only-PB within pagefile.sys may also result in recovering websites visited with the Tor browser. Recovering Internet history in this fashion is not as satisfying as recovering history from non-Tor browsers, but if you can find the specific site that was visited that is needed for your investigation, it may be enough. Searching for any "Tor"-related keywords such as "torproject" throughout the media may also reveal information about Tor's use in e-mails or recoverable Internet history.

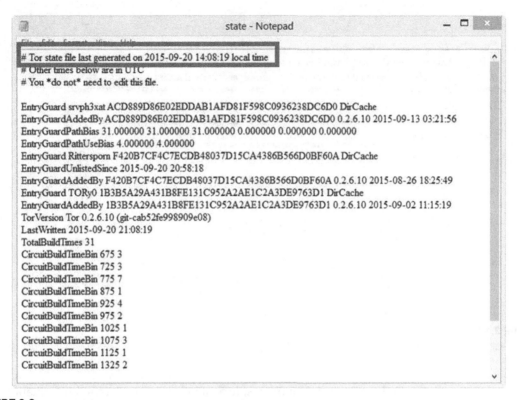

FIGURE 2.9

C:\Users\suspect\Desktop\Tor Browser\Browser\TorBrowser\Data\Tor.

Within the Tor browser folder, you can find the last local execution date and time in the file named "state." If you have multiple Tor browser folders, which is likely for any Tor user, you will have multiple last execution dates and times for each browser's use. This file is viewable through Notepad or other text editors. An example is seen in Fig. 2.9.

Within the same file path as Fig. 2.9, the location of where the Tor browser was run can be found in the file torrc as seen in Fig. 2.10. Again, if the user has multiple Tor browser folders on their system, you can find multiple file paths including the drive letter from which the Tor browser was run.

Looking at the following files in the registry (HKCU) will also show the file path to the Tor Browser Bundle executable:

```
C:\Users\runa\AppData\Local\Microsoft\Windows\UsrClass.dat
C:\Users\runa\AppData\Local\Microsoft\Windows\UsrClass.dat.LOG1
```

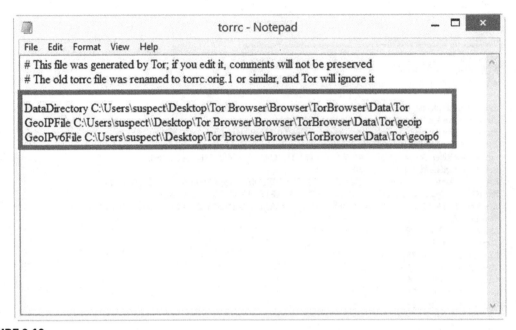

FIGURE 2.10

File path that the Tor browser was run.

Windows Prefetch is another source of information to recover information that may be pertinent to your investigation. One of the main purposes of a Prefetch file is to speed up the loading of applications, and the logging of Prefetch information gives a forensic analyst a wealth of application use information. For example, the following Prefetch example shows that Tor was installed on 9/20/2015 at 12:04:12PM and run about a minute later.

```
Filename     TORBROWSER-INSTALL-5.0.2_EN-U-51B7220A.pf
Created Time     9/20/2015 12:04:12 PM
Modified Time     9/20/2015 12:04:12 PM
File Size     33,676
Process EXE     TOR.EXE
Process Path
Run Counter     1
Last Run Time 9/20/2015 12:05:20 PM
Missing Process     No
Filename     TOR.EXE-4FD90956.pf
Created Time     9/20/2015 12:05:30 PM
Modified Time     9/20/2015 12:05:30 PM
File Size     49,482
Process EXE    TOR.EXE
Process Path  C:\Users\suspect\Desktop\TOR BROWSER\Browser\
TORBROWSER\Tor\tor.exe
```

```
Run Counter    1
Last Run Time 9/20/2015 12:05:20 PM
Missing Process   No
```

Since Tor does not create artifacts that are helpful for analysis, other activity on the system may be related to inferring user activity. If an external drive was attached to this system in the same time period of use and files accessed from that device, it would be feasible that the files may have been e-mails or uploaded through Tor. Any files accessed during this time could be suspect as being infiltrated outside the system through Tor. A corporate network could miss data exfiltration in this manner.

Given the Prefetch sample information above and the below USB connection that occurred roughly 1 minute after starting Tor, a fair assumption that the activity may be related and would be the start of good questions of the computer user.

```
Device Name    USB 2.0 FD
Description    PNY USB 2.0 FD USB Device
Device Type    Mass Storage
Drive Letter E:
Serial Number AAC214A100900336
Created Date 9/20/2015 12:06:30 PM
Last Plug/Unplug Date 9/20/2015 12:08:30 PM
VendorID    154b
ProductID   0059
Driver Filename  USBSTOR.SYS
Device Mfg       Compatible USB storage device
Driver Description USB Mass Storage Device
Driver Version 6.3.9600.17331
Instance ID    USB\VID_154B&PID_0059\AAC214A980000336
```

Although a forensic analysis of Tor does not give you as much information as does that of non-Tor browsers, there is still much value in the analysis. Besides the install/first use/last use/number of uses, the possibility of recovering some URLs exists. The mere existence and use of Tor on any machine should also give immediate cause for concern for all aspects of counter/antiforensics that may have been employed on the system. With the Volume Shadow Copies, an analysis can provide an historical usage of Tor that can be compared with other activity on the system that may be related.

IT'S PORTABLE!
The Tor browser can run from almost anywhere

Remember, the Tor browser is portable, meaning that no installation is necessary. This also means that it can run from external devices, such as a flash drive or external hard drive, and may have never been installed (extracted) onto a system's hard drive. When Tor is run from an external device, you can expect even fewer artifacts to remain, but certainly does not make looking for Tor artifacts less important.

TRACKING CRIMINALS USING TOR

By now you understand the difficulty in tracking Tor users, but do not feel alone because practically every government agency is working on deanonymizing Tor to either find criminals and terrorists or prohibit citizens from accessing the Internet. A few successes have made the national news, but for the most part, the breaks in the cases were not due to breaking Tor but rather exploiting errors made by suspects. Like the majority of investigators, having access to federal resources to investigate criminals using Tor is most likely not possible. Unless you have a terrorist connection to a case, you are on your own to investigate without the National Security Agency.

IT'S POSSIBLE TO BREAK TOR!
The FBI did it…once…at least once…

A child pornography hosting service was identified and taken down by the FBI using an exploit of Firefox. The FBI simply infected the servers at Freedom Hosting, which in turn, infected the Tor browsers of the visitors of the criminal websites. The exploit (Firefox bug CVE-2013-1690 in version 17 ESR) captured the true IP address, MAC address, and Windows hostname from the Tor browser exploit. This information was then sent to the FBI until the exploit was discovered and patched. Linux Tor users and those who had used updated versions of Tor were apparently unaffected (The FBI TOR Exploit).

One of the weaknesses, if not the biggest weakness, of the Tor browser is the user. As the browser is preconfigured with security in mind, customization is not recommended. In fact, the best thing a Tor user can do is not to change any settings of the browser because anyone setting can leak information out of Tor.

A simple example is a geolocation. Some websites ask if you will allow your location to be shared. A Tor user should always choose "never" but as investigators, we rely on mistakes and hope these types of modifications are made by criminals. Other aspects of customization revolve around the entertainment factor of the Internet. Video and animation on the Internet usually require plugins to be installed and active while at the same time, these very plugins can allow the true IP address to be collected. Tor users who routinely allow scripts, java, and any other website requests to run on the browser risk having their IP address captured by those websites. But how does that help you?

The amount of research conducted on Tor to find vulnerabilities, identify users, and decrypt data has been ongoing for years. Some researchers have gone so far as to theorize deanonymizing Tor by attacking and disabling a large percentage of the Tor network to identify users (Jansen, Tschorsch, Johnson, & Scheuermann, n.d.).

Other theories include gaining control of as many entry and exit nodes as possible to correlate traffic and identify users. Even if several entry (guard) nodes are controlled, the Tor network does not automatically use new entry nodes for weeks at a time to reduce the threat of compromised entry nodes. Entry nodes are also rotated regularly. So, to control entry nodes in hopes that your suspect's Tor circuit uses it is slim. On top of that, if the communications are encrypted end-to-end, capturing the traffic does not decrypt the contents of messages.

The man-in-the-middle attack is yet another method to bypass the security of Tor users by interjecting a capture service between the Tor user and destination. Nation-states have the resources for these types of attacks on Tor, but even then, compromising Tor is very difficult.

Each of these methods requires more resources and time than will ever be given to the common criminal unless special situations exist, such as a terror connection. Even then, the number of agencies with access to such resources is very few. Given that, the few remaining methods rely on the suspect and the suspect's errors.

The most common goal of any Internet-related investigation is obtaining the true IP address. With the true IP address, traditional investigative methods can corroborate, verify, and potentially seize physical evidence and suspects at that location. The trick is getting the IP address when Tor makes it extremely difficult.

Depending upon the investigation, you may have access to one end of the communication, such as that of a victim. When a victim receives harassing or threatening e-mails, the potential to capitalize on the suspect's mistakes increase. For example, an e-mail can be seeded with a tracking code, sent by the victim to the suspect. Once the e-mail is opened by the suspect, the tracking code can obtain the true IP address and send it to the investigator. The success depends on a couple of factors. One is that of the e-mail service being used and its configuration. If the e-mail (webmail) allows HTML, then the tracking script should work without alerting the suspect. However, if not, the suspect will be immediately notified that a script has been placed in the e-mail and not be allowed to run. This method is risky as it will tip off the suspect that e-mail may be compromised.

Another method with less risk of notifying the suspect is placing a tracking code in a document that is e-mailed to the suspect. Documents need to be downloaded and opened for viewing, usually outside the browser. When the document is opened outside the browser, the tracking code obtains the true IP address which is sent to the investigator. There are few if any, warnings, given to a computer user that opens a document with an IP address tracking code. Tor does give a warning that downloading documents can be dangerous and recommends to open the documents safely, offline or in a virtual machine to prevent the IP address from being captured.

When these methods are ineffective or may cause too much risk of compromise, identifying the Tor user outside of the Tor network may be possible. In this manner, using all of the information you have of your suspect requires open-source and online investigative methods. Basically, finding your suspect in the open web can help identify the suspect in the Dark Web. Even if the only information you have on the suspect is a username, it may be enough to lead to more information otherwise unobtainable.

ONE MISTAKE RESULTS IN A LIFETIME IN PRISON
One Weak Strand of the Silk Road Caused the Crash

Silk Road found Ross Ulbricht used his personal e-mail address and real name on the open Internet to request help building a Bitcoin-venture, which led federal agents the ability to link directly to his previously unidentified Dark Web identity (Bradbury, 2013). Now he is spending the rest of his life in prison. That wasn't the only evidence in the case, but it is one example of a suspect's mistake making an investigation much easier.

Investigations that involve an internal corporate network are at an advantage of identifying Tor users if the network is being used with Tor. Network administrators can see Internet access using the Tor network, but cannot see the content of messages or websites accessed. However, the mere fact of being able to locate someone using Tor on the network is something impossible to do from outside a network. An example of how this can benefit an investigation is that a victim may have an idea as to who the suspect may be. If the employment can be identified, and the IT staff has the ability to find any local users accessing the Tor network, potentially e-mail traffic can be assumed based on the access date/time to the Tor network and receipt date/time of e-mails sent to the victim. Basically, if a user at the corporation accesses Tor between 3:30 pm and 3:40 pm, and the victim receives a threatening e-mail between those times, the likelihood that the suspect can be tied to a computer is high.

BUT MOM, I DON'T WANT TO TAKE THE EXAM!
How a Harvard student was busted using Tor

In 2013, Harvard student Eldo Kim used Tor to e-mail bomb threats to Harvard staff to avoid taking an exam. The IT staff at Harvard looked at their logs and identified Kim as accessing Tor on the school network during the time of the e-mails (Dalton, 2013). FBI agents asked Kim if he did it and Kim admitted. Tor worked. Kim broke.

The most common method of cases being solved is that from the "breaks" in the case. Breaks in the case are usually found by mistakes made by the suspects. In the case of Tor browser use, a suspect may be using the Tor browser properly, but might inadvertently use another browser falsely believing the non-Tor browser provides anonymity. Any e-mails or Internet connections through a non-Tor browser will show the true IP address of the suspect. In effect, a suspect could mistakenly use a non-Tor browser and not realize it while the victim will receive the true IP address.

USED IN COMBINATION OF OTHER TOOLS AND METHODS

Tor, when used by itself works well. When used in combination with other security methods works perfectly as an anonymous communication tool. As you have seen, the last hop of data in the Tor circuit is unencrypted. Theoretically, this data could be compromised. However, if the data was encrypted, not only is the transmission anonymous, but the information is encrypted. At that point, even if both ends of the communication are identified, the encrypted contents are secure if end-to-end encryption has been employed.

If a Tor user adds an additional layer of protection by using a nonowned computer on a nonowned network, the odds of being identified are even smaller. This would be the case of using Tor on a public computer at a library or hotel lobby as both the sender and receiver of electronic communications.

TAILS

As Tor is a browser that can be used anonymously, Tails (The Amnesic Incognito Live System) is a complete operating system that can be used anonymously. Tails is based on Debian/Linux and runs from a DVD, USB flash drive, or SD card and does not need to be installed. In the context of the Tor browser, the Tor browser is preinstalled and preconfigured in Tails. The operation is the same as described previously with all the benefits of anonymity.

However, Tails adds even more security and anonymity to covert communications and web surfing. To run Tails, a computer must be able to boot to an external device that contains Tails. Once booted to Tails, the user needs to only connect to an active Internet connection and the Tor browser can be used immediately. The most substantial difference in using Tails compared to using the Tor browser in Windows or other installed operating system is that Tails does not leave any trace on the host computer system. A Tails user can prevent any forensic artifacts being created since Tails does not touch the host computer hard drive.

Additionally, you have seen that Tor forensic artifacts and even URLs can be found in memory and the hiberfil.sys file. Tails does not create, use, or write to a pagefile.sys or hiberfil.sys. Moreover, the live memory is wiped on shutdown. Even when run from a writable USB flash drive, data is not saved to the flash drive from the Tails use.

On Linux operating systems, the boot loader (GRUB2) can be configured to bypass the operating system and boot from an ISO that is stored on the host system hard drive. For example, a Tails ISO file can be saved on the hard drive of a Linux operating system, and through the boot loader the system will boot from the Tails ISO instead of booting from the host operating system. There is no need for external media to accomplish this, and trace evidence on the host hard drive will not be created when booting the ISO file. The host hard drive can have as many different ISO files of "live CDs" as desired, and any can be chosen to boot directly. A live CD is an operating system on an external medium that can boot a computer system and run completely from the external medium without use of the computer internal hard drive.

As an investigative point, forensic analysis of the boot loader is important to determine if the system was configured to boot from an ISO on the hard drive which could explain computer use without associated metadata and system changes to the hard drive operating system. Although the host hard drive is untouched (except for the ISO access), an analysis is not going to show user or system activity. However, the user can boot from the ISO and choose to access the hard drive to save, delete, or modify files. In this type of usage, there may be no system activity that matches user-created file creation/modification/access times, which would be indicative that the system was booted from an ISO (or even external bootable medium) and the host hard drive was accessed through the ISO operating system. A detailed instruction guide on booting Linux to a stored ISO on the hard drive can be found here: http://www.howtogeek.com/196933/how-to-boot-linux-iso-images-directly-from-your-hard-drive/. http://www.howtogeek.com/196933/how-to-boot-linux-iso-images-directly-from-your-hard-drive/

Tails provides more than just a Tor browser. It provides tools for encryption, encrypted chat, an office suite, MAC address spoofing, and a virtual keyboard that can thwart key loggers from capturing passwords. Nearly everything in Tails is designed for ease of use, portability, security, and anonymity. Upon booting Tails, the user can choose between the typical Linux configuration and a camouflage configuration that looks like the Windows operating system. Fig. 2.11 is the desktop view of Tails with the Windows operating system configuration.

The same methods to defeat Tails apply to the previous discussion with Tors, but forensically, there will be no forensic artifacts to be found in a host system if Tails was the only method used to run the Tor browser. Tails is limited to the types of computers that can boot to external media. For example, many libraries are configured not to allow booting to external media which require users to run Tor on the host machine.

FIGURE 2.11
Tails operating system with Windows camouflage.

RELATED TOR TOOLS AND APPLICATIONS

The Tor network works well for its intended purpose and because of its effectiveness, Third-party tools capitalize on it. One commercial example is the Anonabox (http://www.anonabox.com). The Anonabox is a hardware router that routes all Internet traffic through Tor, rather than only the Tor browser being routed through the Tor network. Devices such as the Anonabox should be considered when seizing computer systems for analysis.

Devices such as the Anonabox reduce security errors made by Tor browser users by eliminating the risk of using a non-Tor browser connection as the entire Internet connection runs through Tor. By running the entire Internet connection through a device such as this, suspects can use any web browser, not just Tor, without their true IP address being disclosed.

The risk of using devices like the Anonabox may not be worth the effort of just using the Tor browser. In April 2015, Anonabox recalled their devices for security flaws. The Tor network functioned, but the Anonabox was defective (Greenberg, n.d.).

Mobile applications with Tor may also become one of the most popular smartphone applications as the Tor browser can run on the Android operating system. Applications such as Orbot (n.d.) force Internet traffic on mobile devices to the Tor network, encrypting and sending traffic through worldwide Tor nodes. The ability to use Tor on a mobile device adds an entirely new dimension to "burner phones" in that a prepaid phone can be used to send anonymous communications via the Tor network and subsequently discarded. Virtually any and every mobile device may eventually have the option to direct Internet traffic through the Tor network, making it even more difficult to investigate crimes facilitated in this manner.

Hidden Services

An aspect of the Tor network to consider as covert communications is that of hidden services. A hidden service is a server on the Tor network that provides a service, such as e-mail or file hosting. Hidden services are not indexed by search engines and therefore, practically invisible to the Internet. Hidden services also do not use exit nodes. If you remember, exit nodes strip off the last layer of encryption of a message. Hidden services provide end-to-end encryption since exit nodes are not needed. User connects directly to a hidden service with (currently) unbreakable encryption.

Setting up a hidden service on the Tor network is a fairly easy task that can be completed within an afternoon, which makes hidden services a prime candidate for covert communications due to being hidden and providing end-to-end encryption. Many hidden services are listed on directory websites for convenience and marketing, but can also be set up without being listed and known by certain persons for access.

Hidden service websites are most always accessed with the Tor browser with the top-level domain of the hidden services being ".onion". A typical .onion web URL appears as http://dppmfxaacucguzpc.onion/. Browser plugins exist which can allow a non-Tor browser to access a hidden service website. However, there is no viable reason to use a non-Tor browser to access a hidden service, particularly since the hidden service may capture your true IP address. This would not be productive if you are investigating the hidden service and your office IP address is captured. Fig. 2.12 shows one directory on the Dark Web offering drugs for sale. Note that Silk Road 3.0 is listed, which appeared right after the previous Silk Road was taken offline. There are directories of anything you can imagine, including hiring assassins and buying fake identities.

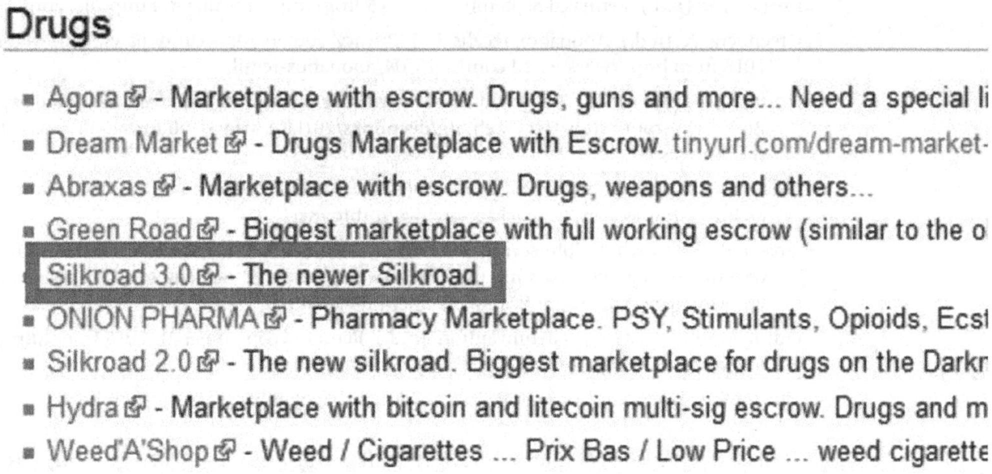

Drugs

- Agora 🔗 - Marketplace with escrow. Drugs, guns and more... Need a special li
- Dream Market 🔗 - Drugs Marketplace with Escrow. tinyurl.com/dream-market-
- Abraxas 🔗 - Marketplace with escrow. Drugs, weapons and others...
- Green Road 🔗 - Biggest marketplace with full working escrow (similar to the o
- Silkroad 3.0 🔗 - The newer Silkroad.
- ONION PHARMA 🔗 - Pharmacy Marketplace. PSY, Stimulants, Opioids, Ecst
- Silkroad 2.0 🔗 - The new silkroad. Biggest marketplace for drugs on the Darkr
- Hydra 🔗 - Marketplace with bitcoin and litecoin multi-sig escrow. Drugs and m
- Weed'A'Shop 🔗 - Weed / Cigarettes ... Prix Bas / Low Price ... weed cigarette

FIGURE 2.12

Directory of illegal drugs for purchase on the Dark Web.

Many, if not most, of the hidden services market illicit or restricted products or services. Drugs, firearms, credit card numbers, child pornography, and anything you can imagine are for sale on the hidden services, otherwise known as the "Dark Web." Considering the anonymity provided by the Tor browser coupled with the hidden service encryption, investigations into the Dark Web require more than IP address capturing. These investigations require a new level of traditional investigative methods to uncover and identify the networks of online criminals.

SUMMARY

Tor is the most commonly used anonymous Internet tool in the world and is used for both legitimate and illicit communication. Although identifying the illicit users of Tor is nearly impossible, any forensics investigation should not discount the possibility of Tor use by a suspect as a means of covert communication. Identifying communications between persons requires more than just identifying the Internet traffic or identifying the persons involved. A complete picture is identifying the suspects as well as the contents of their communications.

REFERENCES

Bradbury, D. (October 3, 2013). *Silk road fell due to a catalogue of errors by owner Ross Ulbricht.* Retrieved September 21, 2015 from http://www.coindesk.com/ross-ulbrichts-silk-road-head-smacking-rookie-errors/.

Dalton, T. (December 17, 2013). *AFFIDAVIT OF SPECIAL AGENT THOMAS M. DALTON 835 1682.* Retrieved September 21, 2015 from https://www.washingtonpost.com/blogs/the-switch/files/2013/12/kimeldoharvard.pdf.

ExoneraTor. (n.d.). Retrieved September 21, 2015 from https://exonerator.torproject.org/.

Greenberg, A. (n.d.). Anonabox recalls 350 'Privacy' routers for security flaws. Retrieved April 7, 2015 from http://www.wired.com/2015/04/anonabox-recall/.

Hoffman, M. (August 24, 2011). *Why IP addresses alone don't identify criminals.* Retrieved September 21, 2015 from https://www.eff.org/deeplinks/2011/08/why-ip-addresses-alone-dont-identify-criminals.

Index of /tor-package-archive/torbrowser. (n.d.). Retrieved September 21, 2015 from https://archive.torproject.org/tor-package-archive/torbrowser/.

Jansen, R., Tschorsch, F., Johnson, A., & Scheuermann, B. (n.d.). The Sniper attack: Anonymously deanonymizing and disabling the Tor network. Retrieved September 21, 2015 from http://www.robgjansen.com/publications/sniper-ndss2014.pdf.

Orbot: Mobile anonymity circumvention. (n.d.). Retrieved September 21, 2015 from http://guardianproject.info/apps/orbot/.

The amnesic incognito live system. (n.d.). Retrieved September 21, 2015 from https://tails.boum.org.

The FBI TOR Exploit. (November 29, 2013). Retrieved September 21, 2015 from http://resources.infosecinstitute.com/fbi-tor-exploit/.

Tor Metrics. (n.d.). Retrieved September 21, 2015 from https://metrics.torproject.org/.

Tor Project. (n.d.). Retrieved September 21, 2015 from http://www.torproject.org.

CHAPTER 3

Triaging Mobile Evidence

In defining a logical and physical exam, it is important to understand some basic information regarding forensic acquisitions on mobile devices. In this chapter, we will primarily be referring to mobile phones. One should also understand that with the popularity of user-installed applications, some devices are not necessarily equipped with internal components (radio) that communicate with cellular towers. These *devices*, however, can communicate through WIFI when properly set up by the user and can still provide calling, texting, web browsing, and other media exchanges. For the forensic examiner, the same types of exams would apply—the challenge often being the decoding of the application itself. Application data will be discussed in more detail in Chapter "Mobile Extraction Issues," so for now, let's briefly explain the logical and physical exam.

LOGICAL DATA

Take out your mobile device right now. Assuming it is powered, you may have enabled some security—such as a passcode or gesture (pattern) lock. Defeat your security if such is enabled. Now navigate to a stored contact. Let's say for this example you locate, "Mom – Mobile number??? - ????." Now locate a picture on your phone. If you have no stored picture, look at your background image on your home screen. These two areas on your phone are examples of stored logical data. Logical data can simply be defined as data (or media) that you can easily see and understood. If you own an Android, iPhone, or Windows device, you have on numerous occasions navigated your graphical user interface (GUI) to get to specific logical data at the swipe of your finger.

Here's some key things about logical data for mobile forensic examiners:

1. It's usually self-explanatory. In most cases it needs no supplementary explanation. For prosecutors, this "tells the story by itself."
2. It does not need special tools, utilities, or specialized training to decode. It is as simple as the old saying within forensics—"What you see is what you get."

3. Most corporations, private investigators, businesses, and law enforcement entities tasked with mobile forensic extractions are ultimately "looking" for logical data. It is the quickest way to understand the answer to the specific reason behind the exam when it is obtainable.
4. Most forensic vendors design their product around the ability to parse— or pull logical data.
5. The cost involved in extracting logical data is generally less than that of physical. It also (generally) costs less time and money to train individuals to understand the "logical" exam. Most logical exams with commercially available tools are more about how the tool interface works, as well as the make and model the tool may support.
6. Logical exams are limited on what they can locate, and not all phones are supported through logical acquisitions.

PHYSICAL DATA

Most people, in general, would never give much thought to what is needed for the screen on their smartphone to display the phone book entry they stored as "MOM." If we look inside the file system with specialized tools and decoders, we will find this entry would look very different within the binary world. Physical data is typically explained as "deleted" data. If we used the previous example of our mom's cell phone number stored on our phone, and then deleted the same entry, we no longer can see it within the GUI. The entry in some cases may still be within the file system. This is definitely a common way to describe physical data—but more needs to be added to the definition.

1. Physical data is the composition of the logical data. Logical data is generally easy to see, but if we look at it within the hex and binary formats, it now becomes much harder to read. Think of a light bulb. You see the light and understand it. Think of the light as logical data. But what creates the light is an inert gas, wires, a bulb, glass mount, treads, isolation, and power. Maybe we don't understand completely how all the components work together—we simply understand it takes the entire bulb for it to put out desired light. As the consumer, we simply flip a switch and the light is on. Logical data that you easily can see also has complex elements within in mobile device making them work.
2. Data obtained from a physical exam requires specialized tools, training, and on many occasions additional time to interpret.
3. The composition of the physical data may have different types of encoding based upon the make and model of the phone. Unlike computer forensics, mobile forensics will have various types of file systems. Each may store their own data in a unique fashion, to include how the date and time stamps appear in physical format.

4. Not all forensic tools support the acquiring of physical data. Physical support will generally require more financial resources. For advanced techniques, this can run into thousands of dollars just in the equipment alone.

EXAMPLES OF LOGICAL AND PHYSICAL DATA

Figs. 3.1 and 3.2 are examples of logical and physical exams. Fig. 3.1 is a common logical exam summary for a text entry that was found with a common forensic tool. In this example, we see the tool located only two sent entries for the phone number 9152081138. However, if we determine the type of encoding that number uses within the file system, we can conduct additional (physical) searches. Fig. 3.2 is a screenshot showing the additional content involving this number that was missed logically because the entries were missed by the logical exam.

☀	Timestamp	Folder	Parties	Body
◉	4/9/2014 3:08:04 PM(UTC+0)	Sent	➡ 3604028812	It was a pleasure getting him off this earth...not so fun burying him
◉	4/8/2014 10:33:38 PM(UTC+0)	Sent	➡ 9152081138	Delete that
◉	4/8/2014 10:31:41 PM(UTC+0)	Sent	➡ 9152081138	Yes

FIGURE 3.1
Logical data example.

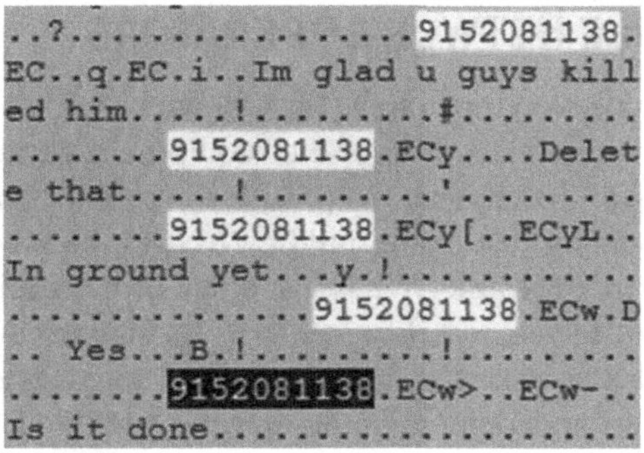

FIGURE 3.2
Physical data example.

IS THAT DATA REALLY DELETED? *WELL...MAYBE, MAYBE NOT*

Just like with computer forensics, many people are under the impression that when they deleted data on a mobile device, it is actually deleted. You may be thinking ahead and answering this by saying that it is *not actually deleted*. The truth is with mobile forensics is *it just depends*. Factors that play into if the item in question is actually deleted can be the type of operating system on the phone (smartphone vs simple bar or flip phone), time involved after the item was deleted, and in some cases the type of data that was deleted. Unlike computer forensics that has a higher probability of recovering deleted data on a standard hard drive, mobile forensics data discarded by the user may

Continued

IS THAT DATA REALLY DELETED? *WELL...MAYBE, MAYBE NOT—Cont'd*

or may not be accessible through forensic processes. Factors such as *wear-leveling* and *garbage collection* will effect if artifacts can be recovered from larger physical memory. This memory is now commonly found on popular phones such as the iPhone, Android, Blackberry, and Windows.

WIRELESS CARRIERS

As we continue to discuss the elements of mobile forensics, one aspect that is often overlooked are the wireless carriers. The reason behind this is many examiners will in most cases acquire the artifact(s) using a forensic tool, and forget about how the wireless carrier may play into what they located. Also, the target number and associated account are not usually thought of when discussing mobile forensics. Many investigators have served subpoenas and search warrants on a particular number, and never had an opportunity to examine the actual mobile device. In the future, this too may be the case for you, but in this chapter it will be explained how they overlap and can be a necessity with regards to the mobile exam and validation. Validation will be discussed later on in more detail, for now, we address how the carriers are divided into two categories.

MOBILE NETWORK OPERATORS

Mobile network operators (MNOs) are wireless carriers that own and maintain their own towers and associated equipment. Most of us have traveled down the freeway or driven next to a cellular tower. The panels at the top, large strands of wires leading to a small building next to the tower, generally surrounded by a fenced in enclosure. This is just some of the equipment involved in the MNO. There are servers, switching centers, base station controllers, and many other components that make this all work. In the United States, the MNOs are AT&T, Sprint, T-Mobile, and Verizon. Some may include US Cellular on that list as they have continued to grow. The point being they have the ability to provide customers with wireless devices as well as service how the device connects to their network.

MOBILE VIRTUAL NETWORK OPERATOR

The opposite are the carriers that don't maintain their infrastructure. These are called mobile virtual network operators (MVNOs). World-wide, MVNOs easily outnumber MNOs. Virtual networks work out deals with the major networks, buying airtime which is in turn bundled around their own plans and handsets sold to consumers. Each MNO may have restrictions with what type of service will be provided and often times may limit some of the make and model handsets that can be sold by the virtual network. The idea behind this is not to compete with their own product or plans. As a forensic examiner over time, you will see specific model devices that are only serviced by the MVNOs.

You may be asking yourself why would you need to know the differences between an MNO and an MVNO? Besides validation, the answer leads into the next topic which has to do who services the target number. In some cases, the legal process may require a subpoena or search warrant to more than one location based on if the number is serviced by an MVNO.

PAY-AS-YOU-GO IS NOT ALWAYS A DEAD END (NO PUN INTENDED)

During a triple homicide investigation, all of the suspects disposed of their smartphones. One of the suspects contacted his girlfriend with his new "pay-as-you-go" phone number. She feared for his safety and supplied the number to law enforcement. A search warrant to Tracfone in Florida revealed very little information regarding who owned the phone. It did supply a store number where the phone was sold. The store was contacted, and it was determined that the Electronic Serial Number (ESN) on the phone was activated at the register during the cash sale. The store also maintains surveillance video for 30 days. Using the actual ESN value, the phone sale was looked up and the video was researched for the date and time of the sale. The video showed all three suspects who were involved in the murder standing at the register. Along with the pay-as-you-go phone, they also purchased cleaning supplies (bleach, mops, etc.). Many investigators can at times locate additional details of the distribution information—even when the device itself is designed for a virtual network.

DETERMINING TARGET NUMBER

Now that we understand the types of networks, we need also to establish who may be servicing the number in question. Law Enforcement can apply for a free account that can aid investigators with this task. This account is not completely necessary, but can save time in some cases. First we will explain free services that can help determine who services the number.

FONEFINDER.NET

This free Website allows a person to search a number to potentially show who may be providing wireless service. It is important to understand, however, what porting is and how it works. In Fig. 3.3, a phone number was entered using the Fonefinder interface. Fig. 3.4 shows the results of the search indicating the number belonging to Sprint Spectrum.

This number actually is being serviced by Verizon and the results from Fonefinder show whom the number was originally ported to. Years ago, phone numbers stayed assigned to the network they originated with, the control and ownership being given to the carrier. The short version of this story is that the government became involved with this and now allows consumers to move their number to any network they choose—as long as they meet geographical

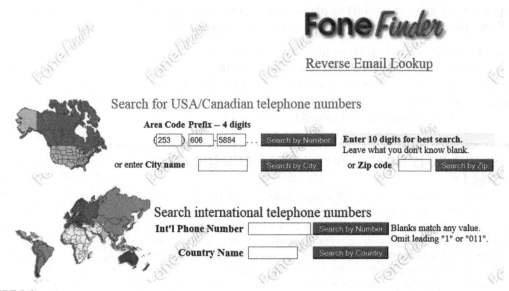

FIGURE 3.3
Fonefinder interface.

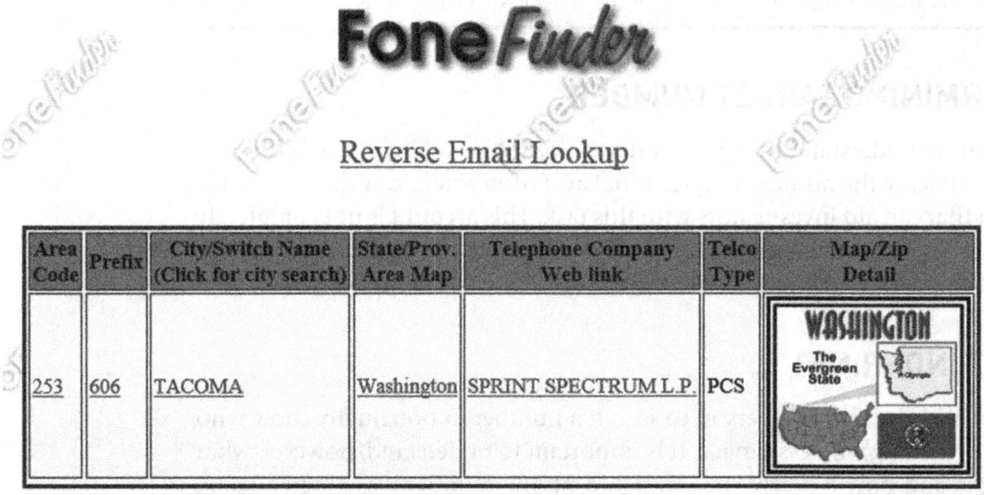

FIGURE 3.4
Fonefinder search results.

requirements. The official name of this is "local number portability," which is commonly referred to as "porting." Porting can apply to Voice Over Internet Protocol assigned numbers as well. When trying to determine who is currently servicing a target number, the investigator must be aware of porting and how it plays into the accuracy of their research.

Fonefinder.net should be used as a general guide, which many times will be accurate. This points a person in a "starting" direction. Before proceeding with legal process, confirmation must be made to the suspected carrier. This is generally completed by phone and is later explained in further detail.

As previously stated, law enforcement can apply for a free account to determine who is serving the number in their investigation.

NUMBER PORTABILITY ADMINISTRATION CENTER

Number Portability Administration Center (NPAC) will assign a PIN number for agencies who complete their online application. Once approved, a phone number to the automated system will allow users to enter the number(s) in question. The automated system will, in turn, provide information regarding the inputted values. Like Fonefinder.net, NPAC may not inform the user of who is actually servicing the number. In fact, if the number has never been ported, it may only indicate through the automated system, "That number has not been ported." This response will require some additional research, and again a phone call to one of the MNOs to determine who is servicing the number. The opposite response from NPAC will be listing who is servicing the number and providing a phone number for law enforcement to call.

SEARCH.ORG

Our next step is taking the results from Fonefinder.net or NPAC and validating the number is actually with that carrier and also confirming their legal information is up to date. The Website Search.org can be utilized to look up the carrier. Fig. 3.5 shows how to navigate from the Resources tab and select ISP List.

This selection will allow access to an alphabetical listing of various providers. This listing is not limited to wireless carriers and contains a number of other useful businesses one may encounter in other types of investigations (Fig. 3.6). Some providers may have more than one section that can be accessed. Fig. 3.7 shows the points of contact for Verizon.

Once the specific business has been located, information will be revealed where legal compliance can be sent and faxed. This information may pertain to more than one area of the business, and in some cases with wireless providers also include exigent contact information. In any case, it is imperative that confirmation is made by phone with an actual "live" representative. The reasons are twofold:

1. Validate that the target number actually is being serviced by the carrier for the specific period requested.
2. Confirm that the address and fax number listed in Search.org is correct.

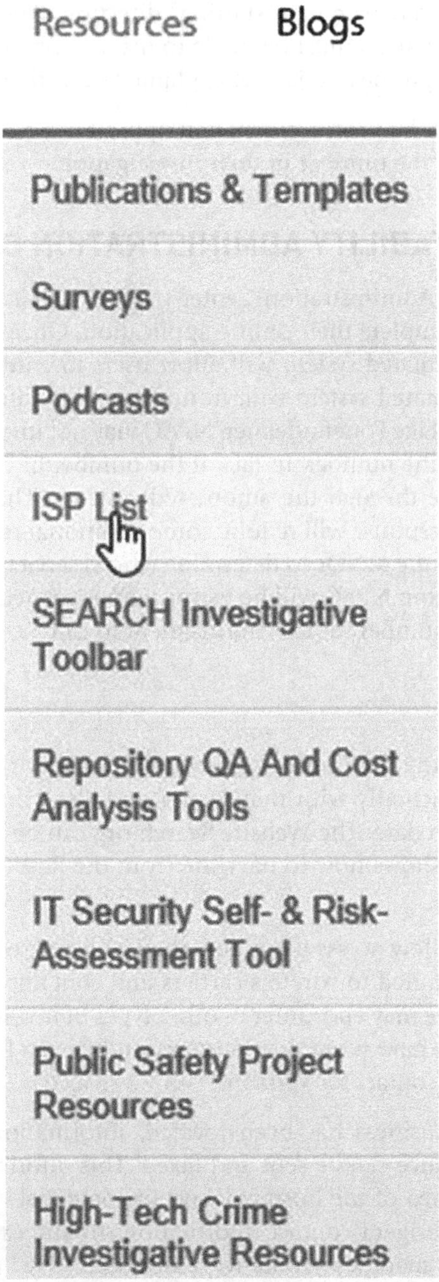

Resources   Blogs

Publications & Templates

Surveys

Podcasts

ISP List

SEARCH Investigative
Toolbar

Repository QA And Cost
Analysis Tools

IT Security Self- & Risk-
Assessment Tool

Public Safety Project
Resources

High-Tech Crime
Investigative Resources

FIGURE 3.5
Search.org ISP list.

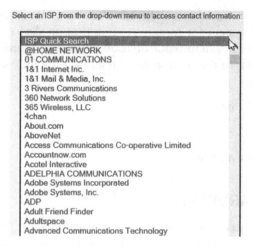

Select an ISP from the drop-down menu to access contact information:

```
ISP Quick Search
@HOME NETWORK
01 COMMUNICATIONS
1&1 Internet Inc.
1&1 Mail & Media, Inc.
3 Rivers Communications
360 Network Solutions
365 Wireless, LLC
4chan
About.com
AboveNet
Access Communications Co-operative Limited
Accountnow.com
Acotel Interactive
ADELPHIA COMMUNICATIONS
Adobe Systems Incorporated
Adobe Systems, Inc.
ADP
Adult Friend Finder
Adultspace
Advanced Communications Technology
```

FIGURE 3.6
ISP list dropdown menu.

Verizon FiOS
Verizon Internet Services
Verizon Landlines (North Central)
Verizon Online
Verizon Online in Vermont, Maine and New Hampshire
Verizon Telematics
Verizon Terremark (Cloud Service)
Verizon Wireless Legal Compliance

FIGURE 3.7
Example of multiple points of contacts.

After confirmation is made, your warrant or subpoena can be faxed. Phone contact with the business should take place a few minutes after the fax is complete. At this point, you will be inquiring if they received your legal request. It is not uncommon for the fax to have to be sent again. Do not rely on the confirmation remarks of the fax machine that was used as this only provides affirmation that it was sent, not necessarily received by an actual person. In some cases e-mailing is also a method of delivery. Providers such as Verizon will in many cases provide the requested data through a secured portal. They require the investigator to set up a password. Once they have compiled the information, they send a link to access the portal where a zipped container is usually located.

SUBSCRIBER IDENTITY MODULE

The subscriber identity module (SIM) has been around for many years. This small wafer-sized device contains information that allows the wireless handset to communicate on a particular network. Years ago, SIM cards would only be located in global system for mobile communication device. Today, with the advent of 4G networks, many code division for mobile access cell phones will also contain a SIM. In this section we will go over the following information related to the SIM:

- Internal (hardware)
- Sizes
- File system
- Stored evidence and values

INTERNAL HARDWARE OF A SIM

SIMs contain an internal chip which has various functions. Today these same sized chips are commonly embedded in credit cards and perform different functions than those located in cellular phones. Internally they work similar to a small computer, and as a computer have a processor, read-only memory (ROM), random access memory (RAM), electronically erasable programmable read-only memory (EEPROM), and an operating system (OS) as shown in Fig. 3.8.

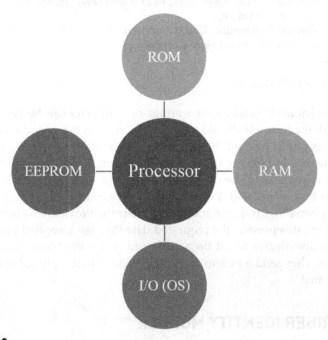

FIGURE 3.8

Diagram of internal SIM structure.

The **ROM** of the SIM holds the firmware, **OS**, and the applications needed. The **RAM** is also used for the OS as well as functionality for the applications. The **EEPROM** stores user data such as phone book entries; dialed numbers; and network information. It is important to understand that not all areas of the SIM allow the user to store information, and some areas have values placed by the carrier. These values in some cases are set during the manufacturing of the SIM. We will discuss these and how they can be used in various investigations.

THE SIM FILE SYSTEM

Internally, the SIM has a logical "parent–child" file system. This is similar to Windows, and the child file can contain artifacts useful to an investigator. Fig. 3.9 shows the logical structure that can be accessed with various forensic tools.

Not all SIM file systems will contain data in each of these folders. In many cases it will be up to the carrier, and with newer 4G phones, common entries such as phone book entries, short message service (SMS) are not by default stored on the SIM.

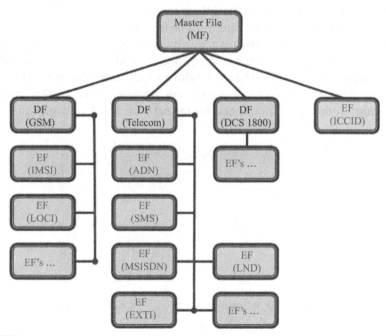

FIGURE 3.9
SIM file system.

SIM SIZES AND EVOLUTION

We will discuss the actual artifacts located with the file system, but first an overview of the sizes and evolution of the SIM will be briefly discussed.

- First form factor—**1FF**. The original SIM card was the size of a credit card. Fig. 3.10 shows an example (not actual) first generation SIM. This card size is no longer used for wireless handsets.
- Second form factor—**2FF**. This SIM is currently the most commonly encountered card today. Fig. 3.11 depicts two SIMs with the integrated circuit card identifier (ICCID) printed on the outside of the card. This practice has become common among many of the wireless carriers.
- Third form factor—**3FF**. This is commonly referred to as the "micro-SIM." This SIM version began appearing to field the need for 4G speeds. It is still very common today. Like previous versions, it still uses the same part of the chip but removes some of the plastic area around the mainboard(Fig. 3.12).
- Fourth form factor—**4FF**. This can also be referred to as the "nano-SIM." Like the version before it, it still utilizes the same chip area and removes even more of the surrounding plastic, Fig. 3.13.
- Embedded SIM—**eSIM**. This has not officially been named 5FF, nor has it began to become commonplace within the US market. Currently, most devices that contain SIM cards allow for user removal. Typically, they can insert another SIM that allows service to the handset. Unless the device is unlocked, the SIM card must be from the MNO or MVNO that services the phone. For instance, removing a 2FF allocated SIM card from a network locked T-Mobile, Samsung phone would allow for another 2FF allocated T-Mobile SIM to be used. With an embedded SIM, the SIM is not removable, and this allows the user to reactivate between carriers without having to purchase a specific SIM for the network. Fig. 3.14 depicts an eSIM.

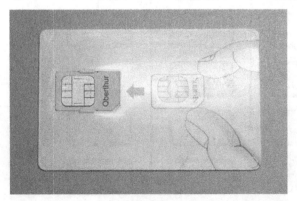

FIGURE 3.10
Example of 1FF SIM size.

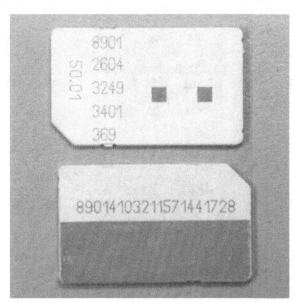

FIGURE 3.11
Example of 2FF SIM size.

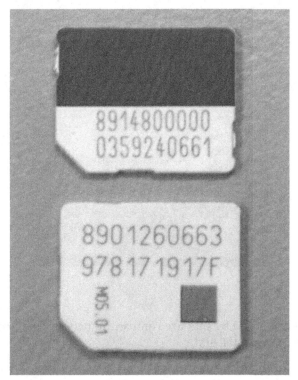

FIGURE 3.12
Example of 3FF SIM size.

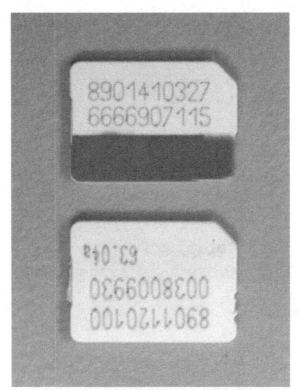

FIGURE 3.13
Example of 4FF SIM size.

FIGURE 3.14
Example of embedded SIM.

Fig. 3.15 provides a side by side size comparison between the first generation SIM size to the current 4FF SIM.

Many users who maintain their original 2FF SIM will typically cut the card down to the appropriate 3FF or 4FF size. Others use an adaptor when they move from one phone that supports the smaller size (4FF or 3FF) back to the

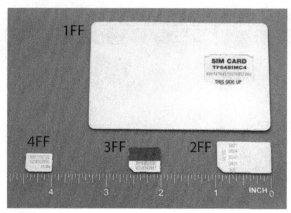

FIGURE 3.15
1FF through 4FF size comparison.

FIGURE 3.16
Examples of 3FF/4FF SIM adaptors.

larger 2FF. Fig. 3.16 shows an example of some of the cheap adaptors available. There are also adaptors that simply have the user cut out the paper holder depending on which size they need to read to.

TYPICAL EVIDENCE

As previously mentioned, not all SIM cards will have evidential data relevant to the investigation. This seems to coincide with the advancement of the smartphone—as the data that typically was found on the SIM file system is now being located within the memory of the phone. As an example, an Apple iPhone would not store the contacts on the SIM by default. The user would need to specify if they wanted the entry moved to the SIM. Also, SIM file systems by today's standards do not hold as much information that is available on a phone file system. Lastly, years ago SIMs were very convenient to the user, allowing them to keep their contacts and other data on the SIM, switch phones as needed and access the information. Today with cloud-based storage, the same transferring of user data applies, but now it

Item	Value	File
☑ Card Identity	8901260650034643690	EF_ICCID

FIGURE 3.17
ICCID value located within SIM file system.

Item	Value	File
☑ International Mobile Subscriber Identity (IMSI)	310260653464369 - United States	EF_IMSI

FIGURE 3.18
IMSI value located within SIM file system.

includes even more space as well as media that can't be stored within the SIM file structure.

If we go back and look at our file system on the SIM, we can find **Elementary File (EF)** areas that may contain potential artifacts that can assist with investigations. Here are the most common ways in which they can assist an investigator:

- **ICCID (Integrated Circuit Card Identifier) = EF_ICCID**

Fig. 3.17 is a screenshot from a forensic tool that utilizes a USB SIM card reader to access this data. The right side indicates the area within the file system the value(s) are stored. This value is typically 20 digits in length. The user can't change this value, and it is set by the manufacturer. Think of this value as the "serial number" to the SIM card. Similar to a vehicle identification number (VIN) on a vehicle, the ICCID value can be broken down.

- 89 represents the standard for telecommunication.
- 1–3 digits after the 89 represents the country code, followed by 1–3 digits for the issuer identifier.
- Remaining digits is the actual account number. Within these values is a check digit which is a calculation using the other values within the ICCID.
- ICCID values are not locked even when a user enables SIM security.

Using proper legal process, the ICCID can be traced back to the account and stays with the SIM even if the user changes cell phones. As long as the SIM is not changed, the ICCID stays the same.

- **IMSI (International Mobile Subscriber Identity) = EF_IMSI**

The IMSI value like the ICCID can be broken down to provide different values. Fig. 3.18 is an example of this value. This 15 digit value is all about "who" is paying for the services. The first three values represent the mobile country code, followed by the next two or three digits indicating the mobile network code. The last digits generally are 10 numbers in length and comprise the mobile

Item	Value	File
☑ Abbreviated Dialling Number 1	Teto : 2533102	EF_ADN
☑ Abbreviated Dialling Number 2	Chio : 8183899	EF_ADN
☑ Abbreviated Dialling Number 3	Nevada : 7752250	EF_ADN
☑ Abbreviated Dialling Number 4	Yolièn : 360540	EF_ADN
☑ Abbreviated Dialling Number 5	Yda : 0115214531	EF_ADN
☑ Abbreviated Dialling Number 6	Bagdad : 206432	EF_ADN
☑ Abbreviated Dialling Number 7	Bld : 831512	EF_ADN
☑ Abbreviated Dialling Number 8	Scrrt : 01152145353	EF_ADN
☑ Abbreviated Dialling Number 9	Cac : 2532328	EF_ADN
☑ Abbreviated Dialling Number 10	Roldo : 2532121	EF_ADN
☑ Abbreviated Dialling Number 11	Rglo : 509440	EF_ADN
☑ Abbreviated Dialling Number 12	B : 253882	EF_ADN
☑ Abbreviated Dialling Number 13	Kta : 12533815	EF_ADN
☑ Abbreviated Dialling Number 14	Trsa : 1253302	EF_ADN
☑ Abbreviated Dialling Number 15	Pn : 2532673	EF_ADN
☑ Abbreviated Dialling Number 16	Clts : 2536830	EF_ADN
☑ Abbreviated Dialling Number 17	Pdno : 3602399	EF_ADN
☑ Abbreviated Dialling Number 18	Mrno : 3607902	EF_ADN
☑ Abbreviated Dialling Number 19	Val : 8317402	EF_ADN
☑ Abbreviated Dialling Number 20	Chls : 408422	EF_ADN

FIGURE 3.19
ADN value located within SIM file system.

subscriber identification number. This value is set by the manufacturer and like the ICCID the user can't change it.

- IMSI values like ICCID values are always different on each SIM card
- Most SIM's will have an IMSI and ICCID value
- **ADN (Abbreviated Dialing Numbers) = EF_ADN** (Fig. 3.19)

The ADN area is also called "contacts" or "phonebook." These entries are set by the user and can be erased and written over. The ADN area is limited to 250 entries. When a user stores an entry and then deletes it, the next entry does not fill the blank slot but goes to the next open "ADN" position. The deleted entry slots are not filled until all 250 slots are used, starting over with the lowest blank opening. As an example from the ADN list above, if "Nevada" was deleted, and "Jimmy" was added, it would fill the highest open slot first. If all 250 slots were used at the time "Nevada" was deleted, then the new entry (Jimmy) would have to be stored in the same slot.

- **LND (Last Number Dialed) = EF_LND** (Fig. 3.20)

The LND area is limited to 10 slots. This can record the phone number that was last dialed on the handset. It is important to note that when a user dials 9-1-1 as the last number dialed, this area may not populate with the same value. Dialing 9-1-1 does not need an allocated phone, and as such may not record typical values to the SIM file system when the call is being routed.

Item	Value	File
☑ Last number dialled 1	2535036	EF_LND

FIGURE 3.20
LND value located within SIM file system.

Item	Value	File
☑ Forbidden PLMN 1	20408 - Netherlands, KPN Telecom B.V.	EF_FPLMN
☑ Forbidden PLMN 2	20412 - Netherlands, BT Ignite Nederland B.V.	EF_FPLMN
☑ Forbidden PLMN 3	20420 - Netherlands, Dutchtone N.V.	EF_FPLMN
☑ Forbidden PLMN 4	20416 - Netherlands, BEN Nederland B.V.	EF_FPLMN

FIGURE 3.21
FPLMN value located within SIM file system.

Item	Value	File
☑ Location Area Identity (LAI) area code	A1 5E	EF_LOCI
☑ Location Area Identity (LAI) network code	31026 - United States	EF_LOCI
☑ Location Update Status	updated	EF_LOCI
☑ TMSI timestamp	FF	EF_LOCI
☑ Temporary Mobile Subscriber Identity (TMSI)	0A 76 CB 3E	EF_LOCI

FIGURE 3.22
LOCI value located within SIM file system.

- **FPLMN (Forbidden Public Land Mobile Network) = EF_FPLMN** (Fig. 3.21)

The FPLMN can record values that either show where the phone tried to obtain network service or areas that are flagged as forbidden directly by the manufacturer. These values may aid an investigator when a device was near a specific network but was denied services. An example would be a phone in the United States but is close enough to a Canadian network. The network in Canada would be able to "see" that the device is requesting service, but would not allow it based on the allocated SIM for the wireless target it was servicing (example: T-Mobile/AT&T). The Canada network values would be stored within the FPLMN area. Again, this value stays with the SIM card even when the user moves the SIM to another handset.

- **LOCI (Location Information) = EF_LOCI** (Fig. 3.22)

The LOCI area retains values as to where the device was last powered down. A Temporary Mobile Subscriber Identity (TMSI) changes as the device moves around or away from the home location registry (HLR). The TMSI is linked to the HLR. With proper legal authority, investigators can determine the tower information that the handset last used before it lost power or was shut down by the user. This information does not always provide an exact location, but can get an investigator in the area where the tower(s) were located.

There is also a visitor location registry (VLR). Within this VLR database is some of the overall information related to the subscriber. This can include the ICCID, TMSI, and services allowed to name a few. The HLR database is a complete profile of the user, containing all the information related to the account. Phones will only have one HLR, but can have numerous VLRs—and thus numerous TMSIs. An examiner can examine a SIM card multiple times after it has traveled to various geographical areas where supported towers reside, and the TMSI value will be recorded different each time.

- **Short Message Service (SMS) = EF_SMS** (Fig. 3.23)

EF_SMS allows up to 30 entries to be stored. The entries can include SMS that is flagged as deleted. Using forensic tools, an examiner can look at the SMS in hex, the first byte will represent the value of the "status flag" for that particular message (Fig. 3.24). In these entries, messages show as (in) or (del) (Fig. 3.24). Within the first byte, those represent 01 (inbox) or 00 (deleted) as depicted in Fig. 3.25.

There are more status flags than just the two depicted. Read, draft, sent, and unread would be examples of some of the others. SMS entries like ADN need to fill 30 slots before deleted entries are written over. Also, messages that do get written over do not contain slack space. The unused bytes of the message are filled with FF's.

- **MSISDN (Mobile Station International Subscriber Directory Number) = EF_MSISDN** (Fig. 3.26)

The MSISDN is also referred to as the assigned phone number. This is the actual number the handset would use for mobile communications. This value and SMS entries are the most commonly requested artifacts from SIM cards. There will be many occasions when the MSISDN value is not located on the SIM. This seems to occur more with the 4FF (4G) SIM cards.

In concluding this area regarding the SIM file system, it is important to remember that there are many other areas within the SIM file system that were not discussed. This content was limited to areas that seem to yield the most evidential data. Also, the technical aspect plays into what investigators may locate. Many of the EF artifacts will pertain to network authentication. In many cases it will be carrier specific. It would take more than just a few pages (and a network engineer) to explain all the common artifacts related to network authentication, with the ending result being that its purpose is just that; to provide service to the device it is inserted into. Again, a reminder not to expect always to find

Item	Value	File
☑ Short Message 1	(in) Como estas tu y tu novia	EF_SMS
☑ Short Message 2	(in) Amor ya bienes x mi	EF_SMS
☑ Short Message 3	(in) Ok amor	EF_SMS
☑ Short Message 4	(in) Oye que pasa con tu cel no se oye nada	EF_SMS
☑ Short Message 5	(in) Hi amor dond andas papi	EF_SMS
☑ Short Message 6	(in) Call......andy	EF_SMS
☑ Short Message 7	(del) Y tambien ya tengo novio	EF_SMS
☑ Short Message 8	(del) Y estas con yolanda todavia?	EF_SMS
☑ Short Message 9	(del) Free T-Mobile MSG: Get unlimited text, video, and...	EF_SMS
☑ Short Message 10	(del) Hola mijo ! How are you?	EF_SMS
☑ Short Message 11	(del) Amor ya bienes con el almuerzo	EF_SMS
☑ Short Message 12	(del) Ok no traigas nancy trajo bienes x mi alas 3 y med...	EF_SMS
☑ Short Message 13	(del) Ok amor	EF_SMS
☑ Short Message 14	(del) Estoy en la escuela d mi hija ok{:J+Jazmin+J:}	EF_SMS
☑ Short Message 15	(del) Ya voy amor	EF_SMS
☑ Short Message 16	(del) Amor no t pueden traer para mi trabajo para ir ala...	EF_SMS
☑ Short Message 17	(del) Ok m avisas	EF_SMS
☑ Short Message 18	(del) Tampoco vas air aq t soben?	EF_SMS
☑ Short Message 19	(del) Porque Colgaste que querias	EF_SMS
☑ Short Message 20	(del) Ok mi amor q dios t acompaÑe	EF_SMS
☑ Short Message 21	(del) Ya le llame mi amor cuidate mucho t quiero muc...	EF_SMS
☑ Short Message 22	(del) Yo tambien amor muchos besitos como ati t gust...	EF_SMS
☑ Short Message 23	(del) Oye llamasterte quieres contesta	EF_SMS
☑ Short Message 24	(del) Amor si t fuiste	EF_SMS
☑ Short Message 25	(del) Esta bien feo y frio mi amor cuidateme mucho ya...	EF_SMS
☑ Short Message 26	(del) Mi amor se t olvido el cell y toda la tarde a estado...	EF_SMS
☑ Short Message 27	(del) Sorry, I'll call later	EF_SMS
☑ Short Message 28	(del) Oye cuando te sobre un minuto para mi me lo pu...	EF_SMS
☑ Short Message 29	(del) Hi amor como andas ?	EF_SMS
☑ Short Message 30	(del) Amorcito x q no m contestas t extraÑo amor	EF_SMS

FIGURE 3.23
SMS value located within SIM file system.

each of these items on every SIM, but instead make a habit out of expanding the file system and determining if they might be there and assist with your investigation.

SIM SECURITY—PIN AND PUK

SIM cards allow the user an option to enable security. This is called a SIM **PIN** (personal identification number). Typically the user would use the GUI of the phone to enable the PIN. Some manufacturers have a default PIN value set with new SIM cards. Numbers such as 0000, 1234, or the last four digit of the

EF_SMS
EF_CCP
EF MSISDN

Short Message 3   (in) Ok amor   EF_SMS
Short Message 4   (in) Oye que pasa con tu cel n... EF_SMS

Hex	Content	
00000000	01 07 91 41 40 54 05 10 F1 04 0B 91 31 06 45 00	..◻A@T..ñ..◻1.E.
00000010	04 F0 00 00 01 21 51 81 13 00 2B 07 CF 35 28 DC	.ð...!Q◻..+.Ï5(Ü
00000020	7E CB 01 FF FF FF FF FF FF FF FF FF FF FF FF FF	~Ë.ÿÿÿÿÿÿÿÿÿÿÿÿÿ
00000030	FF FF FF FF FF FF FF FF FF FF FF FF FF FF FF FF	ÿÿÿÿÿÿÿÿÿÿÿÿÿÿÿÿ
00000040	FF FF FF FF FF FF FF FF FF FF FF FF FF FF FF FF	ÿÿÿÿÿÿÿÿÿÿÿÿÿÿÿÿ
00000050	FF FF FF FF FF FF FF FF FF FF FF FF FF FF FF FF	ÿÿÿÿÿÿÿÿÿÿÿÿÿÿÿÿ
00000060	FF FF FF FF FF FF FF FF FF FF FF FF FF FF FF FF	ÿÿÿÿÿÿÿÿÿÿÿÿÿÿÿÿ
00000070	FF FF FF FF FF FF FF FF FF FF FF FF FF FF FF FF	ÿÿÿÿÿÿÿÿÿÿÿÿÿÿÿÿ
00000080	FF FF FF FF FF FF FF FF FF FF FF FF FF FF FF FF	ÿÿÿÿÿÿÿÿÿÿÿÿÿÿÿÿ
00000090	FF FF FF FF FF FF FF FF FF FF FF FF FF FF FF FF	ÿÿÿÿÿÿÿÿÿÿÿÿÿÿÿÿ
000000A0	FF FF FF FF FF FF FF FF FF FF FF FF FF FF FF FF	ÿÿÿÿÿÿÿÿÿÿÿÿÿÿÿÿ

FIGURE 3.24
Inbox (01) status flag byte value.

EF_SMS
EF_CCP
EF MSISDN

Short Message 14   (del) Estoy en la escuela a mi ... EF_SMS
Short Message 15   (del) Ya voy amor   EF_SMS
Short Message 16   (del) Amor no t pueden traer ... EF_SMS

Hex	Content	
00000000	00 07 91 21 60 13 03 20 F8 04 0B 91 31 06 45 00	..◻!`.. ø..◻1.E.
00000010	04 F0 00 00 01 21 41 51 93 61 2B 0B D9 30 C8 FE	.ð...!AQ◻a+.Ù0Èþ
00000020	CE 83 C2 ED B7 1C FF FF FF FF FF FF FF FF FF FF	Î◻Âí·.ÿÿÿÿÿÿÿÿÿÿ
00000030	FF FF FF FF FF FF FF FF FF FF FF FF FF FF FF FF	ÿÿÿÿÿÿÿÿÿÿÿÿÿÿÿÿ
00000040	FF FF FF FF FF FF FF FF FF FF FF FF FF FF FF FF	ÿÿÿÿÿÿÿÿÿÿÿÿÿÿÿÿ
00000050	FF FF FF FF FF FF FF FF FF FF FF FF FF FF FF FF	ÿÿÿÿÿÿÿÿÿÿÿÿÿÿÿÿ
00000060	FF FF FF FF FF FF FF FF FF FF FF FF FF FF FF FF	ÿÿÿÿÿÿÿÿÿÿÿÿÿÿÿÿ
00000070	FF FF FF FF FF FF FF FF FF FF FF FF FF FF FF FF	ÿÿÿÿÿÿÿÿÿÿÿÿÿÿÿÿ
00000080	FF FF FF FF FF FF FF FF FF FF FF FF FF FF FF FF	ÿÿÿÿÿÿÿÿÿÿÿÿÿÿÿÿ
00000090	FF FF FF FF FF FF FF FF FF FF FF FF FF FF FF FF	ÿÿÿÿÿÿÿÿÿÿÿÿÿÿÿÿ
000000A0	FF FF FF FF FF FF FF FF FF FF FF FF FF FF FF FF	ÿÿÿÿÿÿÿÿÿÿÿÿÿÿÿÿ

FIGURE 3.25
Deleted (00) status flag byte value.

Item	Value	File
☑ Own Dialling Number 1	Msisdn1 : 125329	EF_MSISDN

FIGURE 3.26
MSISDN value located within SIM file system.

cell phone number (MSISDN) are common. Once a SIM has the PIN value enabled, it can affect access to different parts of the operation system on the phone and at a minimum, not allow the SIM file system to be read when it is removed from the phone and examined using SIM forensic tools. Most SIM cards use a four digit PIN. Others can use five or six digits.

FIGURE 3.27
New T-Mobile SIM card with PUK value.

To override a lost, forgotten, or improperly entered user PIN, manufacturers also have a personal unlocking key (**PUK**). This is also referred to as personal unblocking key. Both definitions mean the same. A PUK value is not something a user can enable or change. It is set by the manufacturer. The PUK could be entered to unlock the PIN and allow users to reset their PIN value.

PIN and PUK values play into SIM forensics this way:

- Only the ICCID value can be read on a PIN-enabled SIM card.
- Law enforcement can request the PUK value on a PIN-enabled SIM. There are some stipulations to getting the PUK through the legal process. The phone associated with the SIM must be allocated. This means if the network terminated or discontinued service to the device, the PUK is generally also not retained.
- PUK management can be handled through some forensic tools. This means that examiners can change the PIN value if they get the PUK without having to utilize the GUI of the phone or assistance from technicians employed by the target wireless carrier.

Fig. 3.27 shows a SIM card issued by T-Mobile. The upper left side of the card displays the PUK code. Most users will discard the SIM holder and lose this value. The carrier would, in turn, have this information.

Some SIM cards have PIN1 and PIN2 access. PIN1 is only for SIM security. This would be the area a user stores their four digit number. PIN2, when unlocked, allows the user to access the additional data areas such as EF_ADN.

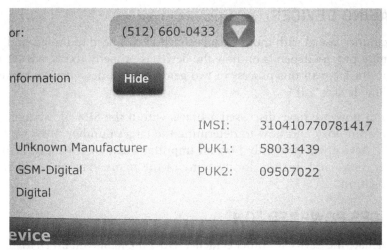

or: (512) 660-0433

nformation   Hide

	IMSI: 310410770781417
Unknown Manufacturer	PUK1: 58031439
GSM-Digital	PUK2: 09507022
Digital	

evice

FIGURE 3.28
AT&T PUK1 and PUK2 values.

Not all carriers have this ability, and many allow users to access the ADN area without the need for managing the PIN2. Some carriers also have cards with PUK1 and PUK2 access. These allow different services to be unlocked on the card. Fig. 3.28 is from an AT&T SIM card. Notice the PUK1 and PUK2 values for this card.

SIM security is generally something the user does not give much thought to until they have locked their own phone and have the need to contact the carrier to regain access (PUK). For the forensic examiner, a locked SIM will require legal process to be served on an active account to reset the PIN through the use of the PUK value. Depending on the account status, there will be times when this is not possible, as previously mentioned.

FORENSIC SIM

There is an advanced process that can be utilized when an examiner encounters a SIM card that has a user-enabled PIN enabled, and the PUK is not available. Many logical forensic tools cannot access the file system unless the SIM is unlocked or the user enables/disables a setting within the phone first. The process reads the ICCID value, which is not locked by the user PIN. The ICCID value contains derivatives of the IMSI and can be created using the values along with the country and network codes. Once the examiner extrapolates the IMSI, the ICCID and IMSI are written to a forensically sterilized card. This card is then placed into the handset, and the phone believes it is "seeing" the correct (original) SIM. This allows the exam to continue and also network isolates the device as the SIM does not contain any allocation data—only the ICCID and IMSI. Of course, the potential data on the evidential SIM is still locked, but at least the handset can be examined using this method if the SIM PIN originally prevented forensic processing.

TRIAGING DEVICES

An examiner tasked with mobile data extraction will need to understand that the entire process depends on how the device is properly recovered. We will explain the steps in this process in two general categories—devices powered "on" and devices "off."

Up until now, we have discussed artifacts within the SIM file system, various terminology and how to determine the target number. How we handle the device will generally play an important role in if we can actually recover data—and in turn, locate some of the items that can assist in an investigation.

DEVICES POWERED "ON"

- Evaluate the device for other evidence. Does the item contain DNA, fingerprints, blood, etc.? If your case dictates, you may want to collect this evidence first. It is important to understand this step and the next step are interchangeable as what may be required as the first, most important step with live devices.
- Remove the device from all wireless connectivity. Network, Bluetooth, WIFI must be deactivated. If the phone does not have internal settings to disable network (example—airplane mode), you must utilize tools to stop the signal. Examples of items that stop signals are aluminum foil (minimum three wraps), Faraday bags, mesh, or Ramsey Box. Empty (new) paint cans with lids can also be used. Based on case law, you do not need a search warrant to enable airplane (or similar) mode, as you are preventing the destruction or altering of evidence.
- Keep the device powered on—and obtain your legal process. This step is intended for devices that have been used in violent felony offenses. It is important to understand that if the device is kept powered on you must get it to a charging source. The reason for keeping it powered on is to ensure you don't encounter a SIM PIN lock or other user enabled security if you were to simply power it off. Generally, the "legal process" is a search warrant, consent (to search), or exigent (emergency aid) circumstances.
- Perform the exam within your means—with the phone kept on. This is meant to address entities that may have no forensic tools, utilities, or hardware as well as those who do. Chapter "Mobile Extraction Issues" will provide examples of various common tools that can be used for mobile forensic exams.
- Power off the device and examine all removable media and SIM—outside of the phone. This again is targeted for those who have

little resources as well as a full forensic lab. The reason for examining removable media and SIM outside of the device is that the result may vary from what was captured with the items examined while inserted in the phone. Also, when examining removable media such as microSD cards, you must use a validated write blocker. The data stored on these cards uses FAT file format and the same steps utilized in computer forensics can be followed. SIM cards have the permission to write data to them removed and write blockers are not necessary.

- Validate your findings. The process of validating is often overlooked. There are simple methods that can be employed to validate the data that you locate.

  1. Visual. An example of visual validation would be when your forensic utility locates 12 SMS entries within its interface. You would in turn manually locate the same 12 SMS entries within the GUI of the device. This is the easiest and quickest form of validation.

  2. Obtain a CDR. A Call Detail Record is obtained by serving the wireless carrier legal process for all connecting and terminating actions. This will only apply if the data you pulled was delivered through an allocated phone that used the towers for "normal" delivery. This will not work on application data that was located.

  3. Cross-tool. Using more than one forensic tool, utility or program can help with this method. For instance, if you have Cellebrite, and it pulled 100 call logs and 12 images, and you also have Secure View Forensics, and it locates the same 100 calls and 12 images, you have just cross-tool validated the findings.

  4. Hand carve. Manually locating artifacts the forensic tool parsed or artifacts that the tool missed is a more complex way of validating. This will in most cases require a file system or physical binary pull. If you are new to mobile forensics, you may need to get additional training on how this is accomplished. Hand carving will also require more time and various understanding on such things as Epoch dates located on phones. Chapter "Mobile Extraction Issues" addresses dates and times located on mobile devices.

- Report your findings. The last step is to create a forensic report on what was recovered. This will include many of the steps listed earlier. An example would flow something similar to this:

> On October 10th 2015 at 1400 hours, I received a "live, powered on" mobile device from a homicide investigation. The device was brought to the lab wrapped in a Faraday mesh. I maintained the Faraday mesh and supplied power to the device while officers obtained a search warrant. At 1630 hours a Superior Court search warrant was obtained to search for stored data and other artifacts on the device. I used three utilities on the powered on device: Cellebrite Touch, Oxygen Forensic Suite and Secure View for Forensics. All three tools located and cross-validated 200 SMS, 36 MMS, 1278 calls, and 346 images. Once this was completed the device was powered off, and the microSD and SIM card were removed and examined outside of the phone. A validated USB write blocker was used to create a forensic image of the microSD. Once this was completed, Cellebrite Physical Analyzer was used to parse various data off the microSD image. The results were visually validated while the microSD card was still mounted to the USB write blocker. Once this was completed, Cellebrite Touch and SIM Card Seizure were used to examine the SIM card. Again, both tools validate the ICCID, IMSI, assigned phone number and 10 stored abbreviated dialing numbers. Once this was completed an overall PDF report was created along with an archive disc.

DEVICES LOCATED "OFF"

Mobile evidence that is recovered "off" may in fact be in standby or "sleep" mode. Individuals tasked with recovering these items should first ensure the evidence is actually off. This can usually be accomplished by touching one of the buttons. If the device screen comes on—then follow the previous steps for a "powered-on" device. Once confirmation is made that the device is off, follow these steps:

- Evaluate the device for other evidence. Does the item contain DNA, fingerprints, blood, etc.? If your case dictates, you may want to collect this evidence first.
- Keep the device off. The rule here is do not turn on the device until you are ready to do so. Exigent circumstances may change this step. If so be aware of Faraday issues.
- Obtain proper authority to access the device through your legal process. Again, this will generally be a search warrant, consent to search or exigent circumstances. If possible, remove the battery and charge it outside of the phone with a generic charger. Be aware that if you charge certain devices that do not have removable batteries such as many Apple products or Blackberry's, they will connect to the wireless network once the battery reaches a certain percentage in its charge. If you are going to charge the device, make certain you follow Faraday steps to prevent this from occurring.

- Search removable media and SIM first—within your means. Just opposite of a powered on device, you need to remove media and SIM if equipped and search them outside of the phone, again using a validated USB write blocker for the media.
- Place original media and SIM back into the phone, power on, Faraday and perform extraction within your means.
- Validate your findings (follow validation steps listed under powered on device).
- Report your findings (follow steps outlined under powered on device).

ALWAYS FARADAY BEST PRACTICES—EVEN WHEN PEOPLE COOPERATE

During a homicide investigation, the spouse of a suspect has been taken to the police station with her smartphone. She was very cooperative during her interview, even implicating her husband. She agreed to allow have her phone examined, signing a consent to search. Based upon the cooperative nature of her, the investigators did not Faraday the device—which was equipped with an internal airplane mode. Halfway through the file system pull, an over-the-air (OTA) wipe command came through the phone—and it began to wipe the phone. Investigators were unable to stop the process in time, and the data was fully wiped from the phone. She later confessed that her husband was going to remotely wipe the phone during her contact with law enforcement.

This should be a reminder that regardless of how cooperative anyone appears to be, always follow proper steps to Faraday devices during forensic exams.

MANUAL EXAMS

Chapter "Mobile Extraction Issues" will discuss various tools that can be used to pull user data and artifacts off mobile devices. Here are common reasons for manual exams or screen shots associated with manual exams:

1. The device is not supported by the tool, program, or utility. Even with a lab that is equipped with every available forensic hardware and software extraction device, some phones will still not be supported. This is very common with simple, pay-as-you-go devices or brand new devices.
2. USB port is locked down. Many pay-as-you-go devices also lock down the data port. The port can only be utilized to charge the phone—not transfer data. The main reason behind this is OTA sales. By locking down the data port, the owner of the phone must purchase extras for the phone through the carrier. Common items purchased will be music, ringtones, screen savers, and applications.
3. Forensic program or tools do not support everything. This is very common. As an example, you connect a Samsung flip phone to Mobile Phone Examiner Plus (MPE+) and it only supports the extraction of call history—missing the SMS that is needed. There is no other tool in your

lab to perform additional extractions and you would need to document *manually* the SMS.

4. Carved artifacts, settings, or a locked file. There will be times when examiners will need to carve *manually* and decode specific artifacts that were either missed by the forensic tool or deleted. Other times the need to show a specific setting as being enabled/disabled/on/ off, etc., will be needed. Some files will also be locked, and can't be opened or don't contain user data. An example would be a pay-as-you-go phone that has no media files in the "media" folder. Documenting the lack of data is just as important as documenting data that is present.

TOOLS AVAILABLE

There are several commercially available hardware and software solutions for manual exams. Here are a few (with descriptions) that are commonly used by law enforcement.

Cellebrite USB Camera

This USB camera is designed to interface with Cellebrite Touch and Cellebrite's Universal Forensic Extraction Device (UFED) 4 PC. It takes both still images and video through the GUI of their programs. It can also be plugged in as a standard PC web camera. Fig. 3.29 shows the optional equipment (not sold) with the camera.

FIGURE 3.29
Cellebrite's USB camera.

Fernico ZRT

Fernico has been in the manual capture business for quite some time. They offer a complete hardware and software kit (Fig. 3.30). The software allows the user to capture images specific to the type of data located on the phone (SMS/MMS/ Calls/Images/etc.). The image can then be stored in that field and saved or printed as a complete report. Included in their kits are a desktop mount, foot pedal, a glare shield with high-resolution digital camera capable of video capture.

Project-A-Phone

Paraben Corporation offers two different manual exam solutions called the *Project-A-Phone Flex* (Fig. 3.31) and *Project-A-Phone ICD 8000* (Fig. 3.32). Both

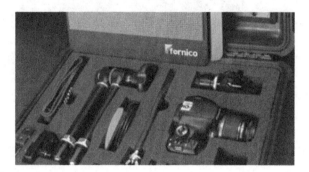

FIGURE 3.30
Fernico ZRT kit.

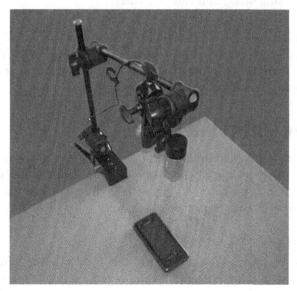

FIGURE 3.31
Project-A-Phone Flex.

FIGURE 3.32
Project-A-Phone ICD 8000.

models interface with software and also offer the ability for the user to document artifacts using image and video capture.

Eclipse Kit 3

The Eclipse Kit 3 is very similar to what users would find in the Fernico ZRT. Eclipse comes with the items pictured in Fig. 3.33 to include their own proprietary software for both image and video capture.

SOFTWARE SOLUTIONS

As previously mentioned at the beginning of this section, examiners will need to document specific settings when they are using a computer that has the forensic extraction installed on it. This will require a software based solution. There are many available. Here are two examples.

ScreenHunter

Wisdomsoft is the company that produces this product. They offer three versions—Free, Plus and Pro. Some of the noteworthy aspects of the free version versus paid are the free version does not allow the user to enable the .jpg

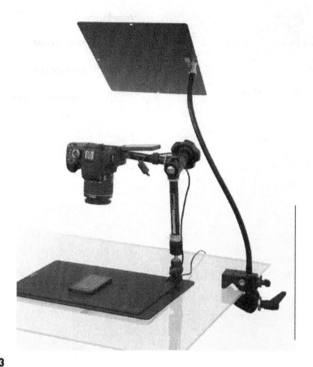

FIGURE 3.33
Eclipse kit 3.

resolution to 100%. It is enabled at 90% and can't be adjusted higher. The free version also prevents adjustment of the capture dialogue box. The user must click and drag over the desired area—getting the image exactly correct (Fig. 3.34).

Snagit
Snagit is one of the more popular screen capturing tools on the market. *TechSmith* makes Snagit and another popular screen video capturing utility called *Camtasia*. Unlike ScreenHunter, Snagit does not offer a free version of their product. Currently, they allow a 15 day full version demo (Fig. 3.35).

Other Options
Many of the hardware solutions covered in the previous pages can cost thousands of dollars. Instead, examiners can elect to utilize a simple digital camera, software such as Microsoft Word or Notepad, and a free PDF writer such as CutePDF. This would allow digital images to be captured, placed in Word (or Notepad), edited accordingly with notes, arrows, etc., and then printed to a lockable file format. The drawback to this is the workflow is much more time-consuming that the proprietary software offered by many of these tools.

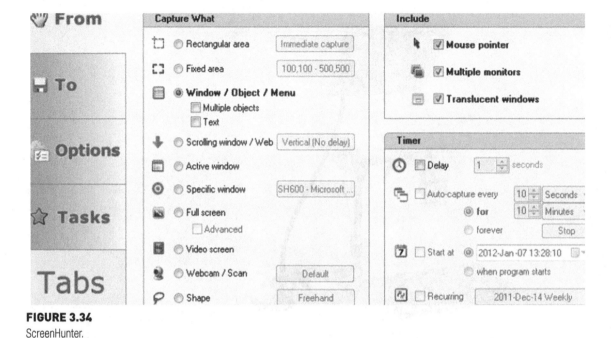

FIGURE 3.34
ScreenHunter.

FIGURE 3.35
Snagit.

CHAPTER SUMMARY POINTS

- Logical data—"What You See Is What You Get" and it generally tells its own story. Physical data—more complex, harder to read, requires more time and training.
- MNO's—maintain their own towers while MVNO's use the towers from MNO's.
- Determining your target number—use free online resources or resources for law enforcement to determine wireless carrier. Always confirm via a phone call before warrant or subpoena service.
- SIM's—Be aware of the various sizes and file system locations for possible evidential evidence: MSISDN, ICCID, IMSI, SMS, LOCI, FPLMN, ADN, and LND. Be aware of SIM security (PIN numbers) and how PUK's can be used.
- Triaging powered "on" devices—evaluate for other evidence processing, Faraday, obtain proper authority through your legal process, perform the exam, remove media and SIM and process, validate your findings and create a report. Powered "off" devices—evaluate for other evidence processing, obtain your legal process, perform the exam on removable media and SIM first, replace media and SIM, power on device/Faraday and perform the exam, validate findings and create a report.

Utilize manual exam tools, utilities or free methods as needed during the triage of powered "on" or 'off' devices.

REFERENCES FOR MANUAL TOOLS

http://shop.cellebrite.com/accessories/ufed-camera-kit-detail.html
http://www.fernico.com/ZRT3.aspx
http://www.project-a-phone.com/
https://www.edecdf.com/promo/eclipse/eclipse.php
http://www.wisdom-soft.com/products/screenhunter_free.htm
http://discover.techsmith.com/try-snagit/?gclid=CKTS9fKOu8gCFQ9rf god_VoEow

CHAPTER 4

Mobile Extraction Issues

In chapter "Triaging Mobile Evidence" we defined logical and physical memory. There are many logical, commercially available forensic tools currently on the market. Such names as **Cellebrite, Micro Systemation (XRY), Susteen Secure View For Forensics, Oxygen, AccessData's Mobile Phone Examiner Plus (MPE+)** are just a few of the commonly used products. These tools are straightforward in their approach at pulling logical data. The problem with logical data is that it is often times just a limited view on what is actually on the device. Most logical extractions are only going to a specific container location or offset and executing a command. If we can think of this analogy as a bucket, on a rope lowered down a well. The bucket is limited in size, and it can only get as much water as it is built to hold. What if we could get all of the water—and in some cases the entire well? Think of this as the physical pull—but first we must understand the well that contains our water.

FLASH MEMORY

There are currently many manufacturers of flash memory. Toshiba was the first inventor of this type of memory. It was called erasable programmable read-only memory, **EEPROM**. Dr. Fujio Masuoka was employed by Toshiba and invented both NOR (1984) and NAND (1987) memory. The original name given was simultaneously erasable EEPROM, but that name was soon changed to "flash" memory due to it being able to be erased like memory cells of a flash camera. Toshiba celebrated its 25th anniversary on the invention of NAND in 2012. Since its start in 1984, it has advanced its technology. It has breakthroughs in larger capacities, multi-level cell (MLC), solid-state drives (SSD), multi-bit per cell technology and in 2012, the world's largest density and smallest die size.

In almost every case, the individual user data such as short message service (SMS), call history, MMS, media (images/video/sound files), application data, chat messages, browser history, GPS data, and much more will reside where on a specific physical memory partition—located on a NAND or NOR chip. Today, most current smartphones will utilize specific types of NAND memory that will store the case artifacts. The path names that point to our typical evidence will be make and model specific, and will be subject to how the OS communicates with the processor and, in turn, the specific data in question. We will explain this in more detail and provide image examples of such like random access memory (RAM), processors, coprocessors, and dedicated video memory. One commonality will be that they all reside on a physical memory *type*. Most examiners who work in computer forensics understand that computers have a hard drive, and the hard drive communicates with the operating system (OS), and when the user deletes data, it generally goes to a location to be written over. Mobile devices in limited ways work similar—but are subject to a smaller storage area, and because of such limitations may require the OS to store and delete data differently. How examiners retrieve the data off mobile evidence is very different from computer forensics. In almost every case there is no "bit-by-bit" exact copy to work with, and forensic tools must be connected to a *live* (powered-on) device. The deleted data may be contained in an application database, or it may reside outside of the original container location. If something is deleted by the user the answer to **IF it can be recovered is always a resounding, MAYBE!** To understand the problems we will further expand on in this chapter, examiners must have some basic knowledge of the memory composition itself. As we go along, we will provide examples of the specific artifacts in question. First let's explain some of the benefits and shortcomings of two common types of memory **NOR** and **NAND**.

Here is a list of the common positive and negatives with NOR and NAND memory:

NOR—positives:

> + *Superior performance with random read and write functions.*
> + *Corrupted blocks is not generally an issue.*
> + *No bad blocks at the time of creation.*
> + *Allows random access to any area of the memory.*
> + *Low standby power needed.*
> + *Easy code execution.*

NOR—negatives:

> – *Long erase and write times.*
> – *Higher costs per bit.*
> – *Higher overall power.*

NAND—positives:

> + *Lower cost than NOR.*
> + *Requires significantly less power.*
> + *Low standby power*

NAND—negatives:

- *Shorter life; degrades quicker.*
- *Higher overall power.*
- *Less stable than NOR.*
- *Error correction code (ECC) required for bad blocks.*
- *Bad blocks at creation.*

After reading this comparison list, you may think that NOR would be today's most common choice for flash memory found in phones, instead it is currently NAND. Cost and function being the main reasons. With regards to function, the names NOR and NAND are derived from the negative-AND and negative-OR gates. Their differences are the way the cells are arranged. NOR provides them in parallel while NAND in series. The efficiency greatly increases when the cells are arranged in series. *Functional completeness* can be achieved when implementing a combination of NAND gates, which allows any Boolean function to be made. Unlike NOR, NAND is not randomly accessible and requires a controller.

EMBEDDED MULTIMEDIA CARD, EMBEDDED MULTICHIP PACKAGE, AND MULTICHIP PACKAGE

Depending on the model of the mobile device, it can contain a specific type of flash memory. Embedded multimedia card (eMMC) will generally contain the user data, to include the applications and OS. This eMMC area can have multiple partitions, and like removable microSD cards can have file allocation table (FAT) partition areas. There is no set size, however, similar to computer hard drives; the space on newer phones is often in somewhat similar increments—8, 12, 16, 32. Furthermore, the memory can reside on different areas. The mainboard can also have RAM, read-only memory (ROM), and a processor. Another way this can be presented is on an embedded multichip package (eMCP). Samsung designed this chip. It combines different configuration sizes of low-power DDR RAM with a NAND chip. It uses less power and takes up less space on the phone's mainboard.

What has also become common on newer phones is the technology that allows the processor (or coprocessor) to be affixed to the RAM. This cuts down on board real estate. This is also referred to as package on package (POP). Fig. 4.1 is an image of the mainboard from a Blackberry Bold 9650. The chip to the left is a Samsung and is a NAND BGA220A socket. The chip to the right is a POP. It consists of a Qualcomm processor and POP Samsung RAM. Fig. 4.2 depicts the RAM after it has been separated from the Qualcomm processor (left side of image) and the removal of the NAND memory (right side of image).

FIGURE 4.1
Mainboard of Blackberry Bold 9650.

In most cases, the NAND memory contains all the evidential information. The processor and RAM contents are not generally read for evidence but do contain data—however, it is typically executable data that generally holds input/output functions.

When examiners use commercially available forensic tools that support a physical acquisition, the tool will generally communicate with the processor or controller, and perform the function through starting and ending offsets in the memory or more common, a boot loader. The boot loader is not typically loaded into an area where it affects typically user installed (evidential) data such as contacts, SMS, call history, images, etc. Once the boot loader is loaded, the user can execute specific commands through the graphical user interface (GUI) of the software that placed the loader on the phone, which results in a binary pull. This type of forensic exam does not destroy the device. There can be system changes to all this. However, the changes are far removed from the partition that contains the items used as evidence. Most examiners can visually validate entries before the exam, and in turn, confirm the same entries were obtained by their forensic process. Actually showing where these changes take place requires a more thorough approach using specific utilities to show how the binary and system areas occurred. This will be discussed when we address validation. Mainboards can also contain coprocessors and dedicated video memory.

Fig. 4.3 is the mainboard from a Motorola XT912 with the heat shields removed. This uses a Toshiba or SanDisk eMMC NAND chip for the main OS and user

FIGURE 4.2
Random access memory (RAM) separated from Qualcomm Processor and NAND memory removed.

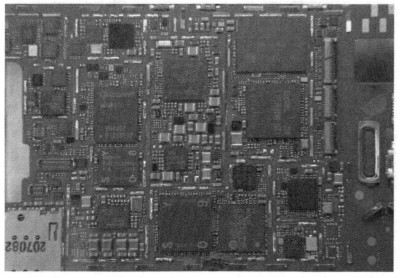

FIGURE 4.3
Mainboard Motorola XT912.

area of the phone. This memory area would contain all the evidence in a case. It also has a POP Samsung RAM chip, which is mounted on a Texas Instruments (TI) dual-core processor. There is also a TI coprocessor with another Samsung RAM chip packaged on top (POP), along with a chip that is used exclusively for dedicated video memory. Fig. 4.4 shows the removal of the RAM from the

FIGURE 4.4
Main Processor with package on package random access memory removed.

FIGURE 4.5
Coprocessor with package on package random access memory (RAM) removed.

main TI processor. Fig. 4.5 depicts the RAM removed from the TI coprocessor. Fig. 4.6 places the removed processors, RAM, dedicated video, and NAND memory side by side. The ball grid array (BGA) sides of each of these chips are shown in Fig. 4.6.

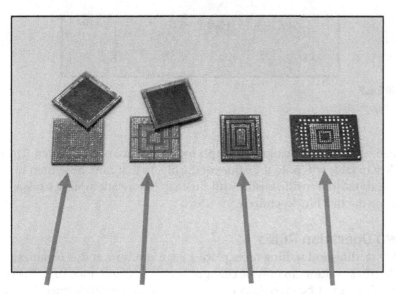

Processor & RAM   Co-processor & RAM   Video Memory   eMMC (NAND)

FIGURE 4.6
XT912 Processors, package on package random access memory, embedded multimedia card (NAND) and Video Memory.

THE FUNCTION OF NAND

We briefly explained some of the typical hardware that can be found on just a couple smartphone examples. Since the user-related data will be located on eMMC or eMCP configurations, we will discuss the function of the NAND. Internally, NAND memory can have a fixed number of blocks; each block has a set number of pages. For example, a small block would have a page 512 bytes of main data with 16 bytes of spare data. A larger block would have 2048 bytes of data with 64 bytes of spare data. Fig. 4.7 shows this correlation. The fixed number of blocks depends on the size of the device. The spare area is used for ECC, wear leveling, and other functions needed by the OS.

Pages are typically 512, 2048, or 4096 bytes in size. Based upon the page size, the corresponding spare areas are $512 = 16$, $2048 = 64$, $4096 = 128$.

The function of read and write is performed on a page basis. Input and output pins receive commands and address for a page to be read—there is specified delay, and then the selected page is loaded into data and spare registries.

"Bad blocks" can be a symptom with NAND memory. The bad block area cannot be written to nor erased. As mentioned previously, bad blocks may exist at birth (creation of NAND) or caused over time. The system is set up to address

FIGURE 4.7
NAND page example.

the bad blocks so that storage attempts to the area are not permitted. The bad block map table will hold the values of the blocks that can't be written to. Software and hardware will consult with the map before attempting storage, thus avoiding the bad blocks entirely.

NAND Operation Rules

NAND reading and writing takes place a page at a time and is organized into blocks. These values can only be changed from 1 to 0 and not 0 to 1. The single cell (1 or 0) can't be erased on its own and the entire block must be erased. Once this is accomplished, a block sets all bits to 1.

The delete and writing executions are subject to two algorithms that NAND flashes use. These are called *garbage collection* and *wear leveling*.

Wear Leveling and Garbage Collection

Flash memory efficiency deploys a process that allows the entire memory to degrade evenly over time. The hardware has a lifecycle; a certain number of read, write, and erase cycles. Wear leveling keeps this spread out, thus ensuring no one area degrades faster than another. This is referred to as *wear leveling*. Because of this, data may be held there until the cycle completes.

An additional controller over this process is the flash translation level (FTL). The various OS commands go to the FTL. The FTL prevents repeated writes to the same memory location. Data can't be written to areas in flash until the section is cleaned. This process sets the area to 1's. This particular function is called *garbage collection*.

Due to wear leveling and garbage collection, deleted data can reside within the hardware area (flash memory). Obviously, there are various conditions to all this. One factor would be when the data was deleted with the timing of the physical exam. A greater period of time that elapses the higher the likelihood that wear leveling and garbage collection has permanently deleted the target data in question. Others include the complexity and size of the memory on the device. Many flip and bar phones are not necessarily "smart" phones and have small (at times NOR) memory chips with OS sizes in the megabyte (MB) range. These types of phones do not have SQLite storage. Because of all this data on some phones can be deleted and not recovered through a physical exam.

SQLite Databases

Mobile OSs, such as those found on certain Blackberry, Apple, and Android devices can store information in SQLite databases. These containers have the ability to retain deleted artifacts within their own specific location for their function. We should think of a database as a small program that performs its own functions for the application it is designed for. For example, sms.db is a SQLite database for SMS. When a user deletes an SMS entry, it can remain at this specific location and in some cases may be recovered.

How Does All This Present Problems?

There are two major problems that face most examiners when attempting to recover physical data. The first issue is something that no one has any control over. That being the way in which the hardware (memory) performs its functions can play in the role of potentially recovering deleted artifacts. Examiners must understand this. There will be times that because of how the FTL works, no deleted data is available. Other times with the correct supported forensic tools (and supported phone) the hardware area will yield deleted results. The other area that may or may not yield results can be the software (databases). FATs such as FAT 12, 16, 32 as well as proprietary systems from such vendors as Nokia, Motorola, and others will serve as the platform for the OS. The FTL implementation, in turn, will communicate with the host OS or proprietary system and can combine functionality to utilize both hardware and software locations for data. Software areas will typically be the most common area where examiners can locate deleted data.

The second problem is the examiner's ability to access *even* the hardware or software areas. Besides not having supported tools and utilities, this is primarily caused by damage to the phone, user-enabled security that can't be bypassed by conventional commercial tools, and of course encryption.

ENCODING

Now that we have addressed the location of where user data may reside, what issues can be expected when we actually locate the data? Unlike computer forensics which generally has specific ways in which encoding can be interpreted, mobile device encoding can vary. This also includes date and times which we address later in this chapter.

The data that is recovered through a physical acquisition will at times need to be decoded. As previously addressed, data may reside in hardware physical memory, or software locations such as the previously mentioned SQLite databases. Here are the common types of encoding that will be found.

- Binary
- Hexadecimal
- Nibble
- American Standard Code for Information Exchange (ASCII)
- Unicode
- 7-bit GSM protocol description unit (PDU)

Binary

The lowest level of encoding is binary. Mobile devices like computers will contain bits that are either a "1" or a "0." This represents if the bit is on or off. 1 means the bit is on while 0 is off. A total of 8 bits equals 1 byte.

Binary to Decimal

The binary value can be converted to decimal, the total of 8 bits in a byte can hold a value if it is on or off. If all of the bits were on (in the 1 position) the total value would be 255. Fig. 4.8 is an example of the binary to decimal conversion in a byte.

Binary numbers can represent letters and characters. Standard ASCII charts can provide the decoded values without the need to manually covert them. It is important to understand that binary is one of the core encoding types, and knowing how to convert *manually* can help with validation.

Binary to Decimal Bit Value Table

(8 Bits in a Byte)

128	64	32	16	8	4	2	1
1 (On)	1 (On)	1 (On)	1 (On)	1 (On)	1 (On)	1 (On)	1 (On)
+ 128	+64	+32	+16	+8	+4	+2	+1

255

FIGURE 4.8

(1) Byte Binary to Decimal conversion example.

Hexadecimal

Four (4) binary digits represent hexadecimal. These four binary digits are known as a "nibble." Two nibbles equal a byte. This equates to eight binary digits. Fig. 4.9 shows two nibbles representing one-byte value. Binary values can also represent both letters and numbers. Fig. 4.10 represents the binary value of the letter "B" and also shows the breakdown of the nibble values for the same value representing the number 42.

American Standard Code for Information Exchange

ASCII tables can reflect all 256 codes (0–255). There will be 95 printable codes. 52 are US English codes with 26 lowercase and 26 uppercase. The remaining codes represent codes from the decimal 128 decimal values. This is commonly referred to the extended table. The most common table is the ISO 8859-1 which is also called the ISO Latin-1. Fig. 4.11 shows an ASCII character to binary table example. Fig. 4.12 is an example of a standard ASCII decimal–hexadecimal–character example. These are just two examples and do not include values from the extended ASCII table.

Unicode

Another type of encoding that examiners may see is called Unicode. Languages other than English were limited to the 256 codes of the ASCII. They could not fit into this limited space and developers created Unicode. This creates a 2 bytes number for every character, no matter what language is used. Using 16 bits (2 bytes), 65,536 characters can be defined, whereas 256 possibilities were possible with 8 bits (1 byte). One way to quickly recognize

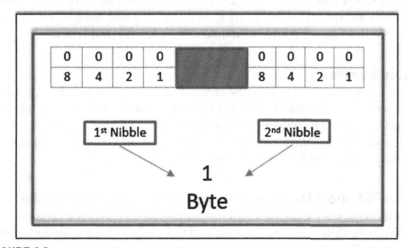

FIGURE 4.9
Nibble to byte value example.

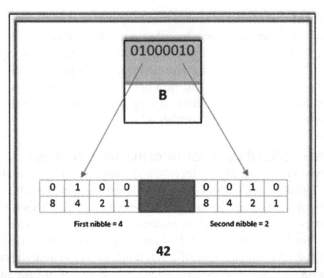

FIGURE 4.10
Binary to letter, Nibble to number example.

Unicode is to look for the 00 padding between the bytes. Fig. 4.13 is an example of Unicode.

Big and Little Endian

Additional formats called Big Endian (BE) and Little Endian (LE) relate to how data can be encoded. Both refer to a specific byte order. BE is the most significant byte being first while LE references the least significant byte being first. Both are read from left to right. Unicode can also have BE or LE byte order. Fig. 4.14 is an example of standard hexadecimal and Unicode.

Nibble Reversed

Nibble reversed is used to describe values that need to be switched in order to be decoded. This type of encoding can commonly be found in mobile file systems and is more prevalent in time some stamps. We will discuss in more detail about time stamps, but for now, Fig. 4.15 is an example to illustrate a nibbled reverse value from a Samsung GSM phone.

Seven-Bit Short Message Service Protocol Description Unit

Short message service protocol description unit (SMS PDU) is a message feature that uses 7 bits per character compared to 8 bits per character of traditional messaging. This efficiency allows 160 characters to fit into 140 bytes. This saves space during the sending and receiving of text messages.

ASCII Code: Character to Binary

0	0011 0000	O	0100 1111	m	0110 1101
1	0011 0001	P	0101 0000	n	0110 1110
2	0011 0010	Q	0101 0001	o	0110 1111
3	0011 0011	R	0101 0010	p	0111 0000
4	0011 0100	S	0101 0011	q	0111 0001
5	0011 0101	T	0101 0100	r	0111 0010
6	0011 0110	U	0101 0101	s	0111 0011
7	0011 0111	V	0101 0110	t	0111 0100
8	0011 1000	W	0101 0111	u	0111 0101
9	0011 1001	X	0101 1000	v	0111 0110
A	0100 0001	Y	0101 1001	w	0111 0111
B	0100 0010	Z	0101 1010	x	0111 1000
C	0100 0011	a	0110 0001	y	0111 1001
D	0100 0100	b	0110 0010	z	0111 1010
E	0100 0101	c	0110 0011	.	0010 1110
F	0100 0110	d	0110 0100	,	0010 0111
G	0100 0111	e	0110 0101	:	0011 1010
H	0100 1000	f	0110 0110	;	0011 1011
I	0100 1001	g	0110 0111	?	0011 1111
J	0100 1010	h	0110 1000	!	0010 0001
K	0100 1011	I	0110 1001	'	0010 1100
L	0100 1100	j	0110 1010	"	0010 0010
M	0100 1101	k	0110 1011	(	0010 1000
N	0100 1110	l	0110 1100	)	0010 1001
				space	0010 0000

FIGURE 4.11
Character to binary.

When an SMS is sent, encoding and decoding must take place. PDU mode uses three special data types: ctet, semi-octet, and septet. 7-bit PDU uses 7-bit septet which has to be converted to the octet string to transfer through the network.

Fig. 4.16 is an example of the binary to lower character representation of the two words: "hellohello." The table shows the lowercase letter at the top, the decimal version of the letter in the middle, followed below by the decimal 7-bit septet.

This message (**hellohello**) consists of 10 characters, called septets when represented by 7 bits each. For SMS delivery, these septets need to be converted into 8-bit octets for the transfer. This takes place by adding the rightmost bit of the second septet. This bit is inserted into the first septet, 1+1101000 = 11101000 (E8). The rightmost bit of the second character is then consumed, so the second character needs 2 bits of the third character to make an 8-bit octet. This

Decimal	Hex	Char	Decimal	Hex	Char	Decimal	Hex	Char	Decimal	Hex	Char
0	0	[NULL]	32	20	[SPACE]	64	40	@	96	60	`
1	1	[START OF HEADING]	33	21	!	65	41	A	97	61	a
2	2	[START OF TEXT]	34	22	"	66	42	B	98	62	b
3	3	[END OF TEXT]	35	23	#	67	43	C	99	63	c
4	4	[END OF TRANSMISSION]	36	24	$	68	44	D	100	64	d
5	5	[ENQUIRY]	37	25	%	69	45	E	101	65	e
6	6	[ACKNOWLEDGE]	38	26	&	70	46	F	102	66	f
7	7	[BELL]	39	27	'	71	47	G	103	67	g
8	8	[BACKSPACE]	40	28	(	72	48	H	104	68	h
9	9	[HORIZONTAL TAB]	41	29	)	73	49	I	105	69	i
10	A	[LINE FEED]	42	2A	*	74	4A	J	106	6A	j
11	B	[VERTICAL TAB]	43	2B	+	75	4B	K	107	6B	k
12	C	[FORM FEED]	44	2C	,	76	4C	L	108	6C	l
13	D	[CARRIAGE RETURN]	45	2D	-	77	4D	M	109	6D	m
14	E	[SHIFT OUT]	46	2E	.	78	4E	N	110	6E	n
15	F	[SHIFT IN]	47	2F	/	79	4F	O	111	6F	o
16	10	[DATA LINK ESCAPE]	48	30	0	80	50	P	112	70	p
17	11	[DEVICE CONTROL 1]	49	31	1	81	51	Q	113	71	q
18	12	[DEVICE CONTROL 2]	50	32	2	82	52	R	114	72	r
19	13	[DEVICE CONTROL 3]	51	33	3	83	53	S	115	73	s
20	14	[DEVICE CONTROL 4]	52	34	4	84	54	T	116	74	t
21	15	[NEGATIVE ACKNOWLEDGE]	53	35	5	85	55	U	117	75	u
22	16	[SYNCHRONOUS IDLE]	54	36	6	86	56	V	118	76	v
23	17	[ENG OF TRANS. BLOCK]	55	37	7	87	57	W	119	77	w
24	18	[CANCEL]	56	38	8	88	58	X	120	78	x
25	19	[END OF MEDIUM]	57	39	9	89	59	Y	121	79	y
26	1A	[SUBSTITUTE]	58	3A	:	90	5A	Z	122	7A	z
27	1B	[ESCAPE]	59	3B	;	91	5B	[	123	7B	{
28	1C	[FILE SEPARATOR]	60	3C	<	92	5C	\	124	7C	|
29	1D	[GROUP SEPARATOR]	61	3D	=	93	5D	]	125	7D	}
30	1E	[RECORD SEPARATOR]	62	3E	>	94	5E	^	126	7E	~
31	1F	[UNIT SEPARATOR]	63	3F	?	95	5F	_	127	7F	[DEL]

FIGURE 4.12
Decimal/hexadecimal/character.

```
00 00 00 00 07 00 00 00-00 00 00 00 A2 F1 5D 40
A2 F1 5D 40 44 00 69 00-64 00 20 00 75 00 20 00
67 00 65 00 74 00 20 00-74 00 68 00 65 00 20 00
67 00 75 00 6E 00 73 00-3F 00 00 00 00 00 00 00
00 00 00 00 00 00 00 00-00 00 00 00 00 00 00 00
```

FIGURE 4.13
Unicode example.

process continues until the entire string is complete and in the case of this example, has fitted the 10 septets into 9 octets. Fig. 4.17 shows the 7-bit septet hellohello SMS example being converted to 8-bit octet.

A completed 7-bit PDU message will generally have the SMS string, a time stamp, and the numbers involved in the message. If we take just the content of a PDU string, "Where did you bury the body?" This sentence would look like this: **00110000910000FF1C5774595E0691D36450FE5D0789EBF-23C888E2E83C46F72FE07**.

BE: 32 54

LE: 54 32

BE: 00 32 54 00

LE: 00 54 00 32

FIGURE 4.14
Big/Little Endian examples (with Unicode).

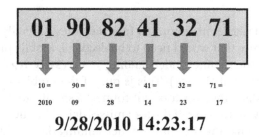

01 90 82 41 32 71

| 10 = | 90 = | 82 = | 41 = | 32 = | 71 = |
| 2010 | 09 | 28 | 14 | 23 | 17 |

9/28/2010 14:23:17

FIGURE 4.15
Six byte Nibble Reversed date and time stamp.

h	e	l	l	o	h	e	l	l	o
104	101	108	108	111	104	101	108	108	111
1101000	1100101	1101100	1101100	1101111	1101000	1100101	1101100	1101100	1101111

FIGURE 4.16
7-bit septet short message service example.

EPOCHS

Epoch has to do with a period or the origin in time. This can be used as the reference point from which that particular time is measured. For cell phone forensic examiners, this origin plays a role on how a particular series of bytes may be interpreted. UNIX dates typically originated in seconds starting since 1970-01-01. These means time that elapsed (in seconds) after January 1, 1970 at 00:00:00 GMT (Greenwich Mean Time). Simply stated, mobile times can have Epoch dates that have origins that differ from 1970, or are a specific format of 1970.

7 bit septets 10 character example start

1101000	1100101	1101100	1101100	1101111	1101000	1100101	1101100	1101100	1101111

8 bit octet converted – 9 character end

11101000	00110010	10011011	11111101	01000110	10010111	1100101		1110100	110111
E8	32	38	FD	46	97	D9		EC	37

FIGURE 4.17

7-bit septet conversion to 8-bit octet.

For investigators tasked with computer forensics, they generally deal with only a few date and times that would need to be decoded. Mobile phones are quite different and as such some understanding is necessary regarding common dates and their original (Epoch). This is one of the problems with decoding physical values. Many investigators will connect a specific tool to a phone and select what they want to parse. If the tool misses deleted values or the examiner needs to validate what the tool pulls, understanding date and time formats is important. A list of common dates and their Epoch periods are provided.

UNIX

A UNIX date is stored as a 32-bit integer and records the number of seconds since 1/1/1970.

Unix 48 bit

This particular Epoch is commonly located on Android devices. It is a date and time that uses a 6-byte integer which records the number of milliseconds since 1/1/1970.

UNIX Decimal 10 Byte

The UNIX decimal 10-byte format can commonly be found in chat messages on some phones. It is a 10-digit decimal representation of the number stored as 32-bit UNIX time. The date is very common in web-based applications and can be read without the use of specialized tools.

GPS

GPS is a UNIX-based time; however, the Epoch is the number of seconds since 1/6/1980.

AOL

The AOL date is just like a UNIX time but records seconds since 1/1/1980. The GPS and AOL dates can mistakenly be decoded as the actual date when hand carving for deleted values related to date and times. These two dates (GPS and AOL) vary in decoding by 5 days.

GSM

GSM, A.K.A: 7-bit PDU time is time format discussed earlier during encoding. It utilizes the septet and octet format. The time zone byte represents 15-min intervals between local time and GMT.

Decimal Format

Decimal format is model specific and is very similar to the GSM date, however, the year can be either 2 bytes of LE or BE.

64 bit

The 64-bit integer value that has 100 ns since 1/1/1601. This will be typical of Windows standard, in a BE format.

File Time Formatted

This has the same Epoch as the 64-bit integer but is represented by two 32-bit integers. There will usually be a separator between the values such as colon or period.

HTML

HTML will have an Epoch of 64-bit, formatted similarly to file time formatted date/time. However, the 32-bit values are swapped.

JAVA

This Epoch is in milliseconds since 1/1/1970 that uses 64-bit integer value.

MSDOS

MSDOS uses a 32-bit date and time which MSDOS and Windows FAT entry uses. The year, month, day, etc. is encoded with specific bits of the 32-bit time stamp. 1980 is the Epoch year and must be added to the date within specific bits which are 25 through 31.

Binary-Coded Decimal

The binary-coded decimal dates show as 6 bytes that represent the year, month, day, hour, minute, and seconds. They do not necessarily decode in the same order.

ISO 8601

An ISO 8601 date is easy to read, and is textually formatted as YYYY-MM-DD hh:mm:ss or YY-MM-DD hh:mm:ss.

Bit Date

This 32-bit integer can typically be found on some Samsung and LG devices that can have different components of the date specified by the integer. There are no seconds in this format and it is similar to the MSDOS/FAT date and time.

MAC Absolute

MAC absolute is also referred to as the Core Absolute (CF Absolute) time. This date is a 32-bit integer using the number of seconds since 1/1/2001 00:00:00 UTC (Universal Time Code).

As we can see, there are many file formats that can be found on mobile devices. This is not an exclusive list of Epoch dates; these happened to be more of the common ones found. Now we understand that a problem may arise when examiners do not understand some of the encoding and possible date formats. Let's address popular tools that are commonly used to locate and parse data and how we can address the problem of decoding what tools may miss that is usually deleted.

CELLEBRITE PHYSICAL ANALYZER

Undoubtingly, one forensics mobile extraction vendor that is extremely popular among law enforcement and private wireless carriers is Cellebrite. This Israeli-based company started its business by offering wireless carriers the ability to transfer data to the consumer when they purchase a new cellular phone. This service still continues, but years back they began offering tools and utilities that address the forensic need for law enforcement. Cellebrite has typically had relationships with the vendors of these phones and is allowed access to phone versions many times before they are released to the public. Law enforcement and other investigators can easily connect supported mobile devices to their products, follow the prompts and instructions, and obtain logical and physical data. But if we go back to encoding and Epoch, we can use parsed values to determine additional where additional artifacts can be found that were missed by forensic tools.

Project Tree Example

The information in this chapter is not necessary directed at investigators who utilize the popular Cellebrite tools and follow prompts to pull data. Instead, we attempt to address issues with how to use the interface to locate more data.

Cellebrite has a software tool that is utilized to parse physical, logical, and file system pulls. This is called Cellebrite Physical Analyzer. When investigators use this tool, it will show what was supported by the Project Tree of the interfaced. Fig. 4.18 shows a Samsung flip phone that was supported by Cellebrite Touch, a very popular tool used worldwide for mobile extractions. The data was then parsed using Physical Analyzer. What we see are the default areas that the tool supports within the Project Tree. Most examiners follow the GUI within Cellebrite, and pull what is supported.

In the example shown in Fig. 4.18, the popular interface shows only five SMS. This tool is very capable of locating deleted data, however, for it to parse the data and display it in the interface; it may still need to be in its original format for the tool to see it.

If we determine a value from the encoding, such as one of the phone numbers, we can search for that particular value and locate values the tool did not parse. Fig. 4.19 shows the same number being searched using ASCII. The search results locate a missed SMS which was related to a homicide and used to communicate with another number—**Kill joey**.

This same type of technique can be applied to any encoded value that investigators locate. Many people tasked with mobile extractions rely on what tool relates back as parsed or in some cases if supported deleted, parsed values. A problem here is that unless the examiner takes the time to determine the encoding, and search further, they may be missing artifacts. Most tools will only flag values as deleted if everything stays together nice and neat for the tool to see.

Multimedia Message Service

Multimedia message service stands for MMS. This is just like texting (SMS) but the user can attach an image, video, sound file, or other forms of media. Another problem that investigators may face is that many robust, expensive tools may not parse MMS. The main problem is that the data needed for parsing can be located in different locations. Also, many vendors concentrate decoding efforts to smartphones such as Android, iOS, BlackBerry, and Windows. Many suspects involved in violent criminal endeavors do not typically purchase these

Timestamp	Folder	Parties	Body	Status
6/4/2014 1:53:16 AM(UTC+0)	Inbox	2536253211	Hello	Unread
6/4/2014 1:51:50 AM(UTC+0)	Outbox	2536253211	Hello	Sent
6/4/2014 1:45:23 AM(UTC+0)	Inbox	2536254407	VZW-FREE-MSG: Your new Mobile number is 2536254407. Your...	Unread
6/4/2014 1:43:05 AM(UTC+0)	Inbox	2536254407	VZW-FREE-MSG: Your Account Security Code has been updated...	Unread
6/4/2014 1:43:02 AM(UTC+0)	Inbox	2536254407	VZW-FREE-MSG: $10.00 has been added to your account.	Unread

Project tree: Samsung CDMA_SCH-U365 GUSTO — Extraction Summary, Device Info, Images, Memory Ranges, File Systems, Analyzed Data (Contacts (7), SMS Messages (5))

FIGURE 4.18
Parsed data shown in the Project Tree of Physical Analyzer.

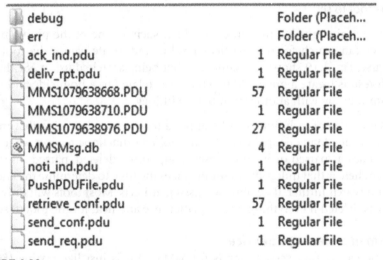

FIGURE 4.19
Values located using encoding from parsed data.

debug		Folder (Placeh...
err		Folder (Placeh...
ack_ind.pdu	1	Regular File
deliv_rpt.pdu	1	Regular File
MMS1079638668.PDU	57	Regular File
MMS1079638710.PDU	1	Regular File
MMS1079638976.PDU	27	Regular File
MMSMsg.db	4	Regular File
noti_ind.pdu	1	Regular File
PushPDUFile.pdu	1	Regular File
retrieve_conf.pdu	57	Regular File
send_conf.pdu	1	Regular File
send_req.pdu	1	Regular File

FIGURE 4.20
File System showing missed multimedia message service entries.

expensive devices. Instead, they typically will buy a "burner" device that can be disposed of and is cheap. Fig. 4.20 is a file system from a simple LG flip phone. A popular expensive law enforcement tool parsed call history, SMS, images, and videos. The tool, however, missed the MMS content.

If we look at Fig. 4.20, we can see that three MMS messages are stored on the phone, each showing with a PDU extension. If we examine these messages on this particular model phone, we can locate some of the content that was used in the message. The problem ,however, is that not all aspects of the message are within the PDU container for each message. Fig. 4.21 shows message titled, MMS1079638668.PDU expanded. Only the top of the message shown in Fig. 4.21.

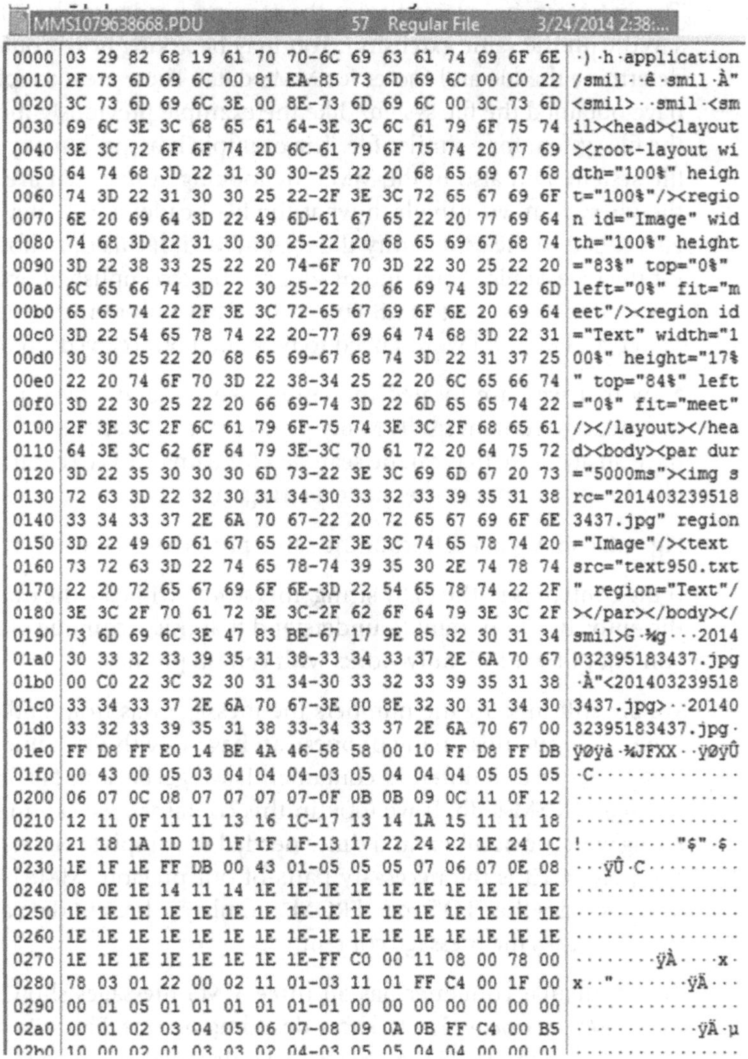

```
MMS1079638668.PDU        57  Regular File     3/24/2014 2:38:...
0000 03 29 82 68 19 61 70 70-6C 69 63 61 74 69 6F 6E  ·)·h·application
0010 2F 73 6D 69 6C 00 81 EA-85 73 6D 69 6C 00 C0 22  /smil··ê·smil·À"
0020 3C 73 6D 69 6C 3E 00 8E-73 6D 69 6C 00 3C 73 6D  <smil>··smil·<sm
0030 69 6C 3E 3C 68 65 61 64-3E 3C 6C 61 79 6F 75 74  il><head><layout
0040 3E 3C 72 6F 6F 74 2D 6C-61 79 6F 75 74 20 77 69  ><root-layout wi
0050 64 74 68 3D 22 31 30 30-25 22 20 68 65 69 67 68  dth="100%" heigh
0060 74 3D 22 31 30 30 25 22-2F 3E 3C 72 65 67 69 6F  t="100%"/><regio
0070 6E 20 69 64 3D 22 49 6D-61 67 65 22 20 77 69 64  n id="Image" wid
0080 74 68 3D 22 31 30 30 25-22 20 68 65 69 67 68 74  th="100%" height
0090 3D 22 38 33 25 22 20 74-6F 70 3D 22 30 25 22 20  ="83%" top="0%"
00a0 6C 65 66 74 3D 22 30 25-22 20 66 69 74 3D 22 6D  left="0%" fit="m
00b0 65 65 74 22 2F 3E 3C 72-65 67 69 6F 6E 20 69 64  eet"/><region id
00c0 3D 22 54 65 78 74 22 20-77 69 64 74 68 3D 22 31  ="Text" width="1
00d0 30 30 25 22 20 68 65 69-67 68 74 3D 22 31 37 25  00%" height="17%
00e0 22 20 74 6F 70 3D 22 38-34 25 22 20 6C 65 66 74  " top="84%" left
00f0 3D 22 30 25 22 20 66 69-74 3D 22 6D 65 65 74 22  ="0%" fit="meet"
0100 2F 3E 3C 2F 6C 61 79 6F-75 74 3E 3C 2F 68 65 61  /></layout></hea
0110 64 3E 3C 62 6F 64 79 3E-3C 70 61 72 20 64 75 72  d><body><par dur
0120 3D 22 35 30 30 30 6D 73-22 3E 3C 69 6D 67 20 73  ="5000ms"><img s
0130 72 63 3D 22 32 30 31 34-30 33 32 33 39 35 31 38  rc="201403239518
0140 33 34 33 37 2E 6A 70 67-22 20 72 65 67 69 6F 6E  3437.jpg" region
0150 3D 22 49 6D 61 67 65 22-2F 3E 3C 74 65 78 74 20  ="Image"/><text
0160 73 72 63 3D 22 74 65 78-74 39 35 30 2E 74 78 74  src="text950.txt
0170 22 20 72 65 67 69 6F 6E-3D 22 54 65 78 74 22 2F  " region="Text"/
0180 3E 3C 2F 70 61 72 3E 3C-2F 62 6F 64 79 3E 3C 2F  ></par></body></
0190 73 6D 69 6C 3E 47 83 BE-67 17 9E 85 32 30 31 34  smil>G·¾g···2014
01a0 30 33 32 33 39 35 31 38-33 34 33 37 2E 6A 70 67  032395183437.jpg
01b0 00 C0 22 3C 32 30 31 34-30 33 32 33 39 35 31 38  ·À"<201403239518
01c0 33 34 33 37 2E 6A 70 67-3E 00 8E 32 30 31 34 30  3437.jpg>··20140
01d0 33 32 33 39 35 31 38 33-34 33 37 2E 6A 70 67 00  32395183437.jpg·
01e0 FF D8 FF E0 14 BE 4A 46-58 58 00 10 FF D8 FF DB  ÿØÿà·¾JFXX··ÿØÿÛ
01f0 00 43 00 05 03 04 04 04-03 05 04 04 04 05 05 05  ·C··············
0200 06 07 0C 08 07 07 07 07-0F 0B 0B 09 0C 11 0F 12  ················
0210 12 11 0F 11 11 13 16 1C-17 13 14 1A 15 11 11 18  ················
0220 21 18 1A 1D 1D 1F 1F 1F-13 17 22 24 22 1E 24 1C  !·········"$"·$·
0230 1E 1F 1E FF DB 00 43 01-05 05 05 07 06 07 0E 08  ···ÿÛ·C·········
0240 08 0E 1E 14 11 14 1E 1E-1E 1E 1E 1E 1E 1E 1E 1E  ················
0250 1E 1E 1E 1E 1E 1E 1E 1E-1E 1E 1E 1E 1E 1E 1E 1E  ················
0260 1E 1E 1E 1E 1E 1E 1E 1E-1E 1E 1E 1E 1E 1E 1E 1E  ················
0270 1E 1E 1E 1E 1E 1E 1E 1E-FF C0 00 11 08 00 78 00  ········ÿÀ····x·
0280 78 03 01 22 00 02 11 01-03 11 01 FF C4 00 1F 00  x··"·······ÿÄ···
0290 00 01 05 01 01 01 01 01-01 00 00 00 00 00 00 00  ················
02a0 00 01 02 03 04 05 06 07-08 09 0A 0B FF C4 00 B5  ············ÿÄ·µ
02b0 10 00 02 01 03 03 02 04-03 05 05 04 04 00 00 01  ················
```

FIGURE 4.21

Expanded multimedia message service example content.

The top area of this entry shows that a .jpg image was embedded in the message. The file name can also be located. Looking at Fig. 4.21, we can see 20140323951183437.jpg, readable to the right starting on offset 01c0 and ending on the next offset, 01d0. As we scroll down one more offset into the same container, we can see the file header of FF D8 which is located on offset 01e0 in Fig. 4.21. This particular image has an FF D8 file header and FF D9 file footer.

The bytes can be selected from the starting header to the ending footer, and saved with the same extension. You may be asking how would an investigator determine the file and footer for MMS data? There are a couple of ways. If you have obtained the file system, like the example previously mentioned, look at the file system for a similar file. The example is a .jpg, but any file can be in the file system, and also in the MMS. By looking at files that are the same within the file system, we can glean what the file header and footer would be that is embedded in the MMS entry the tool missed. If this does not work, searching for the type of file footer and header can be accomplished online. It is important to remember that MMS entries may have more than one file in the container, and both all would need to be pulled out (carved) in the same fashion.

Now that we have located the embedded file and carved it out, what about the message content itself? Many devices that embed MMS in this fashion will have an attribute that can be searched for using Ctrl+F (control find). This will allow investigators to use the text string, *txt>*.

Fig. 4.22 shows a result from the same phone of, "Hey babyx."

If the content is in the PDU string, this search will take the examiner directly to the entry. It is important to understand that this technique of searching for the content of the MMS only works with certain phones.

We are still missing the numbers the message was from and to as well as the time. To locate this, many phones can have it with this same PDU string, but some have it in a different container. If we go back to Fig. 4.20 we see a file labeled MMSMsg.db. If we look in this container, we can match up the PDU string with the numbers and times needed to complete our carving of this message. Fig. 4.23 is the necessary parts of our previous MMS1079638668.PDU. This includes the "TO" and "FROM" numbers, the sent date and time and any in some cases the message content.

This particular container has all three MMS messages showing in sequential order. We are only going to show decoding on one. Fig. 4.24 shows the phone number that the MMS message is from, decoded as Unicode.

```
33 38 37 35 37 2E 74 78-74 00 C0 22 3C 54 45 58   38757.txt·À"<TEX
54 5F 31 30 37 39 36 33-38 37 35 37 2E 74 78 74   T_1079638757.txt
3E 00 48 65 79 20 62 61-62 79 78 00 00 00 00 00   >·Hey babyx·····
00 00 25 00 26 00 00 00-00 00 00 00 00 00 00 00   ··%·&···········
00 00 00 00 00 00 00 00-00 61 70 70 6C 69 63 61   ·········applica
74 69 6F 6E 2F 76 6E 64-2E 77 61 70 2E 6D 75 6C   tion/vnd.wap.mul
74 69 70 61 72 74 2E 72-65 6C 61 74 65 64 00 33   tipart.related·3
00 36 00 30 00 34 00 38-00 30 00 34 00 32 00 35   ·6·0·4·8·0·4·2·5
00 32 00 00 00 00 00 00-00 00 00 00 00 64 00 00   ·2···········d··
00 FF FF 00 00 00 00 00-00 00 00 00 00 00 00 00   ·ÿÿ·············
```

FIGURE 4.22

Using Ctrl+F and *txt>* to locate multimedia message service content.

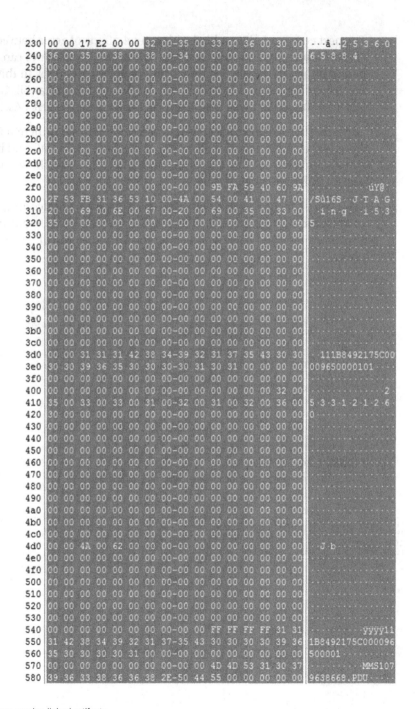

FIGURE 4.23
Multimedia message service linked artifacts.

The next entry which is padded with several offsets of zeros between it and the "From" number are the sent and received times. These values can be the same period or be off by minutes, hours, and in some cases days. In this phone, the first 4 bytes represent the date and times and are decoded as LE, GPS (4 bytes). Fig. 4.25 shows the first 4 bytes being decoded using MFI Hex Assistant.

The next 4 bytes represent a Unix date and time, which is different than the previous. As referenced previously, some of the dates can be affected by UTC. This particular date would be a received time. Fig. 4.26 shows how it was decoded using a different Epoch setting.

Most tools do not decode both times. This type of encoding is common in SMS and MMS entries. Furthermore, there can be different types of date and times present. There is no standard format that will be found on each phone.

```
220 FF FF FF FF FF FF 51 11-FC FF 00 00 00 00 84 E1  ÿÿÿÿÿÿQ·üÿ·····á
230 00 00 17 E2 00 00 32 00-35 00 33 00 36 00 30 00  ···â··2·5·3·6·0·
240 36 00 35 00 38 00 38 00-34 00 00 00 00 00 00 00  6·5·8·8·4·······
250 00 00 00 00 00 00 00 00 00-00 00 00 00 00 00 00  ················
260 00 00 00 00 00 00 00 00 00-00 00 00 00 00 00 00  ················
270 00 00 00 00 00 00 00 00 00-00 00 00 00 00 00 00  ················
280 00 00 00 00 00 00 00 00 00-00 00 00 00 00 00 00  ················
290 00 00 00 00 00 00 00 00 00-00 00 00 00 00 00 00  ················
2a0 00 00 00 00 00 00 00 00 00-00 00 00 00 00 00 00  ················
2b0 00 00 00 00 00 00 00 00 00-00 00 00 00 00 00 00  ················
2c0 00 00 00 00 00 00 00 00 00-00 00 00 00 00 00 00  ················
2d0 00 00 00 00 00 00 00 00 00-00 00 00 00 00 00 00  ················
2e0 00 00 00 00 00 00 00 00 00-00 00 00 00 00 00 00  ················
```

FIGURE 4.24

Multimedia message service "From" number for MMS1079638668.PDU.

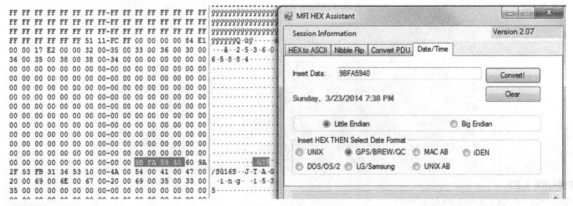

FIGURE 4.25

Decoded GPS date sent.

After the second date and time would be the ASCII values for the message content. Fig. 4.27 shows the message as *JTAGing i535*.

As mentioned previously, the message content may or may not be present in the MMSMsg.db container and may be embedded in the associated PDU string. In this example, the MMS content is in both locations. Fig. 4.28 shows the associated PDU string where Ctrl+F were used with the search entry: *txt>* to locate the exact location of the message.

As we continue to decode this MMS message, the next value of importance is the "To" number. Fig. 4.29 shows this value, again in Unicode. The value that can be seen above the "To" number is part of the message ID and can actually be found in the PDU.

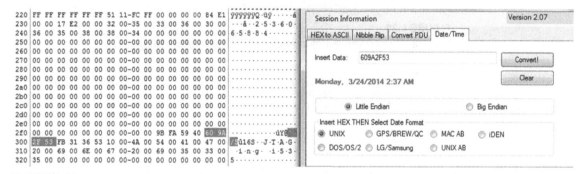

FIGURE 4.26
Decoded Unix date received.

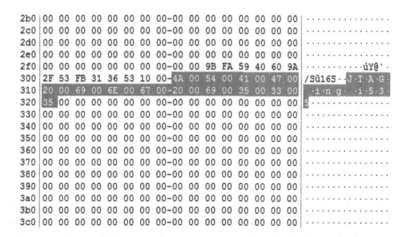

FIGURE 4.27
Multimedia message service content.

```
e0b0 90 0F 27 0A 00 EF 48 4E-14 0E 99 A6 E7 73 67 D2  ··'··ïHN···¦çsgÒ
e0c0 8C E4 93 48 07 13 C0 1D-29 09 E8 3F 3A 68 6C 92  ·ä·H··À·)·è?:hl·
e0d0 69 37 70 4D 20 1C 4E 4E-3B 52 67 24 FA 53 73 C5  i7pM ·NN;Rg$úSsÅ
e0e0 37 38 18 A4 03 F7 73 9E-D4 9B B8 C9 A6 16 ED 49  78·¤·÷s·Ô··É¦·íI
e0f0 BB 27 DA 90 0F CE 07 BD-34 9E D4 DD DD E9 37 60  »'Ú··Î·½4·ÔÝÝé7`
e100 7B 9A 40 3B 39 3E D4 9B-B3 93 4C 27 B5 21 6C FD  {·@;9>Ô·³·L'µ!lý
e110 05 20 1C 5B 8F 73 4D 27-B0 FC 69 BB BA B6 3E 94  · ·[·sM'°üi»°¶>·
e120 D2 DC 7D 69 0C 7E 79 FA-53 77 72 49 A6 96 CF 14  ÒÜ}i·~yúSwrI¦·Ï·
e130 D2 DC FB 52 10 E2 71 C7-7A 42 7B 76 14 CD DF 9D  ÒÜûR·âqÇzB{v·Íß
e140 34 B7 6A 43 3F FF D9 2E-0D 10 83 81 EA 85 74 65  4·jC?ÿÙ.····ê·te
e150 78 74 39 35 30 2E 74 78-74 00 C0 22 3C 74 65 78  xt950.txt·À"<tex
e160 74 39 35 30 2E 74 78 74-3E 00 8E 74 65 78 74 39  t950.txt>··text9
e170 35 30 2E 74 78 74 00 4A-54 41 47 20 69 6E 67 20  50.txt·JTAG ing
e180 69 35 33 35 CB 00 00 00-00 00 46 00 32 00 26 00  i535Ë·····F·2·&·
e190 00 00 00 00 00 00 00 00-00 00 00 00 00 00 00 00  ················
e1a0 00 00 68 74 74 70 3A 2F-2F 36 36 2E 31 37 34 2E  ··http://66.174.
e1b0 37 31 2E 37 31 2F 73 65-72 76 6C 65 74 73 2F 6D  71.71/servlets/m
e1c0 6D 73 3F 6D 65 73 73 61-67 65 2D 69 64 3D 31 31  ms?message-id=11
e1d0 31 42 38 34 39 32 31 37-35 43 30 30 30 30 39 36  1B8492175C000096
e1e0 35 30 30 30 30 31 30 31-00 61 70 70 6C 69 63 61  50000101·applica
```

FIGURE 4.28

Multimedia message service entry located in Protocol description unit string.

```
300 2F 53 FB 31 36 53 10 00-4A 00 54 00 41 00 47 00  /Sûl6S··J·T·A·G·
310 20 00 69 00 6E 00 67 00-20 00 69 00 35 00 33 00   ·i·n·g· ·i·5·3·
320 35 00 00 00 00 00 00 00-00 00 00 00 00 00 00 00  5···············
330 00 00 00 00 00 00 00 00-00 00 00 00 00 00 00 00  ················
340 00 00 00 00 00 00 00 00-00 00 00 00 00 00 00 00  ················
350 00 00 00 00 00 00 00 00-00 00 00 00 00 00 00 00  ················
360 00 00 00 00 00 00 00 00-00 00 00 00 00 00 00 00  ················
370 00 00 00 00 00 00 00 00-00 00 00 00 00 00 00 00  ················
380 00 00 00 00 00 00 00 00-00 00 00 00 00 00 00 00  ················
390 00 00 00 00 00 00 00 00-00 00 00 00 00 00 00 00  ················
3a0 00 00 00 00 00 00 00 00-00 00 00 00 00 00 00 00  ················
3b0 00 00 00 00 00 00 00 00-00 00 00 00 00 00 00 00  ················
3c0 00 00 00 00 00 00 00 00-00 00 00 00 00 00 00 00  ················
3d0 00 00 31 31 31 42 38 34-39 32 31 37 35 43 30 30  ··111B8492175C00
3e0 30 30 39 36 35 30 30 30-30 31 30 31 00 00 00 00  009650000101····
3f0 00 00 00 00 00 00 00 00-00 00 00 00 00 00 00 00  ················
400 00 00 00 00 00 00 00 00-00 00 00 00 00 00 32 00  ··············2·
410 35 00 33 00 33 00 31 00-32 00 31 00 32 00 36 00  5·3·3·1·2·1·2·6·
420 30 00 00 00 00 00 00 00-00 00 00 00 00 00 00 00  0···············
430 00 00 00 00 00 00 00 00-00 00 00 00 00 00 00 00  ················
440 00 00 00 00 00 00 00 00-00 00 00 00 00 00 00 00  ················
```

FIGURE 4.29

To number.

The last item that needs to be decoded in this block of data is the value show-ing in Fig. 4.30 as "Jb." This Unicode value is being referenced as a phonebook entry in another part of the file system. If we were to look into other folders, we would find the stored entry of *Jb* with a corresponding phone number listed as 2536065884. It is important to note that on this phone if the number was not stored in the phonebook, this area would remain blank (all zeros). At the

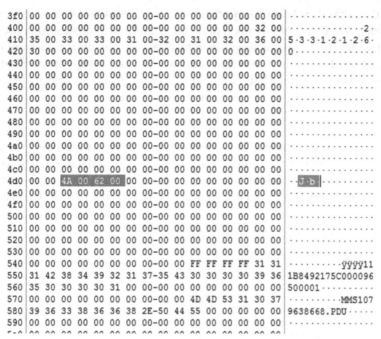

```
3f0 00 00 00 00 00 00 00 00-00 00 00 00 00 00 00 00  ................
400 00 00 00 00 00 00 00 00-00 00 00 00 00 00 32 00  ..............2.
410 35 00 33 00 33 00 31 00-32 00 31 00 32 00 36 00  5.3.3.1.2.1.2.6.
420 30 00 00 00 00 00 00 00-00 00 00 00 00 00 00 00  0...............
430 00 00 00 00 00 00 00 00-00 00 00 00 00 00 00 00  ................
440 00 00 00 00 00 00 00 00-00 00 00 00 00 00 00 00  ................
450 00 00 00 00 00 00 00 00-00 00 00 00 00 00 00 00  ................
460 00 00 00 00 00 00 00 00-00 00 00 00 00 00 00 00  ................
470 00 00 00 00 00 00 00 00-00 00 00 00 00 00 00 00  ................
480 00 00 00 00 00 00 00 00-00 00 00 00 00 00 00 00  ................
490 00 00 00 00 00 00 00 00-00 00 00 00 00 00 00 00  ................
4a0 00 00 00 00 00 00 00 00-00 00 00 00 00 00 00 00  ................
4b0 00 00 00 00 00 00 00 00-00 00 00 00 00 00 00 00  ................
4c0 00 00 00 00 00 00 00 00-00 00 00 00 00 00 00 00  ................
4d0 00 00 4A 00 62 00 00 00-00 00 00 00 00 00 00 00  ..J.b...........
4e0 00 00 00 00 00 00 00 00-00 00 00 00 00 00 00 00  ................
4f0 00 00 00 00 00 00 00 00-00 00 00 00 00 00 00 00  ................
500 00 00 00 00 00 00 00 00-00 00 00 00 00 00 00 00  ................
510 00 00 00 00 00 00 00 00-00 00 00 00 00 00 00 00  ................
520 00 00 00 00 00 00 00 00-00 00 00 00 00 00 00 00  ................
530 00 00 00 00 00 00 00 00-00 00 00 00 00 00 00 00  ................
540 00 00 00 00 00 00 00 00-00 00 00 FF FF FF FF 31 31  ...........ÿÿÿÿ11
550 31 42 38 34 39 32 31 37-35 43 30 30 30 30 39 36  1B8492175C000096
560 35 30 30 30 30 31 00 00-00 00 00 00 00 00 00 00  500001..........
570 00 00 00 00 00 00 00 00-00 00 4D 4D 53 31 30 37  ..........MMS107
580 39 36 33 38 36 36 38 2E-50 44 55 00 00 00 00 00  9638668.PDU.....
590 00 00 00 00 00 00 00 00-00 00 00 00 00 00 00 00  ................
```

FIGURE 4.30

Phone book entry reference for *From* number.

bottom of Fig. 4.30 is the message ID again, and the entire string ends with the PDU MMS number it is referencing. The entire process repeats for the next PDU string and is padded between the entries with several offsets of zeros.

We have provided two very basic problems that examiners may have with physical data that is not always parsed using commercial forensic tools. The first involved a phone that contains additional artifacts that reference the phone number used in parsed SMS messages. The second example involved MMS issues. Let's continue with examples that involve application data.

USER-INSTALLED APPLICATIONS

Many forensic software vendors support the ability to parse various user-installed application data. After each new update to the supported forensics tool, this list grows larger and larger. The problem is that there is no way for any vendor to stay on top of every new application that comes along. There will be times when examiners utilize a popular forensic tool that supports an Android, iOS, Windows, or other smartphone. Their report shows many things supported, such as chats, GPS data, emails, call logs, images, and other common artifacts located on such devices. The case agent, however, does not see the SMS or other data that they know from other evidence should be present on the target phone. What commonly takes place are communications through user-installed applications. This is typically to save money. The device does not even need allocated wireless connection, only a WiFi, and a support application. Examiners should get in a habit of looking at the applications that are installed when they can't find what they believe should be there.

Fig. 4.31 is a look into the database schema from an application called *TextNow*.

At the time of this writing, this particular application was not being decoded by popular mobile forensic tools like Cellebrite. Using database viewers, we can navigate into the various containers. Within this application, we see the actual database and its associated tables. Fig. 4.32 is just part of what can be

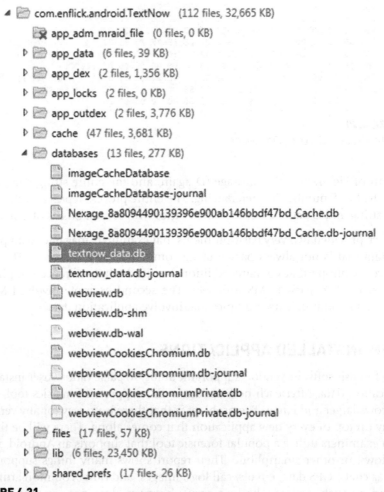

FIGURE 4.31

TextNow application example.

viewed with the messages table. Using the GUI off the actual phone, users can confirm what many of the values are in the various tables off the schema. This will give insight into tables that may indicate a "–1," or might show a "message direction." For example, a sent SMS from the application shown in a table as "0." While a received message from the same application shown in the same table as "–1."

In this particular example, we can navigate to other tables and see what the total messages were that may have been recorded by the application. Fig. 4.33 shows the table that reveals the original number of messages and the number of messages that are actually still within the database.

The content that is still within this database example shows a conversation between users regarding the location of a body that was cut into pieces. There was GPS data on the phone that supported the location listed as "She's in several honey buckets on the mountain highway site." Examiners can in turn also convert the date and time stamp encoding and manually parse incriminating evidence such as what is listed in Fig. 4.34.

We have now covered some of the common problems with the physical aspects of mobile forensics. Understanding the file system encoding, Epoch dates, and unparsed application databases can yield additional artifacts related to the investigation. Let's discuss briefly on user-enabled security problems and possible solutions.

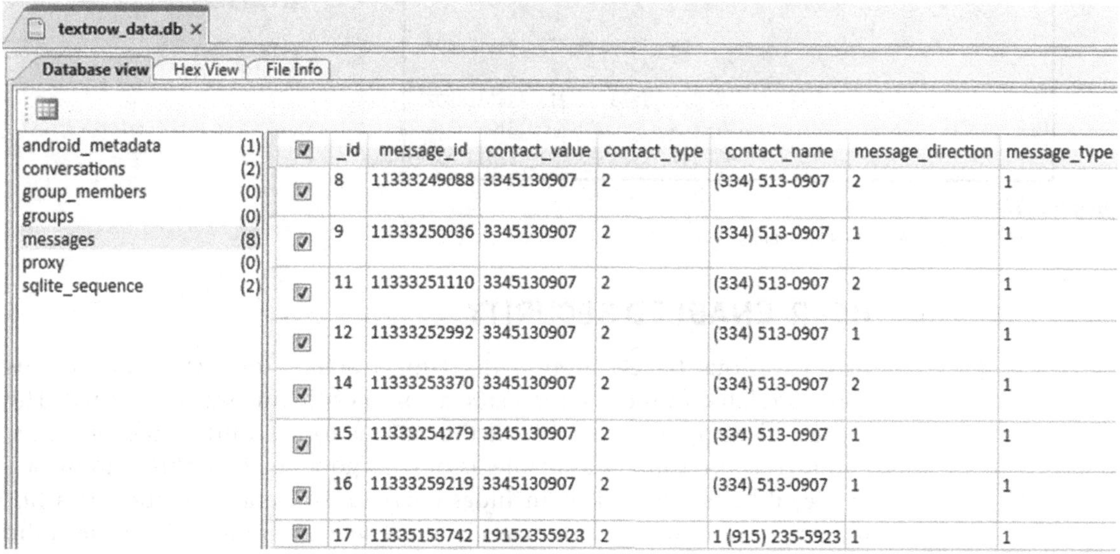

_id	message_id	contact_value	contact_type	contact_name	message_direction	message_type
8	11333249088	3345130907	2	(334) 513-0907	2	1
9	11333250036	3345130907	2	(334) 513-0907	1	1
11	11333251110	3345130907	2	(334) 513-0907	2	1
12	11333252992	3345130907	2	(334) 513-0907	1	1
14	11333253370	3345130907	2	(334) 513-0907	2	1
15	11333254279	3345130907	2	(334) 513-0907	1	1
16	11333259219	3345130907	2	(334) 513-0907	1	1
17	11335153742	19152355923	2	1 (915) 235-5923	1	1

FIGURE 4.32
Database tables.

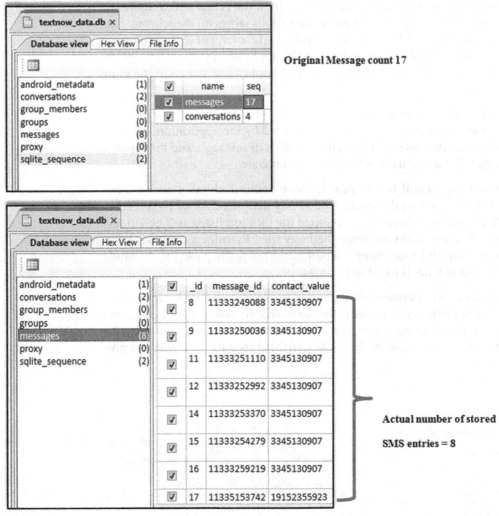

FIGURE 4.33
Short message service deleted from the database.

USER-ENABLED SECURITY

In the various travels around the Unites States, instructing on various courses related to mobile forensics, a common theme was discovered. The most well-equipped lab, with all the various tools, utilities and products, and financial resources available, is only as good as their ability to bypass user-enabled security. This includes encryption. Data encryption is a hot topic right now, with major manufacturers such as Apple and Google at the forefront. Even with the proper legal process, investigators are being denied

contact_name	message_direction	message_type	message_text	read	date	state
(334) 513-0907	2	1	What's up? Angel Ponez	True	1432370778000	0
(334) 513-0907	1	1	It's done -Jimmyjohn-Poopman	True	1432370839000	0
(334) 513-0907	2	1	Good. When Angel Ponez	True	1432370905000	0
(334) 513-0907	1	1	I had to make multiple pieces. He wouldn't fit through the lid on the septic tank. -Jimmyjohn-Poopman	True	1432371026000	0
(334) 513-0907	2	1	Which site did u use? Angel Ponez	True	1432371050000	0
(334) 513-0907	1	1	The new one off Cooper point rd -Jimmyjohn-Poopman	True	1432371087000	0
(334) 513-0907	1	1	I had to take out his wife too. She's in several honeybuckets on the mountain highway site -Jimmyjohn-Poopman	True	1432371415000	0
1 (915) 235-5923	1	1	Angel i miss u. I asked jimmy if you guys took care of everything	True	1432405167000	0

FIGURE 4.34

Unparsed short message service content from an application database.

access to decryption and in turn what evidence may yield from the exam of a mobile device. We'll focus on bypassing security more than decryption in this chapter.

Pattern and PIN—Androids

The ability to bypass a user-enabled PIN or gesture pattern may be a built-in feature on some commercial forensic tools. Cellebrite, for example, allows the examiner to bypass both of these security measures, but it is very much make and model specific. Utilizing special cables and built-in custom recovery exploits, the phones memory is "downloaded." Other Android device can be accessed through specific workarounds using *Odin* or *Heimdahl*. Both Odin and Heimdalh are specific to certain phones. Odin is primarily used to flash a custom recovery firmware to the device, but can be used as a gateway for bypassing OS security.

Heimdahl is an open source tool that works similar to Odin but is very specific for what it supports—mainly some Galaxy S models.

Many of the tools that can bypass security that are not built into commercial mobile forensic programs are not primarily designed for forensic extractions. Their purpose is to usually fix or network unlock the device. If investigators don't use them properly they have the potential to wipe or alter the stored user data, and even "brick" the phone, rendering it useless.

BST

One utility that has grown popular is a program called Best Smart Tool (BST). This utility supports user security unlocking on various HTC, Samsung, Xiaomi, MTK, and some generic Androids.

Like most of the cell phone tools, it was designed for flashing the target supported phone but has a built-in feature that can unlock the security without the use of a setting being enabled called Android Debug Bridge (**ADB**). Androids have this setting disabled by default. Nearly all forensic tools need it enabled to allow the forensic tool to extract data, especially at the logical or file system level. BST on supported models can still bypass the security, without the user needing to know how to use Odin, Heimdahl, or other developer methods. Fig. 4.35 shows the BST interface.

It is very intuitive and allows the user to select the make then model from the drop down. Once this takes place the phone is connected to the computer and the user presses **Scan**. Once the phone is located the **Unlock** button can be used to delete the SHA value for the gesture or PIN security (Fig. 4.36).

FIGURE 4.35

Best smart tool.

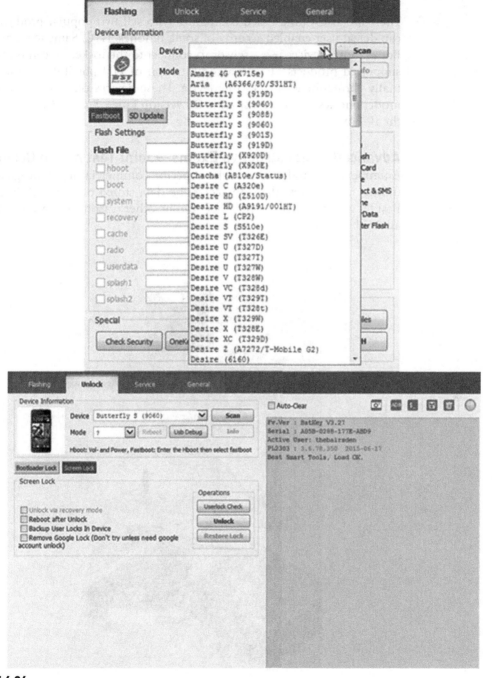

FIGURE 4.36

Best Smart Tool Phone selection and Unlock feature.

IP-Box and MFC Dongle

There are also China-based companies who sell two popular products that can defeat user-enabled security of some iPhones, HTC, Samsung, and Mac-Books. Both devices use a sensor to connect to the locked screen on certain supported products. It runs a combination of PIN possibilities and eventually "brute-force" attacks the device. These devices only work on certain model phones that have a specific OS version range. Fig. 4.37 is an image of the IP-Box.

Advanced Nondestructive Exams—Joint Test Action Group

Examiners will find at times when specific commercial tools, programs, or utilities won't allow them to access the data stored on the mobile device. Besides user-enabled security, there can be other reasons why access was not allowed.

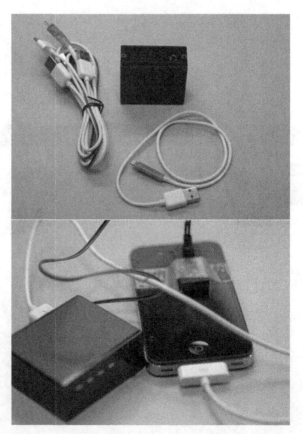

FIGURE 4.37
IP-Box.

- Locked USB ports

Many pay-as-you-go phones can lock down their USB ports. The port is only used for charging. The main reason is to make users pay for services over the air, or the phone's OS is so basic, developers may have felt no need to allow data to be moved off the device. These devices are common for individuals who may be on the run from law enforcement and are using cell phones they can dispose of and are cheap.

- Damaged phone

Devices may need to be examined that have been damaged. The reasons for the damage could have been the environment itself, such as the device was thrown into a lake or ocean. Some are involved in fires. Many devices simply have a damaged screen or USB data port that doesn't allow the connection. Other times examiners may find circumstances they may never have imagined.

WHAT'S THAT SMELL? YOU DON'T WANT TO KNOW!

Recently, a law enforcement agency requested examination of a device that came out of the pants pocket of a deceased individual. The victim had been stuffed into a duffle bag and left for quite some time before discovery. The body fluids had seeped into the phone and exposed all the components of the mainboard. The phone was cleaned as best as possible by the agency but failed to read using conventional commercial tools. The main board was isolated in a cleaning solution within an ultrasonic cleaner. This process was repeated numerous times, each at different frequencies within the ultrasonic bath. Even when the board showed no signs of left over dried body fluids, it still gave off the distinct odor that many in law enforcement are familiar with. By cooking the board each time in the sonic cleaner, the odor grew—similar to thanksgiving but unfortunately, we weren't making a turkey.

- The device is not supported with forensic tools

Many devices on the market may not be supported for any type of acquisition by any forensic tool that is available worldwide. This is especially true with many non-smartphone devices, especially pay-as-you-go.

A technique that may work on some phones is the use of JTAG. JTAG stands for Joint Test Action Group. The simple version of defining this term is that JTAG allows examiners to use specific areas on the phone's mainboard to pull the memory. If there is user security and the phone is not encrypted, the binary pull can be parsed. If the phone is damaged but the board can still communicate with the processor and other memory, it will also work. JTAG for mobile devices was designed to repair, network unlock, or flash the phone. It wasn't until recently that law enforcement began seeing the benefits of using a JTAG extraction for forensic purposes.

There are many conditions to all this. First the board must have these contacts, which are often called TAPs. The term TAP means *test access port*. JTAG is part of the IEEE standard, and many devices will have TAP areas on the board. Examiners must locate and determine how they are mapped back to the processor. The common TAP's used are TCK which is test clock, TMS—Test Mode Select, TDI—Test Data In, TDO—Test Data Out, TRST—Test Reset, VCC—which refers to positive circuit's power supply, NRST—This can also be referred to as NTRST which resets the signal, and GRD—ground. Not all of these will be used on every phone.

The problem examiners will run into is that not all vendors who support JTAG extraction show the map of the TAPs that are needed. There is a multitude of vendors; two popular ones used by law enforcement are RIFF and Octoplus. Fig. 4.38 shows an image of a Samsung that has been conducted to the TAPs and then connected to an Octoplus box. This phone was used in a homicide, and the user had enabled a gesture security pattern.

Once the binary is pulled using the supported box, it needs to be decoded. JTAG extractions pull the data in the manner that suits that particular vendor. This may be an issue during decoding. Thankfully such vendors as Cellebrite allow for these problems and have specific decoding profiles that can be used to rebuild the data.

FIGURE 4.38
Joint Test Action Group extraction using Octoplus

Destructive Exams

There will be times when a device can't be exploited using JTAG, commercial tools, or any mentioned tools or similar products. Again, excluding encryption scenarios, a destructive technique called chip removal may be of benefit.

This technique has inherited risks, costs much more and requires training and substantial practice before attempting it on an actual case. First, the examiner must introduce heat to the memory, and electronic components don't like that! This can be an issue as the chip can actually be "cooked" and damaged from inside. The second issue is the contact area, which on newer chips is called the BGA. This needs to be cleaned and prepared for reading. This process also involves heat and scrapping. The process can damage any one of the BGA points that are already a mess from the chip removal. Cleaning is by far the point in this process where the examiner needs the most practice. Last is reading and decoding. If your removal and cleaning is success, the actual reading of the memory generally only takes additional time. The decoding, however, can be a problem if the examiner does not understand how to utilize commercial tools to help with this process. Also, some devices may require specific ways in which the binary has to be decoded. This all comes back to what we addressed earlier, which is the types of encoding. Fig. 4.39 shows the mainboard on a popular Samsung device. The NAND is removed. In the upper right cover the chip BGA area is a mess and also contains glue along with excess solder on the contacts. This needs all to be cleaned and the surface area prepared for the binary read (pull). The lower image in Fig. 4.39 shows what comes off this area during the cleaning. Care was taken not to press into the chip too far or tear off what is left of the BGA balls.

Once the chip is properly cleaned, it may need to be retinned using a small amount of solder paste so that all of the contacts have equal amounts of solder to contact the pins of the adaptor. The reader can vary. Fig. 4.40 shows the cleaned and retinned chip at the top of the image followed by a two popular adaptors.

Once the process of reading is completed, tools such as AccessData's FTK Imager can be used to create an image of the binary and also view the various partitions that will later be parsed. Programs such as Cellebrite's Physical Analyzer generally supports the decoding using a setting called "open advanced." This allows the examiner to premade profile to decode a specific model phone that has been read through this destructive chip removal. Fig. 4.41 shows the various partitions visible using FTK Imager.

Nondestructive and destructive exams have many variables to their success. There will be times when the examiner for whatever reason can't get the physical memory to read with either technique. Other times the JTAG pull although supported, won't start or when it starts it doesn't complete. The examiner may

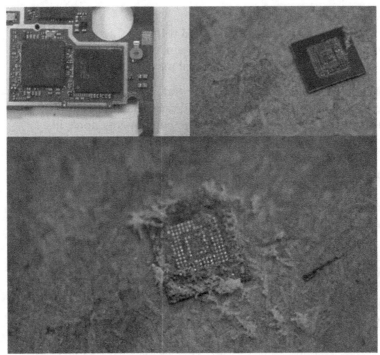

FIGURE 4.39
Chip removal and cleaning.

decide to switch to a destructive technique. It is also recommended that these types of exams are explained to prosecutors or supervisor. In some jurisdictions, if someone is charged or about to be charged with an offense, the prosecutor must address the court and obtain an order allowing a destructive process to take place. Typically the objection by the defense is witnessing the extraction. We remedy this by video recording the destructive removal with a microscope capable of photography and video.

ADVANCED VALIDATION

There may be times when examiners may be asked in court testimony about their forensic tools and what exactly they do to the phone when an extraction takes place. This may have not happened to anyone reading this book, or you may have a profession where your exams are not subject to the judicial process. Either way, we would like to provide some understanding of what may take place to the file system and binary areas when forensic tools extract data.

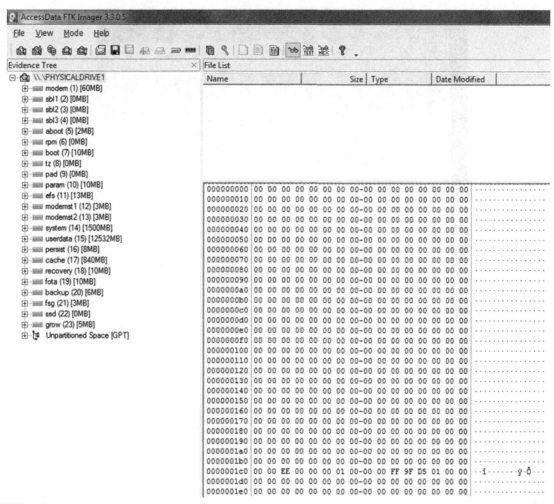

FIGURE 4.40
Cleaned memory and adaptor examples.

If we use an Android for our example, and we are conducting a logical exam, almost every commercial forensic tool used will pull that data using some form of an agent. The agent goes to the phone and executes commands to a container that stores only the data that was requested by the examiner in the GUI of the forensic tool. Some agents remain on the phone, but most are uninstalled after they perform the requested pull. The next exam on the same Android would be a file system pull. Most forensic tools would conduct this pull by going to the container that has all the files contained in the file system. Which files it obtains on this Android example may be subject to if the tool needs *root access*. Some tools use a Shell Root method, and most examiners

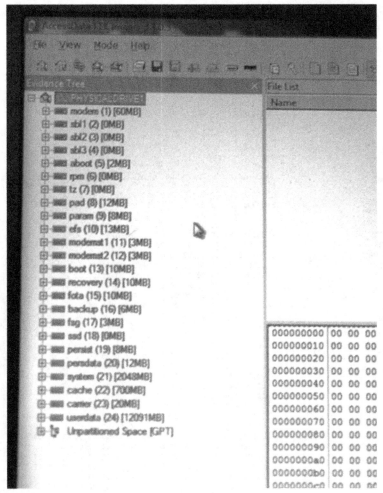

FIGURE 4.41
FTK Imager showing partitions from memory read.

have no idea this is even taking place. A Shell Root is not a permanent root to the device but has all the benefits of a permanent root. The Shell Root state is gone after the phone reboots. Like a permanently rooted device it allows *super user* access to the data folder, thus getting additional stored artifacts.

The last pull would be a nondestructive physical using a commercial tool. This pulls as much off the memory as the vendor supports—getting other partitions that do not necessarily have user data, but may have other artifacts and deleted (unallocated) areas.

Since these methods are destructive and alter electronic data, the methods are discussed last since these are practically used as a last resort to get to the data.

Ultra Compare Professional

Some of you may be saying to yourself that you always validate the data using visual, cross-tool, call detail records, or hand carving. Excellent! That validates the data, but how would you validate what your tools do? One such answer is to locate a tool that can show the changes at each of the levels I described earlier—logical and physical.

There are several vendors who can compare files. One that works well with larger binary and file system compares is Ultra Compare Professional. This allows side by side comparisons of binary and up to three folder compares. Here is an example that was used to illustrate this point. Feel free to replicate it if needed and you have the supported phone and tools.

First, we use a cheap phone that has a relatively small OS and is not a smart-phone. The phone must be supported by a forensic tool that can acquire logically, file system and physical. Any phone can be used that fits into this category, and recommended is a non-smartphone to save time.

Next we conduct a file system exam on the device. When this finishes, we make certain we keep this extraction in a folder we title, "Baseline File System Extraction." You can actually name it whatever you want, but just remember this is your first exam in this process of validating system changes.

We continue, and, this time, performing a physical exam on the same phone. Again we isolate the exam to a folder. This one is titled, "Baseline Physical Extraction" (or whatever you prefer as long as you know where it is located).

Then using other tools that support extraction on the same phone, we perform logical exams. You should perform at least one, and can even use the same tool if you don't have anything else available that supports the phone. This exam does not need to be labeled.

We again pull the file system. This time, we place it in another location and suggest calling it, "Final File System Exam." We repeat this again for the physical, labeling it, "Final Physical Exam."

So far we have a baseline file system, baseline physical, at least, one or more logical exams, and a final file system and final physical exam. We now want to compare our files using Ultra Compare Professional.

We do not have the ability to document how to use completely all the features of this utility, the bottom line is that you would be able to bring the baseline binary and final binary into the interface, and as Fig. 4.42 indicates, the changes between them would show in default *red*(light gray in print versions).

Obviously, it is very difficult to see where these changes are taking place with regards to the areas that may contain our items of evidence, such as images, calls, SMS, etc. To help us see better, let's bring in the baseline file system and final file system. Examiners would want to unzip these file systems first. Fig. 4.43 shows the files. These are much easier to read. Like the binary, changes show in the default color *red*(light gray in print versions).

In this example, we see a change within the *sysinfo* area of the file system. Fig. 4.44 shows the bytes that are affected by this.

This example shows that the other containers were not affected by all these exams we conducted between the baseline and final. The artifacts inside were

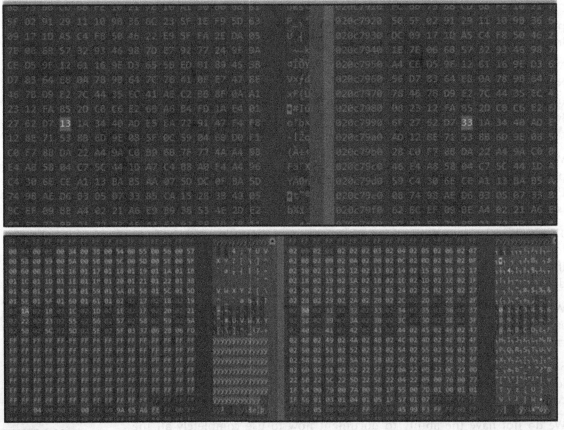

FIGURE 4.42
Binary changes on the same phone.

unchanged. These would include what was on the phone such as SMS, images, calls, videos, GPS, etc. However, at the binary level, we know that areas in will be changed and this will happen any time you connect something that communicates with the device. The important thing to understand is that the communication from the forensic tool does not change our evidence that is inside its container.

There are more forensic tools that can be used to actually watch the date move back and forth between the tool and the phone. One such tool we have used for advanced validation and troubleshooting is HHD Software—USB Monitor Professional. Fig. 4.45 shows the interface of the program. This tool allows the user to select anything that is connected to the computer's USB or Com ports. They can select what type of monitoring they prefer and actually see the offset where the day is written to. There is a higher learning curve with this tool, but it can be used to assist in validating a forensic tool.

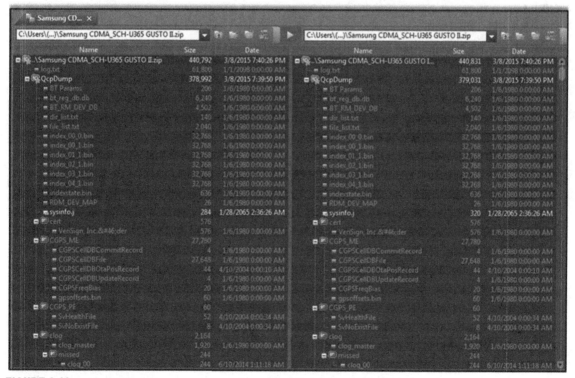

FIGURE 4.43

File system changes on same phone.

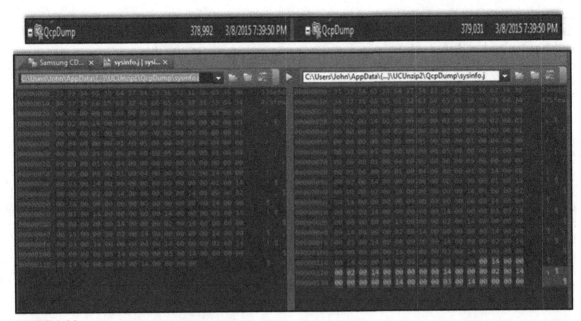

FIGURE 4.44
File system changes *sysinfo* area.

Chapter Summary

Typical evidential data that most investigators are trying to extract can reside in various forms of memory. This may include NOR and NAND. How these memory chips are configured can also vary. Processors and coprocessors will communicate with this memory. Such factors as *wear leveling* and *garbage collection* may determine if artifacts still reside on the phone after they are deleted by the user.

The phone's own encoding and various time stamps many times can be used to locate what a forensic tool may have missed during its parsing. Application databases that forensic tools don't support for decoding can also be manually examined for additional nuggets of information.

On nonencrypted devices, examiners can try and utilize various tools and utilities to try and exploit user-enabled security such as gesture patterns and pin codes. If these methods fail, both advanced nondestructive and destructive exams such as JTAG and chip removal can be utilized on supported phones. Many of these techniques will take additional trying and experience before one becomes proficient. It is important to stress that examiners should practice their craft on nonevidential devices.

Last, in all these processes we must strive to understand and articulate if needed what it is that our various extractions may do to change the phone. You

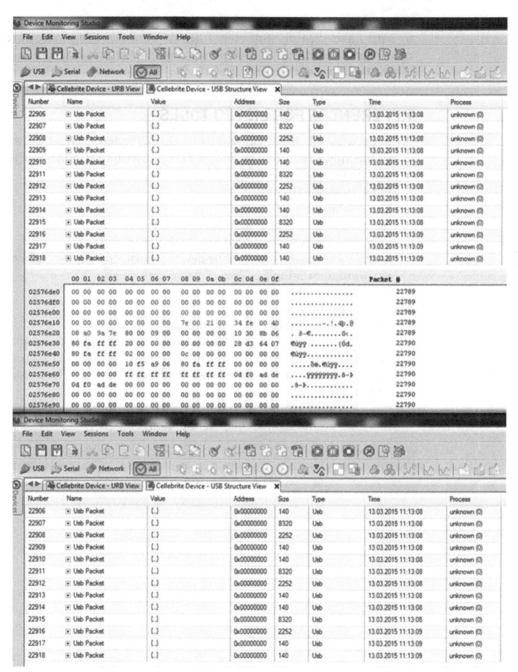

FIGURE 4.45
HHD USB monitoring Professional.

may even be fortunate enough to have a well-equipped lab with the means to obtain and keep up with every forensic processing gadget out there. But remember, the examiner themselves will always be the most important part of the methodology of mobile forensics.

REFERENCES FOR LISTED TOOLS

http://www.cellebrite.com/Mobile-Forensics/Products?gclid=Cj0KEQiA1d WyBRDqiJye6LjkhfIBEiQAw06ITgi-7ZPo0KdWG6mYcGq0RTDIl0QQiU4s iel0tF6QRzQaAk-F8P8HAQ

https://www.msab.com/

http://secureview.us/

http://accessdata.com/solutions/digital-forensics/mpe

http://www.gsmbest.com/en/ShowProduct.asp?Id=4

http://www.teeltech.com/mobile-device-forensic-tools/ip-box-iphone-password-unlock-tool/

http://www.mfcbox.com/

http://www.riffbox.org/

http://octoplusbox.com/en/features/jtag/

http://www.teeltech.com/mobile-device-forensic-tools/sireda-adapter-kit/

http://www.teeltech.com/mobile-device-forensic-tools/up-828-adapters/

http://accessdata.com/product-download/digital-forensics/ftk-imager-version-3.4.2

http://www.ultraedit.com/products/ultracompare.html

http://www.hhdsoftware.com/usb-monitor/compare

CHAPTER 5

Data Hiding

INTRODUCTION

Successful criminals are competent in committing crimes and subsequently getting away with their crimes, even when some evidence is recovered. Many of these successful criminals are well-known through news reports and continually investigated by local and federal law enforcement. Their success hinges on not creating evidence against them even though the crimes may be attributed to them.

The best criminals are virtually unknown. They do not make the news. They do not flaunt their crimes. Investigators are not investigating them. In fact, no one even knows about their involvement in criminal activity because their activity is hidden from view. These types of criminals are the most difficult to find as their communications are secreted behind layers of security, both technical and physical. Not only do they hide their participation in crimes, but just as importantly, they hide the communications that facilitate the crimes.

Hiding communications is such an effective means to facilitate covert acts that it has been used for centuries with criminal intentions, national objectives, and deviant behavior. However, investigators can sometimes find these hidden communications when looking in the right places, at the right time, and with the right mind-set. Rarely will the investigator find hidden data without first looking for it or being told exactly where it resides.

WHAT IS STEGANOGRAPHY

Hiding data and communications have existed since there is a need to communicate secretly with others. Wars from the beginning time require allied nations to communicate with each other while avoiding the contents or context of the communications being intercepted by the enemy. Whether the communication is hidden physically, such as a note with in a hidden compartment of a shoe, or electronically by embedding information in an electronic file, the goals have been the same of hiding the information from being discovered and missions compromised.

If the information is hidden and never discovered, it is as if it never existed. This is a key point of data hiding and criminal investigations. For example, if no one calls the police to report a crime, the crime goes without investigation and without acknowledgment that it ever occurred, except to the victim and criminal. In the context of hiding communications in the criminal realm, if law enforcement does not even know the communications exist, effectively, the criminals do not exist as far as law enforcement is concerned.

The act of hiding data is known as steganography, which simply means "concealed writing." Steganography is derived from the Greek words of "steganos" (covered) and "graphei" (writing). This chapter discusses steganography and not cryptography or encryption, which is discussed in a later chapter. Although cryptography and encryption can be used in conjunction with steganography, it is being kept separate in this chapter for ease of explanation.

Perhaps the best example of steganography is that of writing a message on paper with invisible ink. This technique is widely known, especially since many people have grown up exposed to invisible ink as toys. Invisible ink pens sold as toys work simply by writing a message with an ink that is not visible unless viewed under an ultraviolet (UV) or black light. Another method of invisible writing is using lemon juice or other similar acidic liquid to write on paper. Once the juice is dry, the writing is invisible and can only be seen by holding the paper over a flame or bright light.

The invisible ink method is highly effective today as it was centuries ago. Any piece of paper with innocent and visible markings could hold valuable information written with invisible ink right next to innocent markings. Considering a desk covered with stacks of paper, without knowing or suspecting this method to have been used, finding the one piece of paper that may have secret writings would be a case of luck and labor or sorting through every scrap of paper. Even when suspecting that this method may have been used to hide communications, every scrap of paper would have to be examined under a UV light or held over a flame to find the message.

The above example is brought up to illustrate the difficulty in finding actual physical writing as compared to an electronic file that has hidden data. In a physical crime scene, such as a single room, examining every item for hidden communications will take quite a bit of time to examine. However, on a storage device such as a computer hard drive or external drive, the number of files that can be stored far outweighs that which can be found in a single room. Examining every electronic file for hidden data might not be feasible, especially if the investigator is not suspecting steganography to have been used at all.

HIDING DATA BEHIND DATA

Hiding data in electronic files is quick, easy, and effective. The extent of hiding data depends upon the complexity of the user and intended use. A simple and easily defeated method is using a word processing document, typing the secret message, and changing the font to white in order to match the background of the document. Text can also be added to a document and hidden from view when marked as "hidden" or even through tracked changes with viewing the changes set to off. Fig. 5.1 shows changing font color and giving the text a hidden status to hide text from the viewer.

Obviously, a forensic application can find this text as font color, or hidden text is irrelevant to the applications. Viewers of the document, however, may miss the text, especially not suspicious of hidden information being on the file. For this reason alone, visually looking at electronic documents does not necessarily rule out hidden messages much like looking at a sheet of paper where invisible ink was used.

Although changing font color to hide text is easy to defeat with forensic applications and potentially discovered inadvertently by others for whom the message was unintended, it is a quick and easy method that does not require special software or skills to hide the information. Being that this method is

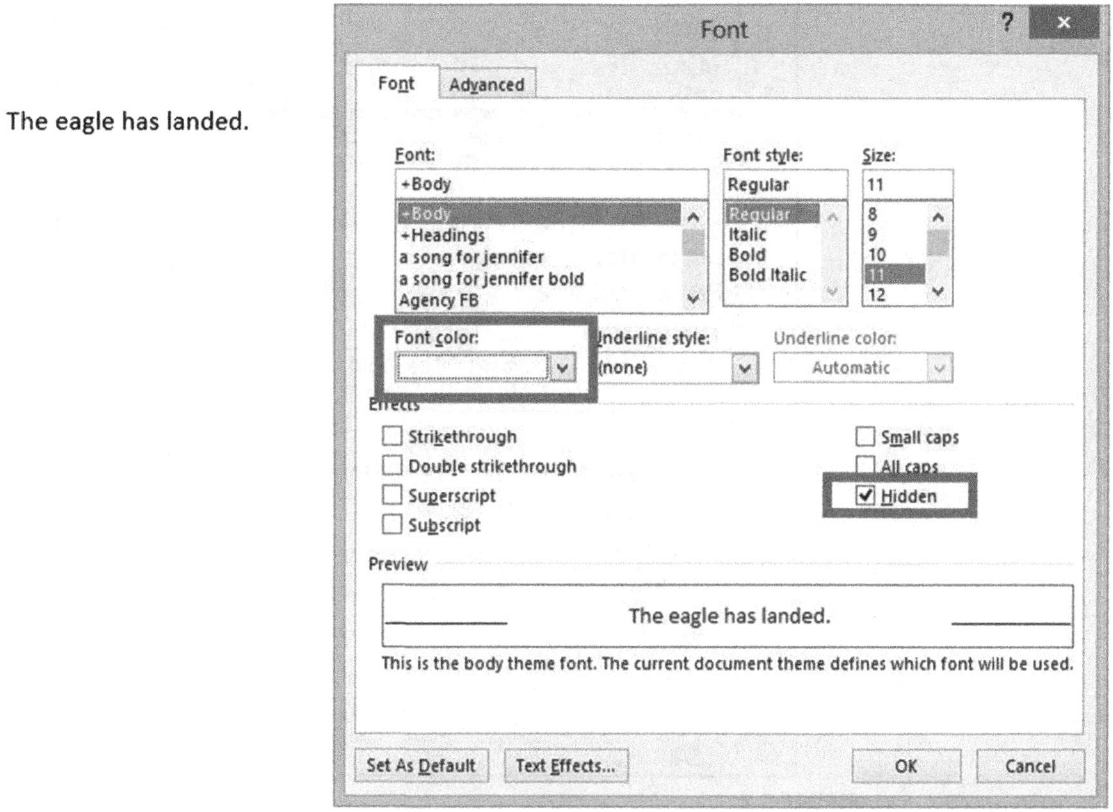

The eagle has landed.

FIGURE 5.1
Hiding text in a Microsoft Word document.

low-tech and low-skill, it stands to reason that it may be of higher use among a wider range of people.

Commonly used file types, such as word processors, have metadata fields that can also be used to hide information. Some of these fields are filled with information by virtue of the program being used with system information such as date and time created. Other fields are open for user-added details as seen in Fig. 5.2. This includes file types such as word processing documents, images (electronic photos), spreadsheets, and so forth.

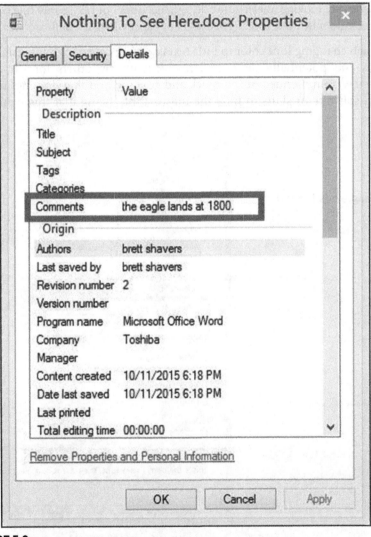

FIGURE 5.2
Metadata within a Microsoft Word document.

Opening a document does not necessarily allow the user to view the metadata without making an intentional effort to do so. But as seen in Fig. 5.3, once a user opens a dialog box to view the metadata, it is clearly visible. In these cases, you may have to expect coded language to be used more than plain language since the information is easily discoverable. Again, forensic applications are able to search and find metadata just as hidden text can be found.

Some native applications do not allow manipulation of metadata as easily as others. However, numerous applications can be freely downloaded which are designed for metadata editing. One example is ProPhoto Tools by Microsoft. As seen in Fig. 5.3, an image can be opened and metadata easily added to the image. Again, the metadata could clearly state the intentions of the user to be read by another person or be a coded language that only two persons know.

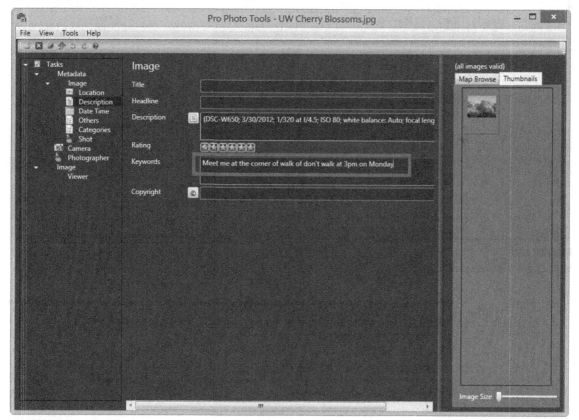

FIGURE 5.3

ProPhoto Tools http://www.microsoft.com.

For one example of the ease to find hidden text and metadata, Fig. 5.4 shows a search for the keyword "eagle" on two files with hidden data using X-Ways Forensics. One file, a Microsoft Word document, contains the text "the eagle has landed." This text was hidden from view in Microsoft Word by formatting the font color as white and selecting "hidden." Visually, the word processing file is empty, but any forensic application will find the text.

Fig. 5.4 also shows embedded text of an image file, which is just as easily found. Although this type of hidden text is straightforwardly uncovered with forensic applications, the work still requires manually reviewing the metadata for every file that may contain relevant information based on keyword search or manually reviewing all hidden text.

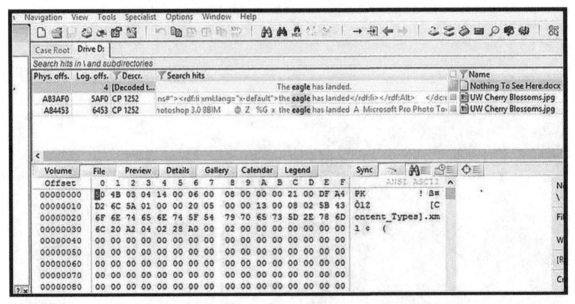

FIGURE 5.4

Metadata and hidden data example using X-Ways Forensics.

INVESTIGATIVE TIP!
Sometimes it really is this easy

In 2012, Higinio O. Ochoa III was identified as the hacker who compromised several federal data-bases (United States of America v Higinio O. Ochoa, III, 2012). His identification was made possible by the metadata in photos of Ochoa's girlfriend that were uploaded to the Internet, which contained GPS coordinates in the metadata. Don't overlook the obvious because sometimes, the evidence yells out to be found as the simplest solution.

Moving forward with more technical data hiding involves some knowledge of file structures or at least, knowledge that data can be hidden inside other data below the user interface of a common application such as a word processor. Data can also be appended to other data. Hiding within data requires commingling the secret data within visible data. Appending secret data is simply adding the text to a file but is not able to be seen with the native application. As an example, secret text can be added to a word processing document but not be visible in the word processing application with simple changes to the text. Secret text commingled in a file, such as an image, can also be hidden from view when using a photo viewer application. Both the word processor file and photo will look undisturbed with a visual inspection as text can be hidden within the files.

Fig. 5.5 shows OpenPuff, a freeware graphical user interface application that places data (target file) into other data (carrier file). A user creates a text file with the secret message as the target, chooses the carrier file, creates a password, and OpenPuff embeds the text file into the image.

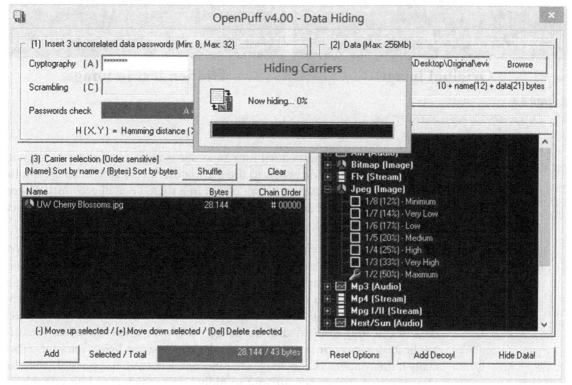

FIGURE 5.5

OpenPuff http://embeddedsw.net/OpenPuff_Steganography_Home.html.

The carrier file can be an audio, video, or image file. As long as the target file containing the secret message is not too large, the carrier file will not show any signs of manipulation. Audio and video carrier files will play as normal, and images will look undisturbed. Fig. 5.6 shows an original, undisturbed image next to an image which has had a text file embedded into it. Visually, the images are indistinguishable.

Original image   **Hidden text in image**

FIGURE 5.6
Original image alongside image with hidden text.

As to how secret text embedded into an image is actually used depends upon the limitations of giving access to the file to other persons. The image can be e-mailed (or left attached to a draft e-mail in a shared e-mail account), placed on an external storage device to be handed to someone, or uploaded online to a Website to be downloaded by others to access the text.

A consideration when viewing images for content is also determining the reason for image corruption. Images that are partially overwritten or corrupted will usually appear to be incomplete or spotty. In most instances this is due to the images being deleted but also may be due to overloading the image with too much hidden data. Fig. 5.7 shows an example of an image having too much secret data (a text file) embedded in the image. On first glance through a forensic application viewer, it is easy to overlook this image as being relevant, especially if the contents of the image are innocent. However, it is possible that the image was an abandoned attempt to hiding data which could be valuable in the analysis to find.

Original Image   Too much hidden data in image

FIGURE 5.7
Overloading an image with hidden data.

The manner in which a file is transmitted to another can indicate if steganography may have been used. For example, if an e-mail between suspects has been sent with an image that seems to be unrelated to the e-mail text, it may be suspect. As an investigator, seeing an out-of-place item such as a blank e-mail with an attachment of an image should give rise to questions about that image.

INVESTIGATIVE TIP!
Sometimes there is no steganography program to find
When you know or believe steganography has been used but cannot find the program used, check the Internet history of the suspect's computer. Many Websites exist where anyone can upload a file (typically an image/photo), type a message in a form, and the image will have the message embedded in the image online, not on the local computer.

Referring back to the hidden text within an image from Fig. 5.6, the receiver needs to read the text for the communication to work. Using the password chosen to hide the data, OpenPuff will unhide the data from the image and create a text file of the secret text as seen in Fig. 5.8. It is important to note that there are only two files needed for this method along with clicking a few buttons to hide completely a message that is created in minutes and can be shared worldwide in seconds. Because of the ease, investigators should expect this method of communication being used.

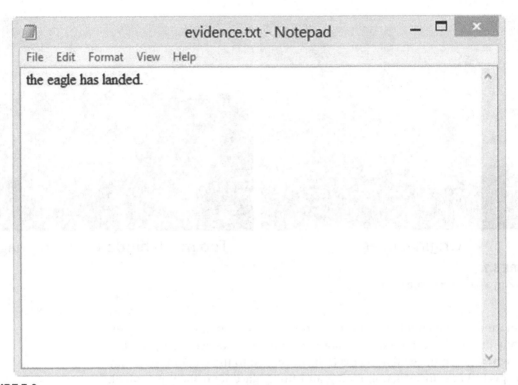

FIGURE 5.8
The unhidden text.

INVESTIGATIVE TIP!
How often is steganography being used?

No one knows, and no one will ever know. Steganography is the art of hiding messages. The only incidents that are known are when steganography fails. No one knows how often this works, because when it works, no one knows besides those communicating covertly. Practically, this means to look for it even when you have never seen it because you may have been missing covert communications for a long time!

As mentioned, OpenPuff is just one of many applications used for hiding data in files. Other programs are similar in operation but can also hide other types of file data (besides text files) into other types of carrier files (besides audio, video, and images). Some software applications can even hide data in executable files. Considering how difficult it is to find hidden data in an image file, hiding data in an executable is exponentially more difficult because it is more cleverly hidden by the carrier file type.

STEGANALYSIS

The first step in analyzing files that contain hidden data is finding the files. Finding the files requires searching through all the files on a system or files specific to a Website or storage device. In a best case scenario, your potential evidence is contained on a small storage device or Website. However, in most cases, your evidence file or files may be intermingled among hundreds of thousands of files on multiple devices. Searching for steganography files has not always been a focus of forensic analysis for several reasons.

One, examiners may not realize that this data hiding method has been used on a machine. Two, even if an examiner suspects steganography, it is quite possible and probable that the hidden data may not be found on the machine. Not finding the files doesn't mean the files don't exist on the machine any more than it means the files exist on the machine or external devices that were attached at one time. Lastly, the time involved to search given investigative priorities and resources may negate the need which will potentially result in overlooked evidence.

One of the best investigative tips is simply asking the suspect about the evidence in the case. Using the best interviewing methods available, sometimes investigators can be guided directly to the specifically sought after evidence, at least to a starting point of evidence, through basic questioning. If a suspect admits to e-mailing files embedded with hidden data, the method of transmission (e-mail) is discovered, and the method of hiding the data may be disclosed by the suspect as well. From this information, searching computer devices specifically for similar evidence files will be more targeted and effective.

Without the suspect's volunteered information, forensic analysis of all files in search of potentially hidden data requires time. Much like searching for a single type of fish in the ocean, searching for a type of file that may have hidden data requires patience and resources. At the basic level of searching, hidden text that has been also encrypted will not be found through keyword searches without decrypting the hidden text. Decrypting the hidden text requires more than just the passphrase, but also the method of encryption and/or software used to encrypt the message in the first place.

By now, you should have started to add searches in your forensic cases for the "Tor browser" as seen in an earlier chapter to find use of covert and anonymous Internet communications. You should also add searching for software applications designed for steganography. Searching the Internet for a list of steganography programs should be done on a regular basis in order to be familiar with the names and also to update hash sets in your forensic applications. Downloading and hashing the programs to create a hash set of steganography programs can save you time in manually searching as well as reducing the odds of missing the programs during an analysis.

In all likelihood, if you find steganography software installed or previously installed on your suspect's machine, you may find the files used that contain the hidden data but is in plain text, such as in a text file. Unless the suspect takes steps to delete securely the original text files, they will remain recoverable and not encrypted.

As a side note, some steganography software is portable, in that it does not have to be installed on the machine to run and can be run from an external storage device. Even more problematic are CD/DVD/USB bootable systems, such as TAILS, in which steganography software can be installed or run on a removable device to hide data on files without any trace on the host computer system.

If there is a reason to believe steganography has been used, the search for hidden data requires a more intensive effort with no method of ensuring all hidden data has been found. Using Nirsoft freeware applications to illustrate methods of determining if steganography may have been used, Fig. 5.9 shows several examples to search. In this example, OpenPuff activity with dates/times

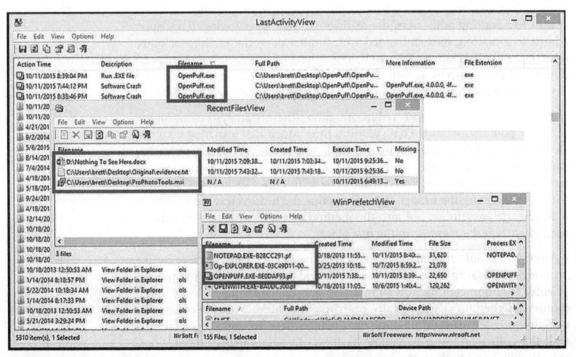

FIGURE 5.9
Nirsoft's LastActivityView shows files with potential hidden data with OpenPuff program use in near access time with several files.

are seen which correspond closely in time with other files and programs such as Microsoft Word, notepad, and ProPhoto Tools. Although this is a simple example that indicates OpenPuff, a steganography application most likely was used to hide data using at least a text file. By creating a timeline of file and program access directly focused on possible steganography use, it is possible to determine some, if not all, of the files, accessed that were used to hide data.

In a best case scenario, the original text files will be found on your suspect's machine, in which case, even without the password or the carrier files, the hidden messages are in plain text outside the carrier files. As seen in this example, it is imperative to know the types of software applications used in steganography in order to realize hidden data most likely exists because of the existence of that type of specialized software.

Keeping along the lines of grabbing the "low-hanging fruit" first, refer back to Fig. 5.7. Both images are visually identical, but of course, their hash values will be different as one of the images has hidden text embedded in the file. Given a case where steganography is certain, a hash comparison of all files (which is usually done anyway) may lead to files suspected of carrying hidden data. Using the images from Fig. 5.6, a hash of both files is seen in Fig. 5.10.

The two images are visually identical, but clearly contain different hash values. By face value, there is some difference. In this example, there is also a size difference. One file is 6,770,660 bytes, and the other file is slightly larger at 6,770,717 bytes. A safe assumption is that the larger file contains the hidden text. This is a very simple example, and realistically, tens of thousands of images can exist on one computer system and any one of the images may contain hidden text, or none of them may contain hidden text. It is in this type of analysis where a timeline of any design will

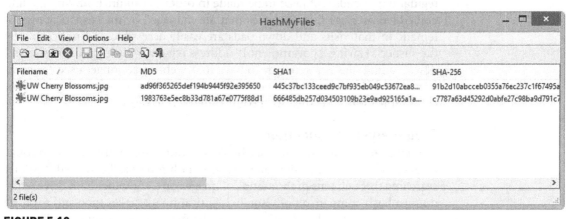

FIGURE 5.10
Visually identical images with different hash values.

be helpful to visualize the files created and accessed in the same period of stegan-ography software applications in order to narrow the focus of analysis.

Intercepted Steganography Files

In cases where electronic evidence files have been intercepted, either through search warrants, informants, or plain view seizure, the suspect's computer system is usually not available for examination. In that situation, the original files and software used to hide the information may be unknown. Discovering files embedded with hidden data is possible, but still difficult. More difficult is reading the hidden data that may be encrypted.

Websites managed by suspects as well as Websites that offer to host images freely can be used to store image files (audio and video) in the public view that contains hidden messages. This is one of the most effective means of communicating covertly without having an obvious electronic connection between two or more persons. In this scenario, one suspect embeds a hidden message into an innocent appearing photo, which is uploaded online among many other photos. The destination Website can be an innocent appearing blog or photo-sharing Website. The receiving party only needs to know which photo contains the embedded message, at which time the image is downloaded and message extracted with the shared password. Making matters worse is the uploading suspect can replace the steganography image with the original (no hidden message) image after a period of time without notice.

Countering this method online image communication requires knowledge of the Websites being used to upload the images. Without knowing the exact URL, images can be uploaded, downloaded, and subsequently replaced with innocent images without detection. However, once these Websites are discovered, to reduce the risk of missing evidence files being used as communication, regular downloads will need to be made in order to capture both original and embedded message files. Websites that are managed by the suspect are problematic in that visits and downloads are easily accessible and noticeable by the suspect. Having a government IP address regularly hitting the Website and downloading files is a sure way to have that Website no longer used for communication. In a later chapter, discussion on methods to uncover this type of communication is detailed with court-ordered intercepts.

Steganalysis Applications

Automation in forensic analysis becomes more important as the amount of data increases and as the intensity of data hiding has been used. Visually searching through tens of thousands of images on a computer hard drive while doing a hash comparison of visually identical images takes time and is prone to error. Given that identification is only the first step as decoding the message may also be next to impossible depending upon the method used to hide the message, the more time saved, the better for the examination.

Currently, there are nearly as fewer software applications that can detect steganography than there are applications that are used for steganography in hiding information. Additionally, not all steganography detection software can detect every type of steganography method used. Practically, there is virtually no way to be absolutely certain that any detection software will find every file with a hidden message just by the reasoning that you may never know you missed a file if you actually missed a file. But even given the odds that any (or every) steganography detection application most likely will miss some files, it is still the most efficient means of finding files that most likely have hidden information when the number of files to examine is overwhelming.

INVESTIGATIVE TIP!
If one suspect uses a certain software, then...

Identifying the software and method used to hide files within files is crucial to gaining access to the hidden data. Since this is necessary for the examiner, it is also necessary for both ends of the communications. So, if you believe steganography is being used by one suspect using a specific steganography application, the other end of the communication needs to use the same software. Identifying the software used at one end practically identifies what is being used on the other end.

An example of the problematic discovery of files containing hidden data can be seen with a detection software illustration. StegExpose (http://www.darknet.org. uk/2014/09/stegexpose-steganalysis-tool-detecting-steganography-images/) is a software application designed to detect files with hidden data. However, it only detects steganography in lossy PNG and BMP images using the least significant bit type of steganography. Outside of those two file types and method of steganography and this tool misses it. To be thorough, using multiple detection software applications is necessary on top of visually inspect files you believe may contain hidden data.

How Much Information Can Be Hidden

From Fig. 5.6, the short text file containing the words "the eagle has landed" increased the hidden message file by less than 60 bytes. It is possible to add data without any noticeable increase in file size at all, especially depending upon the manner of embedding the data. If an audio or video carrier file is used to carry hidden data, the amount possible is much more, so much in fact, that an entire encyclopedia set and more could be embedded without the user of the video or audio file knowing hidden data existed as the file will play without a problem. Simply, the larger the carrier file, the more data that can be hidden.

Although images, such as seen in Fig. 5.7, can show degradation with large amounts of data embedded, visual inspection may often times overlook the possibility of steganography and attribute the degradation to corruption or partial deletion (overwriting) of the file. Countering this limitation only requires using multiple images containing embedded data in each image or in selected images among thousands of images.

STEGANOGRAPHY METHODS

Investigative Steps

Depending on the type of evidence to be examined, there are certain steps to be taken to identify data hidden in files. From the easiest, a search of known steganography software applications should be conducted. The search is not only for active installations, but also previous installations, remnants of installations, and indications of use through forensic artifact analysis of the operating system used. For example, in the Windows operating system, program information can be found in locations such as the registry, Prefetch, and even installation files in the download folder of programs downloaded from the Internet. If steganography applications are not discovered on the suspect's computer system, a search of Internet history and search terms may show the intention of using steganography based on sites visited and keywords searched through the Internet browser.

Once evidence of steganography applications has been determined, computer files should be examined for anything out of the ordinary, such as file sizes seemingly too large than expected or duplicate image/video/audio files with different hash values. Correlating file access time to the steganography program use can help narrow the potential evidence files. Also, depending upon the specific steganography application found, the types of files and method of steganography can be narrowed down to the limitations of that program. Other steganography programs could be used, but going with the known programs narrows the search for files. Depending upon the method used, simple signature detection will find anomalies of appended data to known file types.

When files suspected of containing hidden data are found, the extraction of the data remains to perhaps the most difficult part. In most cases, the software applications provide for some form of cryptography or encryption that will prevent seeing the plain text messages (or other forms of hidden data). If the program used to hide the data has been discovered, the odds of obtaining the hidden data are better, but not certain. Using brute-force or dictionary attacks may yield access to the hidden data, but success depends on the complexity of the passphrase, computer power available, and time. Without knowing how the data was hidden, it may be virtually impossible to recover unless there is a flaw in the manner hidden that can be overcome through various attacks.

RELEVANT CASES

As stated previously, it is practically impossible to determine how many instances of steganography have occurred simply because it is easy to overlook in any investigation. Even when suspected or discovered, accessing the text may be impossible due to encryption. In those types of cases, investigators may never know if the data was relevant to an investigation or completely innocent.

In Berlin, May 2011, a suspected al-Qaeda member possessed storage media containing pornographic videos. After the arrest, forensic experts found that the videos contained hidden data in 141 separate text files related to terrorism operations and plans (Gallagher, 2012). Fortunately, the hidden data was unencrypted, but had it been encrypted, the contents may have been impossible to access.

Over a period of several years, alleged Russian spies lived in the United States can communicate using high-tech means including hidden data in electronic files. In 2010, 11 suspected spies were arrested after a long investigation by the FBI (United States of America v. Anna Chapman and Mikhail Semenko, 2010). During the examination of seized evidence, a steganography program was found installed and used on a computer system that required a 27-character password. In most every situation like this, brute-force and dictionary attacks are unpredictable. However, in this particular case, the password had been written on a piece of paper and found during searches by the FBI.

SUMMARY

Every chapter of this book intends to serve to increase investigative thinking and reasoning in order to build better cases. Data hiding is one of the most elusive acts to uncover when the methods are secure. Preventing evidence from being found in the first place is the primary goal of any criminal or terrorist that wishes to remain undiscovered. Steganography is just another method of hiding evidence that investigators must add to their list of things to look for in a case. For more information on data hiding, Chet Hosmer and Michael Raggo have written a fantastic book titled *Data Hiding, Exposing Concealed Data in Multimedia, Operating Systems, Mobile Devices and Network Protocols*. Hosmer and Raggo cover many aspects of data hiding including use of mobile devices, and would be a good desk reference for any investigator.

REFERENCES

Gallagher, S. (May 2, 2012). *Ars Technica*. Retrieved October 11, 2015, from Ministry of Innovation http://arstechnica.com/business/2012/05/steganography-how-al-qaeda-hid-secret-documents-in-a-porn-video/.

United States of America v. Anna Chapman and Mikhail Semenko (Southern District of New York June 25, 2010).

United States of America v. Higinio O. Ochoa, III, 1:12-M-163 (Western District of Texas February 15, 2012).

CHAPTER 6

Cryptography and Encryption

INTRODUCTION

Several aspects of encryption overlap with that of steganography, but as in the steganography chapter, the focus will be on encryption in this chapter. As an analogy, steganography can be considered protecting an object (data) by hiding it behind a bush (example: embedded in an image). The bush only hides the object from view but is easily viewed if found.

With encryption, the object isn't hidden from view, but rather placed into a locked container. The container can be in plain view and not hiding because without the key, the container cannot be opened and the object is safe. Some of the overlap between steganography and encryption are when an object is placed inside a locked container and hidden behind a bush. Not only is the container hidden from view, but even if found, is virtually impossible to unlock.

This chapter focuses on the locked container, not the hiding spot behind the bush, so to speak.

INVESTIGATIVE TIP!
Malware hides the same way

Malicious software can be hidden (steganography) and protected (cryptography) in commonly used electronic file types such as video files. Although this chapter focuses on cryptology, the intention is that of uncovering communication, not malicious software. Software hidden in files is known as Trojan horses but is beyond the scope of this chapter.

BRIEF HISTORY OF ENCRYPTION AND CRYPTOGRAPHY

For as long as people and nations have had the need to communicate secretly, cryptography has been used to protect the communications. Considering that Julius Caesar had a cipher with his name (The Caesar cipher), cryptography has been around longer than imagined (Bauer, 2013). Through every war and peacetime, cryptography has been used and is continued to be used as a method of protecting communications within and between countries.

Cryptography is not only used for secret communications but also used to convey a great amount of information through codes we use everyday. For example, a zip code is a relatively short string of numbers, but it describes a geographical area that can be as large as 10,000 square miles or as small as 1/10 of a mile. Some driver's license number formats represent dates of birth and other personally identifiable information with only a few characters. The police 10-code is another cryptography system where a short string of numbers is used to communicate multiple words. An example of the police 10-code of "10–28" translates into a request for a dispatcher to check a vehicle's registration, stolen status, and owner information.

These types of codes used openly are not necessarily meant to hide information but is illustrative of how specific information can be changed to an unrecognizable form unless you know the cipher or decryption key. This chapter discusses the use of cryptography and encryption as a means to protect illicit communications that investigators are tasked to decipher using cryptanalysis.

Tell Me What I Need to Know

The main point of a brief history lesson is to show that cryptography and encryption are not a recent means of hiding communications. Quite simply, communications have always needed some form of secrecy and protection from others for whom the communication has not been directed.

This chapter points out methods of identification, decryption, and creating inferences from communications that cannot be broken. Most of this work can be done without an advanced degree in mathematics only because those with advanced mathematics ability have provided the tools to do the work for the examiner.

BASIC WORKING KNOWLEDGE

As a forensic analyst, do not expect to become an expert in cryptology overnight, or perhaps ever. However, the name of the art of figuring out cryptic communications is cryptanalysis, which is as complex and interesting as it sounds. The next examples easily show how simple cryptology becomes exponentially more complex with each small step.

Using the most basic and fundamental method of cryptology of substitution, Fig. 6.1 shows a simple change of plaintext letters to numbers. Using

a	b	c	d	e	f	g	h	i	j	k	l	m	n	o	p	q	r	s	t	u	v	w	x	y	z
01	02	03	04	05	06	07	08	09	10	11	12	13	14	15	16	17	18	19	20	21	22	23	24	25	26

FIGURE 6.1

Basic substitution.

a	b	c	d	e	f	g	h	i	j	k	l	m	n	o	p	q	r	s	t	u	v	w	x	y	z
f	g	h	i	j	k	l	m	n	o	p	q	r	s	t	u	v	w	x	y	z	a	b	c	d	e

FIGURE 6.2

Simple substation by shifting letters left.

the substitution cipher method seen in Fig. 6.1 simply replaces letters with numbers. A numbered string such as 0805121215 is easily deciphered as "hello."

Any party communicating with the intention to change plaintext to unintelligible characters most likely will not use simple substitution without additional layers of cipher involved. However, even with a simple substitution, communications can be overlooked when intermingled with legitimate or innocent looking communications. As an example, a handwritten letter that contained numbers within the context such as, "Did you know that on Jan 25, Alice turns 14?" could be the answer to a previously asked question. In this case, the answer would be "no" when 25 and 14 are replaced with their original letters. A simple substation that is overlooked when intermingled with innocent data is effective but only until the system is discovered.

Substitution can be exchanged letters with letters just as much as letters with numbers. In Fig. 6.1 example, each letter is substituted with a set of two numbers. Adding complexity to this method is substituting letters by shifting the letters a certain number of places to the left or right. Fig. 6.2 shows an example of shifting letters five places to the left. In this case, "hello" becomes "mjqqt." Using Fig. 6.1, "hello" becomes "0805121215." Substituting characters with symbols adds another layer of complexity due to a general unfamiliarity of reading symbols rather than alphanumeric characters.

Another substitution method that adds to complexity in a simplistic manner arranges the alphabet in a square and substitutes letters for numbers. Fig. 6.3 shows this method to be easy to use, difficult to decipher without knowing the method. Using this method, the reader must know the manner of encoding. Letters can be chosen either from the top or side and alternated. For example, "coke" could be "3311" if starting from the top numbered row to encode or it could be "1535" if starting from the left numbered column.

	1	2	3	4	5
1	a	b	c	d	e
2	f	g	h	i	j
3	k	l	m	n	o
4	p	q	r	s	t
5	u	v	w	x	y/z

FIGURE 6.3
Substitution cipher arranged in a block.

In this example, both y and z share the same value in order to have an even numbered square. Any two letters could share a single value. Additionally, the alphabet can be randomly arranged in the square for more complexity in decoding. Of note is that this method was designed by the Greeks over 2000 years ago and since then, many more methods of simple substitution have been invented and used, some based upon this method.

This is the basic knowledge of cryptography, where plaintext is changed into something that is unreadable. Although the introduction into cryptography used the example of the substitution method, there are other methods such as Transposition Ciphers, Playfair Ciphers, Vigenére Ciphers, Product Ciphers, and more. Each uses its own system to encrypt messages and does not require much more than paper and pen to create secret messages. From this point forward, the complexity increases exponentially with easy to use manual and technical methods.

TRY IT, YOU MIGHT BREAK IT

Coming across an encoded note frightens some and excites others. Any encoded message requires effort, patience, and time to decipher. Based on profiling your suspect (high tech or low tech), you may be able to decipher the message if simple substitution was used by a low-tech suspect. Correction Officers have the best opportunities to gain experience in finding secret messages in prisoner mail and attempt to decipher the messages to break illicit communications (or solve crimes!) every day.

FIGURE 6.4
The Jefferson cipher (http://en.wikipedia.org/wiki/Jefferson_disk).

HARDWARE

Hardware has made cryptography easier to create secret messages and more difficult to crack the codes to the messages. The first hardware devices were not computers as these were invented well before electricity or electronics. The first hardware cryptography devices were spindles and wooden discs which eventually evolved into the most complicated cryptography devices of the century. In 1790, Thomas Jefferson used a device consisting of a set of wheels and discs, with each disc having the alphabet imprinted in random order on each disc (Norman, 1989). Fig. 6.4 shows Jefferson's cipher.

The Jefferson cipher requires the message writer to line up all the discs to create a message. As each disc's alphabet is random and the order of discs can be changed, the order of the discs must be known to decipher the message. The message creator lines up the discs to create the words to the message and copies any row of text on the cipher. The note is virtually unreadable without having a duplicate device and knowing the order of the discs.

Today, a similar device can be purchased online or from a toy store for a few dollars to create cryptic messages quickly and easily. Children have been exposed to this type of cryptography for decades in the form of secret decoder rings used by their favorite cartoon heroes and cipher wheels that work and look very similar to the Jefferson cipher wheel.

During investigations in which any item like the Jefferson cipher or even a child's secret decoder ring toy is found, consider that communications are being encrypted with codes and that the key to cracking the code is having the device used to encrypt the message.

Big Boy Encryption Toys

World War II took cryptography to a new level of complexity. As with any war, the ability to communicate covertly and secretly can be the decisive factor in the war's outcome. Fig. 1.1 shows the German Enigma machine, which is fairly well known due to depictions in recent movies. However, more countries than German employed this type of device. For example, Japan had its own encryption device known as "Purple" which operated similarly in principle and complexity (Kippenhahn, 1999). However, with current technology, it would be a surprise to find a device such as the Enigma or Purple in use today.

The design complexity of current day encryption is difficult to comprehend because technology makes encryption quicker, easier, and more secure than ever in the past. No longer are encoder rings, cipher wheels, or suitcase size contraptions needed to encrypt messages. Today, any computer device, including a smartphone, can create a message, encrypt it with the strongest method available, and send anonymously anywhere in the world.

Today's encryption systems are so secure in fact, that not only is online banking and shopping secure for individuals but money is transmitted 24/7 worldwide securely. But like any technology, encryption methods are created, broken, and improved constantly.

Here Come the Computers

During the early 70s, the Data Encryption Standard (DES) was developed. At the time, DES was the strongest encryption in existence and believed to have a long useful life of decades before being broken. DES used a block cipher, which is an algorithm that transforms plaintext into ciphertext through a series of operations. The block size of DES is 64-bit. However, 8 of the 64 bits are for parity checking which reduces the usable block to 56 bits. In 1998, DES was proven to be cracked in less than 3 days by a brute-force attack on 90 billion keys per second (EFF DES Cracker, 2015).

Over the next decade, several improvements over DES were tried until reaching the Advanced Encryption Standard (AES) in 2001. AES is still used today and believed to last for some time to come. As a comparison to DES, AES uses a block size of 128 bits and three different key lengths of 128, 192, and 256 bits. Grasping the basic operation of AES is that AES uses substitution and permutation. Substitution has been demonstrated, however, permutation is bit shuffling.

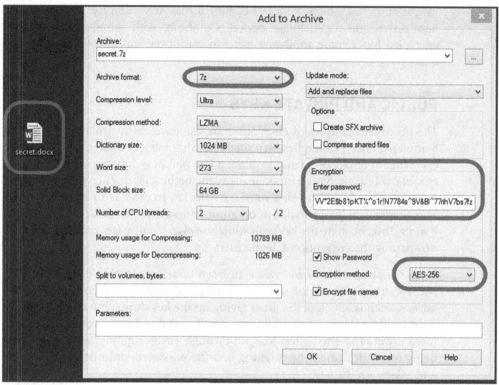

FIGURE 6.5
7-zip interface (http://www.7-zip.org/).

The key size chosen for encryption with AES determines the number of cycles to convert plaintext into ciphertext. A repetition of 10 cycles requires 128-bit keys, 12 cycles requires 192-bit keys, and 14 cycles require 256-bit keys. Clearly, AES encrypted data is unbreakable with current computing power, and even in the future, very unlikely to succeed.

Ease of Use Makes It User-Friendly

Any person with good or bad intentions desiring to send an encrypted message today with assurances of being protected will choose a combination of the easiest and securest encryption method. Given that AES is among the most secure of any encryption method, the assumption is that using it may not be convenient or easy. That is a false assumption. Fig. 6.5 shows an open source compression software (7-zip) which also provides AES-256-bit encryption along with compression.

Considering that AES-256 is virtually and practically the most secure encryption available and that 7-zip can encrypt a file in seconds with a few clicks, any investigation has a high chance of coming across AES encrypted files in e-mails, hard drives, and small storage devices. Combined with strong passwords, AES encrypted files require another method to crack over brute-force and dictionary attacks.

PUBLIC AND PRIVATE KEYS

The previous examples of encryption are examples of symmetric encryption. Symmetric encryption relies on a single key that must be shared with someone else. The mere fact of having to share a key makes symmetric encryption vulnerable. If Bob encrypts a message using the highest grade encryption available in order to send to Alice, Alice must have the key in order to open the message. This results in at least two points of failure in security. Should Bob or Alice mishandle, lose, or share the key with someone else, security weakens regardless of how strong the encryption scheme used.

From the perspective of an investigator, symmetric encryption provides at least two locations to look for the key (sender and receiver). If both persons are known, each is at risk of the other giving up the key during interviews or being found written down on paper during search warrants. Other avenues of obtaining a symmetric encryption key are through eavesdropping, as in physically being near Alice when she is telling Bob the password, or under fake pretense and asking for the key.

The advent of public and private keys (asymmetric encryption) has eliminated the risk of encryption key disclosure from everyone except for the sender of encrypted data who maintains the private key. With asymmetric encryption, senders of encrypted communications (e-mails as an example) use the public key of the recipient. The recipient uses a private key to decrypt the communication. In this manner, anyone can use a public key to encrypt e-mail and know that only the intended recipient will be able to decrypt the e-mail.

An analogy that is useful is that of lockboxes and a key. Imagine that you have a single key (private key) and an unlimited supply of lockboxes (public key) for which only your private key can open. The lockboxes are available for anyone to take, place messages in, close the box, and give back to you. Once the lockbox has been locked, it cannot be opened by anyone without the private key. In this manner, once a message is placed in your lockbox, the sender knows that only you have the key to open it. To reply to the message, you use the lockbox of your recipient to place a message, close the door, and give it back. Fig. 6.6 is a visual depiction of the asymmetric public–private key encryption, where only one person has the key to open an unlimited number of safes in which anyone can use to lock (encrypt) messages.

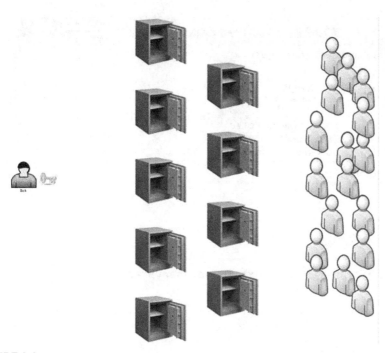

FIGURE 6.6

Visual depiction of public–private key encryption, where anyone has access to use a safe to lock a message, but not able to unlock it.

With asymmetrical encryption, the public key is publicly available to anyone to use for encrypting messages to be sent to the one person with the one key to decrypt the message. Asymmetrical removes the risk of key sharing and reduces the chances that someone will be able to decrypt a message, even if intercepted. Pretty Good Privacy and GNU Privacy Guard are two examples where public keys are shared to restrict one private key.

Perhaps the most common reason asymmetrical encryption is not used as much as it could be is that the perception of encrypting communications is complicated and along the lines of spy movies. But in practical use, encrypting communications with this method is a simple process. Fig. 6.7 shows a screenshot of an e-mail client (Thunderbird) with Enigmail extension added. The sender only needs to press one button (icon of a lock) to encrypt the contents of the e-mail. An option to attach the sender's public key is available to give the receiver the public key to encrypt e-mails to this particular sender.

As you can see, the encryption process using an e-mail client seen in Fig. 6.7 is nearly user-error proof. The receiver of the encrypted e-mail needs only to enter

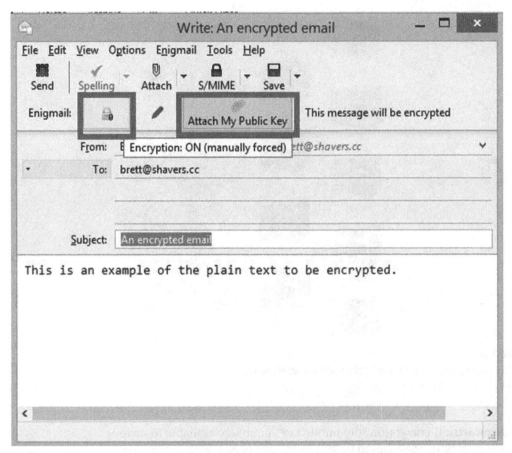

FIGURE 6.7
Thunderbird e-mail client with Enigmail (https://www.mozilla.org/en-US/thunderbird/ and https://www.enigmail.net/home/index.php).

the decryption key (password) to read the contents of the e-mail. Without the password, the contents of the encrypted e-mail will be unintelligible text, such as the example seen in Fig. 6.8.

INVESTIGATIVE TIP!
Only the contents are encrypted

Fig. 6.8 also shows a public key attached to the encrypted e-mail. Additionally, it shows the subject line in plaintext! Investigators may not be able to decrypt the message, but sometimes the subject line may give enough information to help build a case. Users not realizing the subject line is not encrypted provide information in the open unknowingly.

From Brett Shavers <brett@shavers.cc>
Subject **An encrypted email**
    To Brett Shavers <brett@shavers.cc>

```
-----BEGIN PGP MESSAGE-----
Charset: utf-8
Version: GnuPG v2.0.20 (MingW32)

hQIMA2oPDhYUvI/nARAAzmnEKKxL2SvcsZzBijbvaFnMQ7eVsBBjKXSSOARLysPE
2n79WZZZJbxciLTRy5nvbzBT1STQFWCjvaMJN00eQ0Uu/mYZ8yHq3rdnuNxZyVz1
5WNMuebBG0LlRB4LCF+uCsagB8IknU35fznXMoO7yu7tn0xZYDODJkWS8bTDfzL/
5gzXP3COae7JabsUZ/02DNLsjT/xgrlyt3roR4m6dC755Vy4MWlqjwHbvpVvBlL3
inOFLocMetxR700pSa6y/COSEAf/K9ejBOU0a9/LS/ljhWIpSSbl3/SlfCToQQa0
YEiod2P9bmI3hxMjBbz1rmUXD0jNPptrPQmJfZW94aFUFqPakHt8nzVhz0/v3iVo
swJ3r3eYuhHsDcKxeFV/K23AXfpe4vsE+z6PubRH1RVa9AAqUuinQ4njU5HGS6IQ
yjglMJqmmytZeTNNdpA8UFMrebFGLjm0PPFTN6nLTEor2j4pVpgPeoFUxi8uCUXU
K2LuwGKEkYcHGhZjCVvMqLDGBdqN6cGoTXYQK4enjHJAjPqOBYdKPXWR+za+SVwg
NeWFnHT0pAsmfF7VTrsoVgnYXtpT7VrM189gnwFdpfVibDQbkWb13Hwaga+SAHNR
Cmv9bfEwjhECU6P1Z9rjsG525eGa6KynTC9kK3aag+BH9PoZrscocU2NJbxdPPjS
RAEyg7pDIqHssAkg9YMTBZ8MapfjVafHizAobiEEMDXxEiw/hiAfgtYZtcMVGGBz
R7nQcy3xhi5zSAUMUf+OoLA+3o8Y
=0Cs6
-----END PGP MESSAGE-----
```

▷ 📎1 attachment: 0xC6DD3C1B.asc 3.1 KB

FIGURE 6.8
Encrypted e-mail example with attached public key.

Communications sent using asymmetrical encryption using a locally installed e-mail client are as secure as most e-mail service providers offering encrypted webmail with one major difference: the key. With asymmetrical encryption where the users physically possess the key, practically any e-mail provider can be used to send encrypted messages using most any e-mail client such as Mozilla Thunderbird. However, with an e-mail service that provides encryption at the server side (compared to the client side with asymmetrical encryption), a risk exists of compromise at the server side. Users must inherently trust the webmail service provider to encrypt correctly e-mails without creating backdoors or ability to open by others.

A server-side encryption provider is an option to consider during an investigation to obtain decryption keys when used by suspects. Depending upon the jurisdiction and cooperation of a webmail service provider, e-mails may be provided decrypted without the suspect's assistance or knowledge. Interesting enough, many of the webmail providers offering encryption service are based in countries with strong privacy laws making it difficult for law enforcement cooperation

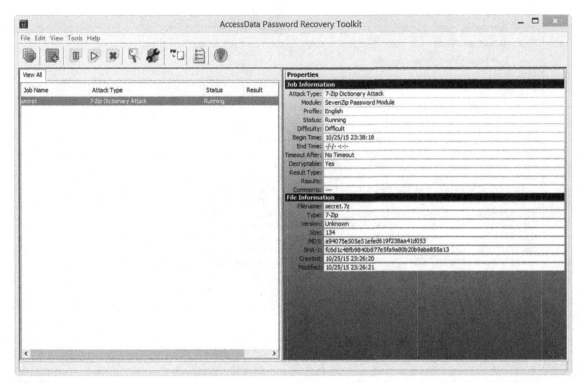

FIGURE 6.9

Accessdata Password Recovery Toolkit (http://www.accessdata.com).

from outside those countries. On one hand, this provides strong privacy protection for individuals, but can also provide protection from criminals.

Breaking Encryption

Several commercial vendors and open source applications provide methods of bypassing passwords. Fig. 6.9 shows Accessdata Password Recovery Toolkit running a dictionary attack on a 7-zip AES-256 bit encrypted file. In this specific example, the file's password is "VV*2E$b81pKT%^o1r!N7784s^9V&Bl^77 rihV7bs7fz." Knowing that AES-256 is extremely secure to cracking attempts, recovering the password requires time, computing power, and luck that a dictionary or brute-force attack will find an easy password. Strong passwords increase the likelihood, if not guarantee it, that the encryption will not be broken.

Breaking any encryption system can be done with unlimited time and unlimited computing power, both of which do not exist. Anything less than that unlimited power and time will require chance and good investigative skills. Several methods to break encryption include dictionary attacks, brute-force attacks, and rainbow tables. A dictionary attack tries variations of words found in dictionaries.

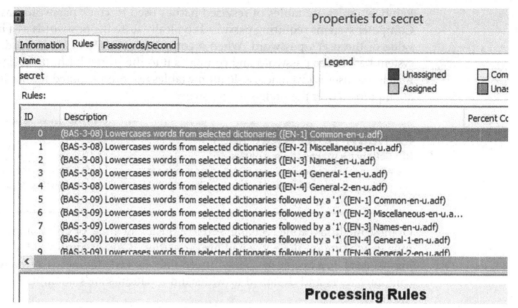

FIGURE 6.10

Accessdata Password Recovery Toolkit "Rules" (http://www.accessdata.com).

The speed at which passwords are tried depends upon the computing power. Millions of passwords can be tried each second using a basic computer system with higher end systems able to try even more passwords per second. Fig. 6.10 shows an example of some of the dictionaries used to attack using Accessdata's Password Recovery Toolkit. Considering that a password may not even be in a recognizable word format, a dictionary attack will be ineffective in some instances.

However, dictionary attacks should not be overlooked because of not knowing the password. As an example, by changing the password used in the test file seen in Fig. 6.6 to a commonly used English word, the password was recovered in less than 3 minutes. Although using the highest grade AES-256 bit encryption is easy, quick, and effective, a flaw remains with the user in choosing a strong password. The password can make a seemingly impossible to crack file easily done in minutes.

Brute-force attacks are similar to dictionary attacks in that guessing is the key method. Brute-force attacks try variations of characters of various lengths that could be the password. The amount of time and computing power required depends on the complexity and length of the password. Short passwords can be recovered fairly quickly, but longer passwords increase the time exponentially according to password length and complexity. Dictionary attacks are generally the chosen method over brute-force attacks.

Rainbow tables are tables of reversed hashes used to crack password hashes. Computer systems requiring passwords typically store the passwords as a hash value of the user's password. When a computer user enters a password, the system hashes the password and compares it to the stored hash. If the hashes match, the user is given access. Rainbow tables use precomputed hashes in an attempt to recover the prehashed password.

RAINBOW TABLES ARE EASY
But Cellebrite makes it even easier
The Android gesture security is a SHA 1 value which can be decoded using a rainbow table. The decoding is now built into Cellebrite's Physical Analyzer which uses Python to decode the value.

Of these methods, none is guaranteed to work all the time, or even some of the time depending on the encrypted file properties. If AES is approved for securing national Top Secret data, then it certainly exceeds the needs of everyday computer users and designed to withstand a nation-state's attempts to crack the encryption.

THE KEY IS THE KEY

In all that has been covered, the most important aspect of cracking codes and encryption is the key. Having the key used to encode the message can make the difference between being able to read the contents of a message and never being able to do so. Depending upon the type of method used, a single key may unlock an entire string of communications. During the course of months or years of encrypted communications that are stored on a computer device, once the key has been obtained, the entirety of all communications can be decrypted. Much like one pull of a zipper can open a coat, having the key can open the strings of communications otherwise not decipherable.

Without the key, cryptanalysis is much a physical feat as it is mental. And luck. Don't forget about luck.

INVESTIGATIVE TIP!
Suspects having access to numbers and letters can communicate secretly
Even prisoners use cryptography to communicate within prison and with the outside world. Physical letters are sent and received with secret messages intermingled with innocent appearing communications. Going beyond looking at the obvious contents of a letter, consider that numbers and letters can have a meaning unseen to the casual observer. All you need is the key to unlock the secret message in the cover content.

SO TELL ME SOMETHING I CAN DO ABOUT THIS!

On the face of strong encryption coupled with strong passwords, decryption with technical resources is many times unable to break encryption. Then again, a password cracker could find the password in a reasonable amount of time. For this reason, try to break the encryption with an application designed to find passwords. Hook it up and let it run. Having access to distributed computer systems or even clustered computer systems will give more computing power to run more password attempts at a faster rate. Both distributed and clustered networks are basically a group of computers connected together to work in conjunction on a problem. Distributed network systems can even use computers from the cloud, which can be a nearly unlimited resource of computing power. If your resources are lacking, colleges and universities may be able to help with computing power in your investigation.

Not every investigator has access to a distributed network system using dozens or hundreds of computer systems to crack a password. Also, time may be of an issue that trying passwords with any system is not going to work. In these situations, the password has to be obtained with other measures. Perhaps the fastest, easiest, and most effective is simply asking for the password. Situations with the suspect in custody, or simply being questioned and not in custody, just asking for passwords might result in being given the password.

The human condition includes forgetfulness. Passwords are in an area where remembering long character strings is incredibly difficult for most people. Even remembering short passwords can be forgotten if not used regularly. This is the main weakness of any encryption method: the user. Users who write passwords on paper, save passwords in electronic files on their electronic devices, use the same passwords for more than one account, or use passwords that are based on some aspect of their lives increase chances that the password will be found or recovered with password recovery applications. Quite simply, finding the password written down anywhere could be the deciding factor in whether or not an encrypted file or e-mail can be decrypted. This applies to encrypted passwords as it does to physical safes. If the combination is written down and found, the strongest safe can be opened without (brute) force.

One method used to reduce forgetting many passwords is to use one password for many accounts. Again, this is a user flaw of encryption and basic computer security. As an example, rather than using different passwords for social networking Websites, online banking, and encrypting e-mail, a suspect may use one or few passwords. So, before trying to brute-force or dictionary attack an encrypted file, search for any plaintext or easily obtainable passwords on the

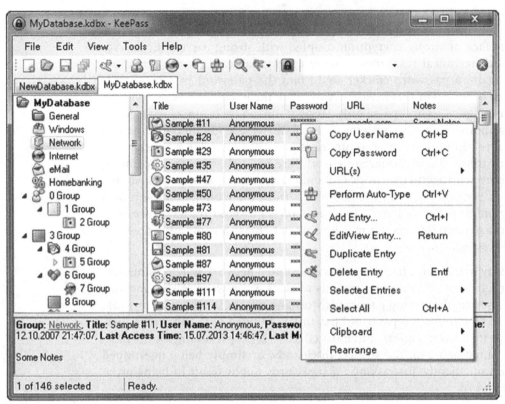

FIGURE 6.11

Keepass password utility (http://keepass.info/).

suspect's systems as the one password found easily on a device could be the password to many encrypted files on multiple devices.

Password storage applications are a good source of passwords if you can access the application. The convenience of being able to store the most complex passwords in one database means that none have to be remembered or written down anywhere, yet still be protected by a single login of the storage application. Fig. 6.11 shows Keepass, a freely available password storage system. Accessing the password database can supply the passwords for all encryption used by the suspect. By default, most password storage systems require a password to access stored passwords. But as mentioned, complacency is a weakness, and if the password storage program is set to open without a password, all passwords are available as if written on a sheet of paper. Again, the key is gaining access to the application, in which the same methods can be used as discussed in this section. Having more sources of passwords increases the odds of obtaining the password needed.

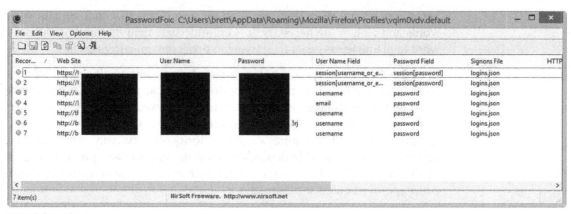

FIGURE 6.12

PasswordFox (http://www.nirsoft.net).

Fig. 6.12 shows Nirsoft's PasswordFox recovering multiple passwords stored in the Firefox browser. Potentially, any of these passwords could be reused with other logins, encrypted e-mails, or individual encrypted files. In this type of situation, regardless of the length and complexity of the password used, if recovered with this method, the encryption is broken. Each Internet browser may have passwords saved, as does the Windows registry, and most importantly, live memory on a system that has not been shut down. In the case of live memory, even if the password has not been saved anywhere else (on or off the system), if it was used during the current session, it is possibly recoverable from live memory.

Another option is creating a word list from electronic devices owned, controlled, or used by suspects. By culling all words, numbers, and strings of words and numbers into a list to be imported into a password recovery program, it is possible that even an extremely complex password can be recovered. This method works on the user point of failure in that perhaps at some point, the user typed the password into an application or stored e-mail on the device, and that the password was collected into the word list. In this manner, a simple word list can be more effective than the most powerful computing machine to recover a password.

When searching a suspect's residence or workplace, the electronic devices are important, but may become useless if not able to be accessed. When the field of digital forensics was in its infancy, the physical seizures of computer systems were extensive in that not only were the computers seized, but also the keyboard, monitor, mouse, and every attached wire. Gradually this has been reduced to seizing only relevant items and photographing irrelevant items unless necessary for the investigation. With encryption, the seizure of every component does not become necessary again, but searching for documents that may contain passwords and ciphers are necessary. It is an understatement that finding the password in plain view is easier than trying to break into an encrypted file.

In cases where the suspect is not yet arrested, and contact will compromise an investigation, asking is not a viable option. Covert acquisitions would provide word lists from storage devices and potentially saved passwords in browsers as previously discussed. However, covert acquisitions may not be easy without case compromise, requires a legal authority on personally owned devices, and might not be possible depending upon the location and physical security of the devices. In a later chapter, legal authority and investigative tips with court-approved orders are discussed.

Barring asymmetric encryption, when shared keys are required to communicate, there must be a point in time when the key(s) are shared. Whether this is done face-to-face, over texts, phone calls, or e-mail, in order for secret communications to be delivered in encrypted files is through delivering the key to the receiving party. If the key is changed, or rather, every time the key is changed, this process must occur each time. Being able to intercept listening to the key/password through wiretaps or other means requires physical investigative work to gather probable cause for legal authority. Intercepts are discussed in a later chapter in more detail. However, the takeaway in this section is to remember that there must be some unencrypted communications between suspects to pass encryption credentials when asymmetric encryption is not used.

When Nothing Works

Encryption works when the user correctly uses it. In situations where the password has not been recovered anywhere, and the suspect refuses to produce the password, don't give up yet. Depending on the time needed to close a case, hold onto the evidence as at some point, the password might be obtained.

One thing to avoid in any investigation is following false leads. Following a false lead wastes time, energy, resources, and can negatively affect a case from being successfully closed. With encrypted evidence, accepting that breaking into the evidence is practically impossible, work on some other aspect of the case. Focusing on an unsolvable problem will take away from productive work. Even when there is only file of interest solely because it is encrypted, that one file may be unimportant in the totality of the case if other evidence exists to make a case.

False leads can be created by suspects using encrypted files to draw intentionally attention away from the real evidence, or to plainly waste an investigator's time. If hundreds or thousands of encrypted files are seen on a system, the possibility exists that the files do not contain any information of importance, other than random data, intentionally encrypted by a suspect to draw attention and time to a meaningless endeavor. Again, in this type of situation, focus on the evidence you can find now and then the tougher to crack potential evidence later unless you know that most important evidence resides in a file that must be decrypted.

BACK TO STEGANOGRAPHY

As mentioned, steganography and cryptography cross paths in some aspects, but are different. But even being different, both can be used in conjunction with each other. Encrypted data hidden in an electronic file more than doubles the chances of not only being not decrypted because not being found in the first place.

However, even if an encrypted file has been found to be hidden behind other data, it is still important beyond its contents. Discovering the methods of communication can show intention, level of technical knowledge, and add overall value to an investigation. Although any encrypted file may or may not contain evidence, the manner and use of encryption to thwart an investigation goes toward showing the complexity of crimes committed.

SUMMARY

Cryptanalysis is not easy. Nation states have invested greatly in the resources to create and break encrypted communications. With the brightest minds and most powerful computer systems, the key to cracking encryption and codes is having the key. Otherwise brute-force attacks are used as the last resort. Investigators must know enough about encryption in order to recognize it as containing potential evidence. Being unable to access encrypted files, including e-mail, today does not mean these will be inaccessible tomorrow. The encryption keys may be found at any point of an investigation, either through the suspect's error, a brute-force/dictionary attack, or chance of coming upon the password. Put the inaccessible evidence aside and work on other aspects of the investigation until keys and passwords are recovered. If all that exists are encrypted communications and encrypted files, work on obtaining the keys, knowing that unless lucky, it may be impossible to access.

REFERENCES

Bauer, C. P. (2013). *Secret history: The story of cryptology*. Boca Raton: CRC Press.

EFF DES cracker. (October 26, 2015). Retrieved from Electronic Frontier Foundation https://w2.eff.org/Privacy/Crypto/Crypto_misc/DESCracker/.

Kippenhahn, R. (1999). *Code breaking a history and exploration*. Woodstock: The Overlook Press.

Norman, B. (1989). *Secret warfare: The battle of codes and cyphers*. New York: Sterling Publishing.

CHAPTER 7

Antiforensics

INTRODUCTION

Criminals are acutely aware that if their communications are discovered, their plans will be compromised, and they will be at risk of arrest based on their spoken or written words. However, they are also aware that future crimes require communication with conspirators to plan their criminal activity even when at risk of discovery.

We have discussed methods of hiding communications using cryptography and also hiding IP addresses while on the Internet to stay anonymous online. This chapter discusses analyzing electronic storage media that have been seized for analysis which may have been tampered with antiforensics (also known as counterforensics) techniques. Just as a forensic analyst will never know how many times they have overlooked evidence hidden through steganography methods, it is also likely that analyst will not know how many times evidence has been obfuscated through antiforensics methods.

One aspect of antiforensics this chapter does not cover is the subject of intruders covering their tracks in networks. The reason for this is that intruders covering their tracks do not have the same purpose in mind that criminals or terrorists do when protecting their communications with each other. Another aspect not covered is all the methods of antiforensics used to hide evidence. The focus is targeting that which is used for communications, such as e-mail and Internet use, not specifically hiding evidence files such as child pornography, although many of the same methods are used for both.

Digital forensics is no longer seen by the public as a mysterious art that magically brings deleted electronic files back to life. Movies and television commonly incorporate, if not focus completely, on the technology capabilities of forensic analysts. Although the Hollywood version may embellish some aspects of forensic analysis, much is based on actual forensic capabilities. Criminals using technology to communicate are acutely aware that if their devices are seized, their communications are at risk of being discovered as seen in the movies. They understand that chats, e-mails, and webmail can be recovered from electronic storage devices, including mobile devices. Methods of countering antiforensics discussed in this chapter are those methods that can be employed by the vast majority of investigators without the need of top secret software and supercomputers, which the vast majority of investigators are unable to access anyway.

THE EASY AND VERY EFFECTIVE METHODS

Sometimes the best way is the easy way, and sometimes the easy way is the most effective. Depending upon the time available, opportunity, and determination of criminals, antiforensic methods can be used that will thwart any and all forensic attempts. Some of these are so effective that they require only a brief statement of discussion.

Hiding the Evidence

If the evidence does not exist, neither can a forensic analysis exist. Simply disposing of the electronic evidence prevents disclosure of the contents of the device. Criminals wishing to prevent any recovery of electronic evidence need only enough time and opportunity to dispose of the evidence. In the case of electronics, evidence usually consists of electronic storage devices since this is where the actual information resides. A common fear is that once electronic storage devices are in the hands of investigators, chat/video logs, e-mail threads, and other communications will be recovered.

The quickest antiforensic method is disposing evidence in an area where the likelihood of its being found is unlikely at best. Whether at the bottom of a lake, river, cliff, or buried in a remote location, preventing the device from being found at all means practically no evidence exists to examine. The smaller the device, the easier to quickly dispose of it, such as tossing it out the window of a car on the freeway.

Whole Device Encryption

Encryption is an antiforensic method employed legitimately and illegitimately. When computing devices are lost or stolen, and the owner employed encryption on the device, criminals are generally unable to access the data. This is legitimate for businesses and persons. Criminal use of encryption is generally for the purpose of preventing law enforcement from accessing electronic evidence in their investigations. As discussed previously, encryption works very well when employed correctly. Many mobile devices are encrypted by default, which gives almost certainty that access will be problematic at best.

Encountering encrypted devices in which there is no known method of bypass-ing the encryption does not mean the data is inaccessible forever, only that it is inaccessible today. For example, whole disk encryption effectively makes the data on the disk inaccessible. Whether decryption keys/passwords can be obtained later may or may not be known, but it is certainly possible that a password can be discovered through traditional means, such as having been written down or divulged by the suspect during interviews. What is impossible today may be possible tomorrow, so hold onto the evidence and keep trying.

Data Wiping

Data wiping, or more accurately "overwriting data with other data," is an effec-tive antiforensic method in that overwriting electronic evidence effectively makes the data unrecoverable. The negative aspect of data wiping for criminals is a positive aspect for investigators. The time required to wipe data increases in relation to the storage size of the storage device, in which small media can be wiped in minutes but larger disk drives can take many hours to complete. Since the time involved is so great, the odds that criminals will regularly wipe all of their storage devices are not great.

Physical Destruction

Data propagates when active, that is, when online, data is created, dupli-cated, and manipulated constantly. However, when taken offline and physi-cally destroyed, the data is gone unless copies exist on other devices. Physical destruction of a device can be as simple as drilling holes in a hard drive or smashing with a sledgehammer, or both. Either way, once the device is phys-ically destroyed, the data is effectively destroyed as well. Physical destruction also requires a time factor to consider if using blunt objects such as a hammer. Even a drill may require several minutes before completely drilling through a hard drive casing and platters. Hard drive shredders, however, are extremely effective and fast in turning a hard drive into scrap metal pieces. Given the prices of hard drive shredders, the odds of the average criminal or terrorist pos-sessing such a large, heavy, and expensive machine would be slim.

Destroying devices means that new devices must be acquired, configured, used, and subsequently destroyed, only to create the need to acquire new devices. Mobile devices, such as cell phones, are easily replaced but also require time to obtain and configure new ones for use. The more devices used, the more the chance a single device may be overlooked for destruction or simply tossed in a drawer or left in a closet. Destruction is effective, but do not assume everything is always destroyed or buried in a secret location. Criminals and terrorists are humans. Humans make mistakes and succumb to the same rules of human nature, such as laziness and complacency. The errors made by the criminals often create the breaks in your investigations.

THE BEST METHODS AREN'T THE MOST COMMONLY USED METHODS

The most effective antiforensic method is a combination of data wiping, encryption, physical destruction, and remote disposal for every device. When all of these are used on any device, that device is no longer a threat to the criminal as evidence. But as mentioned, it is the time, energy, effort, and motivation for any criminal to do this every single time for every single electronic device that makes the most effective method unlikely to succeed due to the sheer amount of effort and time involved.

Additionally, to communicate electronically, including with cell phones and the Internet, criminals must make use of their devices regularly, if not constantly. To dispose of their devices requires new devices to be acquired, in a never-ending cycle in which complacency and mistakes are made. The main point being that even if your targets are disposing their devices, they are certainly keeping some devices active at any given time, reusing devices, and due to the sheer number of devices used, they overlook devices that may be left in a closet, café, or simply lost to be found again as evidence at some point.

ANOTHER SIMPLE METHOD

Disposing of every device is one method; another simple method is collecting as many devices as possible to overwhelm forensic attempts. For example, collecting hundreds of CDs, DVDs, flash drives, hard drives, cell phones, and other storage devices will create an immense volume of items which results in a time delay for investigators to examine each item should a seizure occur.

Potentially, and realistically, any one of the devices may contain actual evidence and just be hidden among hundreds of nonevidence storage devices; however, to find that one device that may contain evidence requires examining every item, which takes time. Compounding the time is the data stored on the devices. It is possible, but not very likely, that the suspect could use the devices regularly to create ongoing data creation on the devices, giving the appearance that the devices may contain evidence. But in all likelihood, using hundreds of storage devices on a regular basis to create fake evidence would leave no time to commit or plan crimes.

There are methods of seeding data on the devices by merely copying thousands of electronic files to all the storage devices. The more files on the devices, the more time needed to sort through each device to determine if evidence exists. In the case of many items, forensic imaging of the storage devices may not be the best method when time is crucial, thereby delaying examination until the devices are triaged for low-hanging fruit (easy-to-find evidence). Even with the best triage methods, evidence can be overlooked resulting in an evidence item being discarded from an evidence container temporarily or permanently.

One forensic application that can greatly decrease triage time is Bulk Extractor (http://digitalcorpora.org/). Bulk Extractor is a multithreaded search utility that scans storage devices for specific types of strings at a speed that far surpasses most forensic suites. For example, Bulk Extractor can scan storage devices and extract e-mail addresses, telephone numbers, ethernet media address control (MAC) addresses, IP addresses, Internet domains, and other relevant information that may indicate potential evidence based on the content desired several times faster than forensic application suites. Focusing on these specific types of data that can be extracted to individual lists after scanning terabytes of data may quickly point to modes of communication in minutes rather than hours or days of triaging manually.

Adding to the methods to overwhelm the forensic examiner with many devices is encryption of many nonevidence electronic files. As an example, one storage device such as a 1-terabyte external drive can be seeded with hundreds of thousands of files in which all or many are encrypted. On first glance, it would seem that this particular device must contain evidence since files are encrypted, but in reality, instead of evidence the encrypted files are meaningless and only created to waste the investigator's time with decryption attempts and computing time.

As an antiforensic method, intentionally collecting hundreds of devices is not the most practical or effective way since it is easily defeated by examiners through triage. It is also not likely to be used by criminals due to the time involved to collect and send data on a large number of devices. This antiforensic method is really only a delaying tactic, as an investigator can go through every item given enough time until real evidence is found. However, a cache of storage media should not be overlooked as a potential source of evidence, hidden or not.

FILE SIGNATURE MANIPULATION

Electronic files have file signatures (file header signatures) which are needed by operating systems and programs in order to select the appropriate program to open or run the file. For example, an image file will be opened in an image viewer. The image viewer program recognizes the header signature as an image file and will correctly open it. Fig. 7.1 shows the header of a typical image file known as a JPEG with the first 4 bytes of a JPEG noted.

The antiforensic method using file signature manipulation is simply changing the header to a different file type. An example would be using the JPEG image file shown in Fig. 7.1 and changing the file signature to a system file or any file

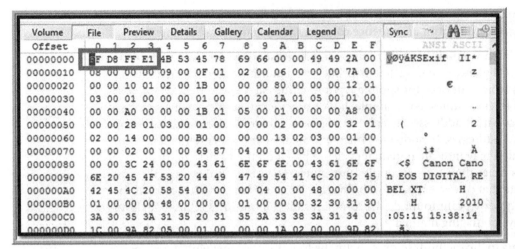

FIGURE 7.1

JPEG file signature header.

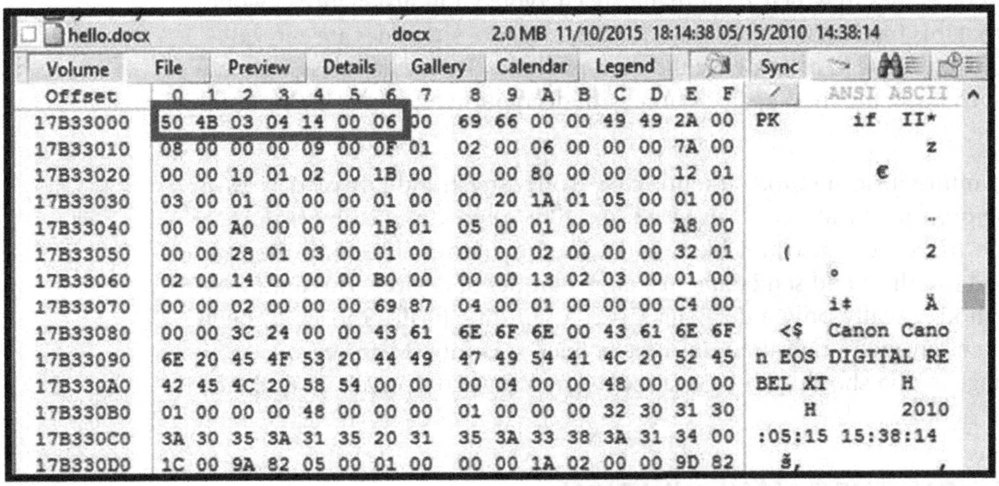

FIGURE 7.2

JPEG file signature changed to a DOCX file signature.

type other than an image file type. The file will not be able to be opened by an image viewer, nor usable as the changed file type, yet can contain electronic evidence such as a text message. Fig. 7.2 shows the same file from Fig. 7.1, but the file header has been changed from a JPEG to a DOCX using a hex editor. The file contents remain the same since only the file header has changed.

Attempting to open a file that has had its file signature changed results in an error as seen in Fig. 7.3. Fig. 7.3 shows that when trying to open the

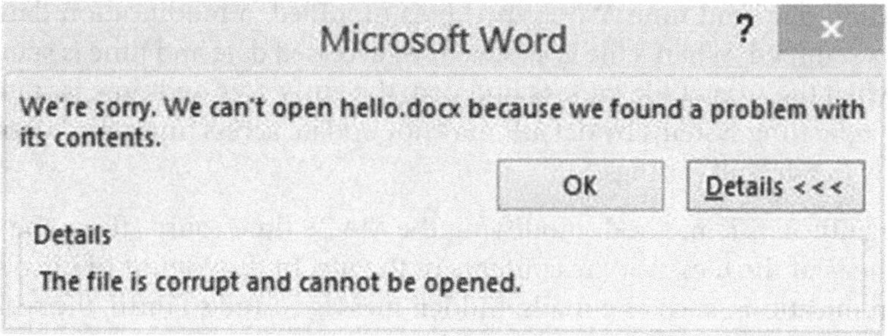

FIGURE 7.3
Program error in attempt to open a file with a manipulated file signature.

manipulated file, Microsoft Word is chosen based on the changed file header, but since the file is actually an image file, an error dialog box gives a corruption notice. Forensic software applications easily defeat this type of antiforensics, but as a simple method of exchanging data with others, it can be easily over-looked with just a visual inspection.

In practical use, one suspect can create a file with a message detailing criminal plans, change the file header, and give the file to another suspect via e-mail, peer-to-peer transfer, or by copying onto an external storage device such as a flash drive. The receiver simply repairs the file header to open and read the message as intended.

A forensic analysis method useful in triage to counter this antiforensic technique is to look at the use of recent programs and the files opened by them. For example, if a text editor was recently used to open a JPEG file this would be suspicious. A text editor is generally used with text files, not image files. Potentially, if a text editor is seen to have been used with a JPEG file, it is possible that this antiforensic method is being used to hide data in a text file, but in reality it has manipulated the text file to appear as an image file.

Changing the file extension of a file, such as changing a .jpg to a .sys does change the appearance of the file name in Windows Explorer and camouflages the true file type. However, the file can still be opened with the intended pro-gram without issue, thereby allowing anyone to read the contents if they know which program to use. However, changing the file header prevents the file from being opened at all, even by the original program used to create the file.

TIME STAMP MODIFICATIONS

The modified, accessed, created, and entry file times (MACE) are time stamps on electronic files, whether system/program files or user-created files. Basically, when files are created on a storage medium, they are "stamped" with a creation date and time. When the file is modified, a modification date and time is stamped. When a file is accessed, an accessed date and time is stamped, and when the master file table is updated, the entry date and time is stamped. Some operating systems by default may not update access times, and users can modify the default settings.

As an antiforensic method, modifying the MACE times only affects the dates and times of the files, not the contents of the file. In the context of uncovering communications, such as e-mails, hidden messages, and so forth, the real date and time may not be as important as the content of the file. However, if a file signature of a text file has been changed to mimic a system file, and the file's MACE times have been predated by months, this method adds to hiding data that can be overlooked. Of note is that not all time stamp manipulation programs alter the entry time stamp.

Several software applications are available to modify any or all of the MACE date/time stamps on single files or an entire storage device. It is important during an analysis to keep that fact in mind when using forensic applications and sorting by file dates. If a chat record or file containing correspondence occurred within a certain period of interest, sorting files by date would potentially miss relevant evidence if the MACE stamps have been altered. Countering this method requires looking for evidence of time stamp modification applications. Review of log files is helpful as log files are sequential, and out of sequence logs show manipulation of MACE time stamps.

Some tools to modify MACE time stamps are seen in Table 7.1. The ease of manipulating file time stamps using software designed for manipulation needs little explanation. Fig. 7.4 shows the dialog box for a graphical user interface for Timestomp, where a file or folder simply needs to be selected and date/time chosen to change. Timestomp is not currently maintained by the developers but has been archived on several Websites for download.

Determining whether or not a MACE time stamp tool was used should be part of most host-based forensic examinations. Windows artifacts (registry, Prefetch, lnk files, etc.) should be analyzed to determine if any of the Table 7.1

Table 7.1 Selection of Software Applications Designed to Alter MACE Time Stamps

TimeStomp	http://www.bishopfox.com/resources/tools/other-free-tools/mafia/
TimeStomp GUI	http://sourceforge.net/projects/timestomp-gui/
BulkFileChanger	http://www.nirsoft.net/utils/bulk_file_changer.html
Funduc Software Touch	http://www.funduc.com/fstouch.htm
AttributeMagic	http://www.attributemagic.com/attributemagic-free.html

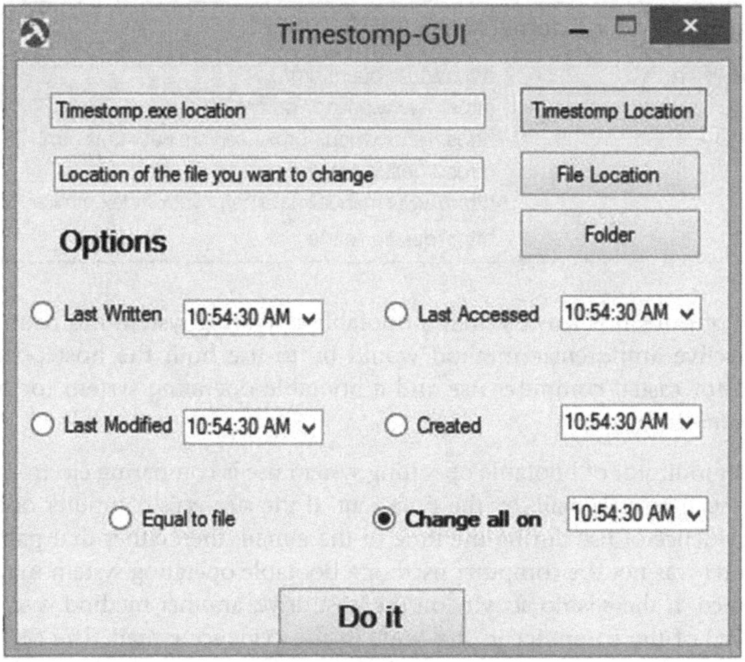

FIGURE 7.4
Timestomp GUI.

applications or similar programs have been used, installed, or searched for with Internet browsers. If any similar application has been found on the device, all dates and times on the device are in question. Randall Karstetter has one of the better slide decks on time stamp detection on Windows operating systems that addresses time stamp manipulation issues (http://www.slideshare.net/ctin/time-stamp-analysis-of-windows-systems).

DECOY STORAGE DEVICES

Bootable operating systems, activated either from CDs, DVDs, or USBs are an effective means to avoid creating local electronic evidence. By booting any computer to an external medium containing an operating system, the host hard drive is not touched, preventing any evidence being created on the host hard drive. Table 7.2 shows a list of several bootable operating systems specifically designed for online privacy and communications, with built-in applications to hide IP and MAC addresses while also providing secure encryption.

One method to determine if a suspect has been using a bootable operating system instead of the host operating system is to simply look at the computer use. If there is no use on the host drive, or very little use, or no use for a long

Table 7.2 Bootable Operating Systems for External Media (CD/DVD/USB)	
Tails:The Amnesiac Incognito Live System	https://tails.boum.org/
Ubuntu Privacy Remix	https://www.privacy-cd.org/en
Jondonym	https://anonymous-proxy-servers.net/index.html
IprediaOS	https://geti2p.net/en/
Privatix	http://www.mandalka.name/privatix/index.html.en
Liberté Linux	http://dee.su/liberte

period of time, it is feasible that a bootable operating system has been used. An effective antiforensic method would be to use both the host operating system for casual computer use and a bootable operating system for online communications.

Another indicator of bootable operating system use is comparing electronic evidence, such as an e-mail, by the time sent. If the suspect's computer does not have evidence of use during the time of the e-mail, then either that particular computer was not the computer used or a bootable operating system may have been used. If there is no activity on the host drive, another method is to check the MAC of the computer to the MAC in the evidence e-mail. The MAC is a unique identifier for communication devices, such as a network adaptor. As MAC addresses are unique to the hardware and part of an e-mail header, if the computer was booted to an external storage medium, the MAC address will be that of the computer used. MAC addresses can be spoofed (altered) and some bootable operating systems such as Tails make spoofing MAC addresses fairly easy.

Another antiforensic method for hiding the computer MAC is to use an external network device, such as USB WiFi device seen in Fig. 7.5. By plugging an

FIGURE 7.5
USB WiFi adaptor with MAC address noted.

external WiFi adaptor and using the adaptor to connect to the Internet, the MAC address will be that of the adaptor, not of the machine being used. The seizure of computer evidence should also include external adaptors such as seen in Fig. 7.5 in order to decipher MAC address conflicts in cases. Without having all MAC addressable network devices, communications with different MAC addresses may seem to originate from different machines, when actually it may be only one machine using different network adaptors.

Log files from the suspect's router may contain information on devices used, particularly if the suspect has entered the MAC addresses of all devices for MAC filtering on a home network.

PORTABLE APPS

Portable applications are programs which do not need to be installed in order to run. Portable apps can be run from external storage devices, such as a USB flash drive, leaving minimal remnants on the computer used. As an antiforensics method, portable apps are effective in keeping most of the evidence on the external device and not on the host system, but it will still leave the external device as a source of evidence.

One of the more popular portable apps Websites is http://www.portableapps. com. Dozens of portable applications are available as freeware, in which practically any software needed for computer use is available. From word processing to Internet video chat, an entire suite of applications can be stored on a single USB flash drive. One of the freely available portable apps is Pidgin Portable. Pidgin Portable is an instant messaging client that supports AOL, Yahoo, MSN, ICQ, and Jabber networks. Most interesting is that Pidgin Portable can use Off-The-Record (OTR) messaging, which is an encrypted messaging service that provides encryption and authentication along with deniable authentication. In other words, OTR encrypts chats between users and authenticates the users without using public keys. Since the chat messages are encrypted, only the users can read the messages, since even the service providers are not able to bypass the encryption.

The use of OTR messaging with portable devices prevents a serious forensic dilemma in that the chats are encrypted (thereby unable to intercept), and the data is not stored on the devices (thereby unrecoverable). In this type of situation, there are few solutions other than obtaining legal authority for key loggers, screen capture applications, or video cameras to record the suspect at the computer. Portable devices with portable applications are inexpensive, easy to hide, and easy to dispose of. Fig. 7.6 shows an example of a 16 GB MicroSD card with USB adaptor. The MicroSD card cannot only have a portable application suite of utilities such as Pidgin Portable on it, but it could also contain

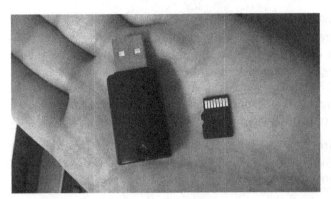

FIGURE 7.6
MicroSD with USB adaptor.

an entire operating system such as Tails. The miniature size allows for ease of disposal, even by ingestion or hiding inside the mouth.

SIZE DOESN'T MATTER!
Big things can come in small packages

The capacity of storage media is not necessarily tied to the physical size of the media. A 32 GB MicroSD card can hold an entire operating system and hundreds of thousands of files, yet be small enough to hide anywhere, even between the pages of a book on a shelf. Don't overlook the little things when searching for electronic evidence. Your entire exam could rely on a storage device that is smaller than a postage stamp!

HIDDEN OPERATING SYSTEMS

The strongest defense to getting caught with incriminating evidence or potentially incriminating evidence is plausible denial. Hidden volumes, hidden operating systems, and hidden files all make for plausible denial for those in possession of incriminating evidence. An extremely effective measure of plausible deniability is the hidden operating system. We have discussed operating systems that can run from external media, such as USB devices, but those types are not hidden operating systems. An operating system can be hidden on a host computer that has a second (nonhidden) operating system. A computer setup in this manner does not need an external storage device with an operating system as it can use the host drive for both the hidden and nonhidden operating system.

One example is VeraCrypt (https://veracrypt.codeplex.com). VeraCrypt enables a user to employ whole disk encryption, which as discussed, is already a very effective method of making data inaccessible. However, VeraCrypt also provides the ability to install another operating system within a hidden volume.

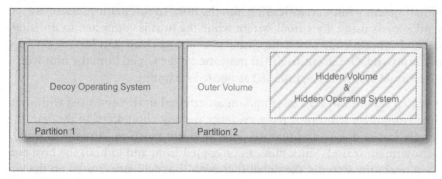

FIGURE 7.7

Example layout of system drive containing hidden operating system (http://veracrypt.codeplex.com).

Upon boot, the user chooses between two login credentials to boot one of two systems. One system (the decoy) contains no evidence and is not used for any communications involved in criminal activity. The other system (hidden) is used for all communications that are intended to be secret, such as Internet chats, video conferencing, e-mails, and so forth. Fig. 7.7 shows a visual of both the hidden and decoy operating systems on a hard drive. The hidden volume appears as random data, not an operating system, and therefore is safe from forensic analysis.

Countering this type of antiforensics is extremely difficult without cooperation from the suspect or access to credentials to the hidden operating system. Encountering any system where whole disk encryption is employed should raise concerns about the possible existence of hidden operating systems, especially if the method used allows for hidden operating systems (such as VeraCrypt). A forensic analysis of the visible operating system may not yield evidence, but the device may yield pertinent information such as the physical MAC address of the computer. At least with the MAC address, the potential of tying e-mail communications which were seized elsewhere to this computer is a possibility.

VIRTUAL MACHINES

A virtual machine is simply a guest operating system running a host operating system. The guest (or host) can be Windows, Linux, DOS, Solaris, OpenSolaris, and others. Most activity that occurs within the guest system stays within the guest system. Most activity that occurs outside the guest system (on the host system) stays outside the guest system. Several different virtual machines can be running at the same time on one host system.

As an antiforensic method, the host system is used to run the virtual (guest) system. Communications via chat, e-mail, or other means can occur within the virtual system without data leaking into the host. In this manner, a suspect can send e-mails using the virtual system while the host is connected to the Internet and subsequently revert the virtual system to a clean start leaving no trace of the activity. Or the entire virtual machine can be wiped from the host with a new virtual system being installed as needed each time.

A virtual system can also be stored on an external device and used with multiple computers without leaving evidence on any computers, other than the connection and use of virtual machine software (such as VirtualBox; http://www.virtualbox.org). Since files can be copied from and to both the host and guest operating systems, the possibility exists that evidence created on the virtual machine could be found on the host if the suspect chose to save the data on the host system. Conversely, evidence files could be created on the host system and copied into the guest system to be e-mailed through the guest system in an attempt to avoid the communications being recorded on the host (even though artifacts of file creation will remain on the host system).

Countering the use of virtual machines is problematic for several reasons. As a virtual machine is a guest on a host machine, examiners need not only access the host machine, but also access the guest machine. Since any folder or file can be encrypted, a virtual machine file or folder structure can also be encrypted when not in use, making it practically impossible to access the virtual machine for examination. If the virtual machine is located on external media, it too can be encrypted or not available if the storage device is hidden (think back to the MicroSD card).

Another problematic issue with virtual machines is the amount of volume added to each device containing one or more virtual machines. As each virtual machine is a complete operating system, every system may need either a complete forensic analysis or, at a minimum, a triage to determine if evidence may exist. Given that today's computers are being sold with terabyte-size hard drives, it is possible to have dozens of virtual machines on one computer hard drive, any or all of which may be used for covert means. Fig. 7.8 shows an example of four virtual machines consisting of Linux and Windows operating systems. Diane Barrett has written a book targeted solely on virtual forensics (*Virtual Forensics: A Digital Forensics Investigator's Guide to Virtual Environments,* 1st Edition) which should be required reading before undertaking analysis of virtual machines.

Not only can a number of virtual machines prove problematic for analysis time, but each virtual machine can have multiple snapshots. A virtual machine snapshot is just that: a snapshot of the operating system at a specific moment in time. A snapshot can be saved periodically, and at the desire of the computer user a virtual machine can be restored to a previous snapshot. The number of virtual machines and the number of snapshots for each virtual machine can result in more time needed to exam for evidence than may be available for any

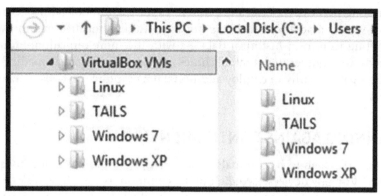

FIGURE 7.8
Example multiple virtual machines on a single host computer.

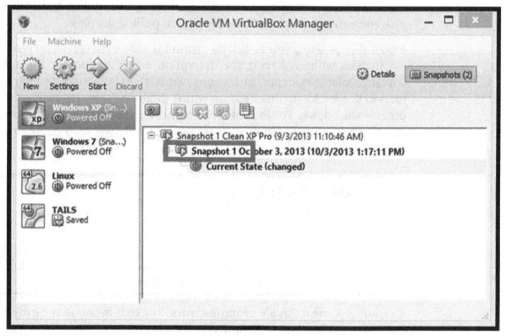

FIGURE 7.9
Virtual machine snapshot information.

one case. Fig. 7.9 shows a virtual machine with one snapshot saved with a current state that is different from the one snapshot. A new snapshot can be saved at any time and virtually any number of times, and in any state of the operating system as desired. Diane Barrett and Greg Kipper wrote a book titled *Virtualization and Forensics: A Digital Forensic Investigator's Guide to Virtual Environments* by Syngress Publishing which contains a wealth of information on this topic.

Monitoring network traffic is an option to capture communications occurring from a virtual machine, but this is not a typical investigative method when attempting to recover historical data. As with the more difficult antiforensic methods, the counter to virtual machines used as an antiforensic method may require legal authority to employ additional data capture methods such as key loggers.

PLANNING AGAINST ANTIFORENSICS

Investigating high-tech criminals assumes that antiforensic methods are employed on any devices used. Before the common use of whole disk encryption, computer systems were shut down by pulling the plug from the back of the machine and creating a forensic image of the internal hard drive. Using this method today on an adversary would most likely be the best antiforensics method because shutting down the computer will lock the data with whole disk encryption, courtesy of the investigator pulling the plug.

Practically speaking, whole disk encryption is secure enough to prevent forensic analysis without having the decryption key. Additionally, live memory contains volatile evidence, such as passwords, chats, and more pertinent information needed for an investigation which should be captured before the computer is shut down. For these reasons alone, the best counter is to protect the machine when it is on and unprotected, especially when an entire investigation hinges upon a single device.

HEY, LOOK OVER THERE!
Sometimes, low tech beats high tech

The undercover operation to seize the laptop of Silk Road's Ross Ulbricht (United States of America v. Ross William Ulbricht, 2014) involved staging a distraction at a public library behind Ulbricht to divert his attention away from his unencrypted laptop. As soon as Ulbricht turned away from his laptop to look at the distraction, a plainclothes agent grabbed his laptop, preventing Ulbricht from turning it off or locking it. A simple grab of the laptop beat whole disk encryption (Greenberg, 2015).

To counter some methods of antiforensics, low-tech means may be the best or only way to defeat high-tech protections such as data wiping and encryption. A good interviewer can sway a suspect to cooperate, confess or admit to crimes, and give up passwords. The better method is gaining access to evidence without relying on the suspect's cooperation, such as in Ulbricht's case where his cooperation was not guaranteed and unknowable. The difference between seizing an unencrypted device and an encrypted device is the difference between having all the evidence and no evidence.

Seizing a computer device is not like seizing any other type of evidence item. An encrypted computer is virtually useless as evidence if the data cannot be accessed. Such as in the Silk Road case, where Ulbricht's laptop was seized when unencrypted, operations to serve warrants must consider the same type of distractions and methods to seize devices when in use or unencrypted. This is certainly easier to do in public than in a private residence. A suspect at the keyboard may have to be physically pulled away from a computer if the computer cannot be pulled from the suspect. An example would be at a desktop computer at a library, hotel lobby, or workplace. Even then, effort must be taken to ensure the computer is currently unencrypted and unlocked by either looking at the monitor or perhaps monitoring the suspect's activity in a chat forum or other online activity that can be seen online from another location.

FINDING COMMUNICATION RECORDS ON HARD DRIVES

Basic host forensics can find nearly anything and everything that is recoverable and viewable. Whether full forensic suites are used or specific applications to target specific types of data, if the data exists, it can be recovered partially or fully. When looking for communications on a seized computer system, one of the most popular forensic applications is Magnet Internet Evidence Finder (IEF). IEF is an automated software tool designed to pull specific data from storage devices, including mobile devices into a format usable for analysis and reporting. Fig. 7.10 shows a screen capture of IEF in which many types of instant messaging applications can be selected for analysis. As a triage tool, IEF does a fantastic job of targeting many types of messaging services quickly and conveniently.

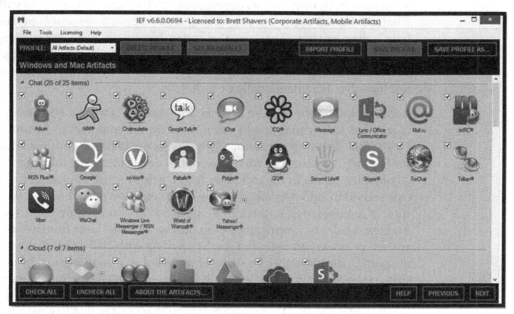

FIGURE 7.10

Magnet Internet Evidence Finder (http://www.magnetforensics.com).

Locked Computers

Considering that whole disk encryption is employed with high-tech suspects, and that entire cases depend upon seizing computers in an unencrypted state, the window of opportunity to successfully seize the systems in unencrypted states is small. Even when a computer is being used by the suspect, such as in a library, the odds that the suspect will detect surveillance and activate antiforensic methods such as encryption or locked screens are great. A computer system can be locked with a keystroke or set of keystrokes in less than a second, and in that second, the entirety of threads of communications in chat logs, e-mails, and other electronic evidence can be locked, encrypted, or wiped.

Just as investigators gauge their actions by predicting the reactions of suspects, the opposite is also true. Suspects plan their reactions based on their predictions about investigators. Some examples include the obvious measures of entering a set of preplanned keystrokes to lock or shutdown a computer (even pressing the power button), or ejecting the operating system if running on a DVD such as Tails when confronted by law enforcement. Ejecting an operating system on CD/DVD will usually cause a crash or automatic shutdown of the system, with some systems able to wipe the live memory to prevent capture as evidence as it shuts down. The takeaway here is that the suspect's hands must not touch the system or mouse at all, regardless of any promise to provide passwords later.

Antiforensic methods to encrypt or lock the computer can also be inadvertently set in motion by investigators during seizure. One example is a laptop without a battery. Laptop users routinely use laptops without power cords because of long-lasting batteries. However, if a laptop battery has been removed by the suspect and the power cord is disconnected during seizure by investigators, whole disk encryption effectively has been activated by the investigator when unplugged, either intentionally or accidently.

Another antiforensic method or locking computers is using a USB device that is required to be connected to a computer for the computer to be unlocked. One such device is Predator (http://www.predator-usb.com/predator/en/index.php). Predator is a USB access control device that, once unplugged from a computer, results in the computer screen being locked. Similar USB devices can be used to automatically shut down the computer or start wiping the hard drive if removed. Again, this can be intentionally initiated by the suspect or unintentionally by investigators. Even pulling a suspect away from a computer to prevent any keystrokes could result in pulling out a USB device that has been attached to the suspect with a string or wire used as a safety measure by the suspect. In the case with Ross Ulbricht, had he used a USB protection device while at the library, the agent grabbing his laptop could have inadvertently activated antiforensics if such a USB device had been there and pulled out.

Mobile Devices

Mobile devices are probably the most commonly used device for communications, such as texting, e-mail, and of course, phone calls. The antiforensic methods on mobile devices are not as extensive as on computer systems, but they are certainly just as problematic depending upon the type of mobile device and encryption employed. Although some of the same applications can be used on a mobile device, such as the Tor browser, a computer displays the information to the computer user in a friendlier manner.

Computers and laptops still remain primary targets along with mobile devices for seizure in order to obtaining communications, for several reasons. The methods to communicate covertly using a laptop or computer are simply easier as a matter of convenience for the computer user. Large monitors, full-size keyboards, easier access to forums chatting, video conferencing, and creating user files are more convenient with a computer than a smartphone or tablet. Messages are easier to create, encrypt, or hide in other files on a computer system using a word processor rather than on a mobile device.

WHEN ALL ELSE FAILS OR IS LIKELY TO FAIL

In cases where monitoring communications is impossible due to anonymous Internet access methods such as the Tor browser or virtual private networks, other means have to be considered. Undercover operations in which an investigator or informant infiltrates a criminal network (online or in real life) may be able to obtain access to encrypted channels of communication and be part of the evidence in e-mails, chats, and forums located on hidden services on the Dark Web.

Where an undercover or informant operation is impractical or impossible, measures to directly infiltrate the computer system may be possible. This could range from injecting spyware on the suspect's computer remotely or by physically placing physical key loggers and video cameras in the suspect's residence or business under authority of covert search warrants that do not alert the suspect. Either of these methods can capture passwords and view computer activity.

SUMMARY

Antiforensics encompasses anything prepared by a person to make forensic analysis difficult, time-consuming, or practically impossible. As not all antiforensics can be detected, investigators have to consider nontraditional methods of device seizures in order to have access to data. The intention of criminals and terrorists regarding communications is to prevent anyone other than the intended recipient to have access. The methods to encrypt, hide, and destroy recorded conversations and messages are as varied as the means to transmit the communications.

Intercepting the many types of electronic communications is beyond most investigators' capabilities due to limitations of authority and technology available. Local law enforcement generally will not have access to the technology used by the most secretive government agencies to capture Internet traffic or active e-mail content. However, once electronic storage devices have been seized, historical communications can be recovered as evidence and are very useful for additional investigative leads.

REFERENCES

Greenberg, A. (January 1, 2015). *Undercover agent reveals how he helped the FBI trap Silk Road's Ross Ulbricht.* Retrieved from Wired http://www.wired.com/2015/01/silk-road-trial-undercover-dhs-fbi-trap-ross-ulbricht/.

United States of America v. Ross William Ulbricht, S1 14-cr-00068-KBF-1 (Southern District of New York February 4, 2014).

CHAPTER 8

Electronic Intercepts

INTRODUCTION

Intercepting electronic communications has been around as long as electronic communications have existed. Even during the US Civil War, intercepting telegraphs was a source of intelligence on the battlefield. Wiretaps have been used in criminal investigations from the beginnings of law enforcement, such as bootlegging investigations in the late 1800s (Funderburg, 2014). Although it has only been in recent years that the general public has learned that nearly any electronic communication method can be compromised, the ability to do so has existed for well over a century.

Obtaining covert communications typically take two forms in an investigation. Analyzing seized devices, such as computers and smartphones, is one form that can provide a historical source of communications. Intercepting communications is another that provides for real-time analysis and actionable intelligence. Both sources of communication data are important; however, with intercepted communications, past crimes can not only be corroborated in conversations, but future planned crimes can also be discovered before being committed.

Compared to recovering communications from electronic devices, electronic intercepts are easier, quicker, and more reliable since recovering data from electronic devices may be problematic due to encryption, corruption, or destruction. But the option to intercept communications with real time, relevant, and actionable information may not be available due to jurisdiction, authority, or lack of necessity or technical feasibility. In many cases, electronic intercepts are only authorized when all other methods have failed or are anticipated to fail.

This chapter gives a high-level view of electronic intercepts for investigators to consider implementing in cases. Although Hollywood tends to show wiretaps to happen at the flip of a switch as needed by just asking for it, authorized intercepts require more than what Hollywood leads you to believe. However, for investigators who have not yet tried electronic intercepts out of fear of not knowing what to do, when to do it, or how to do it, this chapter is for you. The information easily gleaned from an intercept more than just makes investigations easier; it makes them better and more solid.

VALUE OF ELECTRONICALLY INTERCEPTED COMMUNICATIONS

Few types of evidence are more persuasive and compelling than the spoken word of a criminal suspect. Electronic intercepts can provide the spoken word (and typed words) of suspects and co-conspirators in a manner that captures admissions, confessions, and conspiratorial planning of crimes. It does not get much better than that.

Also, interception of electronic communications may be the only method of obtaining evidence of communications and associations between suspects. Because of the technical ease of intercepting communications coupled with the heavy weight placed on evidential value, this investigative method should be considered when appropriate; however, it should be used judiciously as not to overuse such an effective investigative tool. As a tool of last resort, judges can become leery of every investigation needing a wiretap when other less intrusive means are possible and practical.

Although the content of communications is valuable, the metadata of the communications may be just as valuable or, in some instances, more valuable. Metadata of electronic communications include the email addresses sent and received; telephone numbers dialed and received; dates and times of calls; call lengths, and even geolocation data based on cell phone tower locations and IP addresses. By the use of metadata alone, investigators can place suspects at specific locations and determine relationships based on call record analysis. By adding metadata of Internet use, investigations can get a picture of the intentions of a suspect based on Internet surfing habits, searches made in browsers and visited websites.

AUTHORITY AND NECESSITY

Intercepting electronic communications in any manner requires the authority to do so in order to avoid violating any number of laws restricting or forbidding interception. In the broadest of explanations of obtaining approval for any interception, each investigator has to confer with legal counsel with the process set by each jurisdiction. This is not only to prevent losing valuable evidence that may be deemed inadmissible later, but also to prevent breaking state or federal laws in the process.

LAWS? WHAT LAWS?
Yes, the laws apply to the government, too

In the late 19th century, the New York Police Department (NYPD) discovered that they could tap into any phone line of the New York Telephone Company as well as tap into the trunk lines of hotels (Landau, 2007). Although laws preventing illegal wiretaps existed at the time, the NYPD did not feel the laws applied to their investigations.

Generally, a court order, such as a search warrant or agency administrative approval is needed to intercept communications. Depending upon the type of intercept, a higher level of approval, such as from a federal district or circuit judge will be needed. A wiretap, also known as a "Title III," involves a process of collecting enough data to show evidence of crimes along with supporting information that a wiretap may *be* the only method to obtain additional evidence, as other methods have failed or are expected to fail. On the other end of the interception scale, obtaining authorization for a body wire recording may only require administrative approval from the investigating agency.

Exceptionally, there are circumstances that fall out of the usual process of obtaining authorization for intercepting communications. These situations are typically exigent circumstances where there is an immediate or imminent threat of physical harm.

The investigator is responsible for knowing the authorization required in the jurisdiction of the investigation. Beginning a "wiretap" case is not simply turning a switch, but rather embarking on an essential procedure filled with checks and balances to ensure citizen privacy is not unreasonably intruded into. Where a basic search warrant needs only a judge's approval, a wiretap generally needs the approval of the investigating agency and several levels of prosecutorial approval before reaching a judge for review.

WHY IS A WIRETAP CALLED A TITLE III?
It's a name that stuck

A wiretap is commonly referred to as a "T3" or "Title III" since it was first passed as Title III of the Omnibus Crime Control and Safe Streets Act of 1968. Police talk: "We're up on a T3."

TECHNOLOGY

When considering an intercept of electronic communications, it is not as easy as it had once been. In the days of the telegraph, the only source of electronic communication was the telegraph, which makes the decision easy. Today, the types of electronic communication grow as technology grows. No longer are communications only by landline telephones, but by wireless phones with Internet connectivity, e-mails, text messages, peer-to-peer, video conferencing, and more. Once one finds the methods of communications that suspects are using, the planning of intercepting each type or a specific type of method begins.

Insofar as the physical efforts to install and collect electronic communications are concerned, for the most part, simply serving a provider (Internet Service Provider, cellular service provider, and so on) with the proper authorization will set the provider in motion to configure, capture, and provide the information to investigators. In some instances, the law enforcement agency will be the party to install devices and monitor communications directly.

Capture Communications at the Source

Depending on the technology used by a suspect, capturing the communications at the source may be the best or only solution. An example would be placing a listening device on a physical phone at a physical office. This may be a practical method if intercepting the line is not physically possible or practical. Fig. 8.1 shows the installation of a physical device placed into a phone, similar to that used at the Watergate Hotel in Washington DC in the Watergate Scandal (James McCord Demonstrates a Wiretap, 1973).

Another example of capturing communications at the source is installing a hardware key logger on a computer to capture keystrokes of the computer user. Software key loggers might be possible to install remotely, but success is dependent upon factors such as being able to access remotely the computer and install a key logger without detection.

Capturing communications at its source is problematic for several reasons. Compromise of the device is an obvious issue if discovered by anyone with access to the device. Whether the device is a hidden video camera or

FIGURE 8.1
James McCord Demonstrates a Wiretap c. 1973. *Copyright: The WPA Film Library.*

audio transmitter, the mere discovery can compromise an investigation or, at least, make future attempts more difficult. Installation is risky as well. Although it is possible to delay suspects from entering their premises with subterfuge (such as a downed power line ploy), being caught in the act of installing any device not only compromises the investigation but can present a safety issue as well. Another concern is power for the device. Unless the device is hardwired for power, the useful life of the device will depend upon its portable power source, such as a small battery, which can be limited to hours or days.

Capture Communications at the Receiver

Options to capture communications at the receiving end of a conversation can be as low tech as overhearing a phone call of a suspect (aka "phone tip") such as when the suspect speaks over the phone to an informant standing next to the informant's handler. Or it can be covert by trying to be within earshot of a phone call conversation made in public without being compromised.

Overhearing conversations, whether it is face-to-face between suspects or when suspects communicate by phone in public, can be done with technology to enhance the sound. "Bionic ears" or bidirectional devices designed to amplify sounds are effective if the environment is conducive; that is, not so crowded and noisy as to make the conversations unintelligible.

Depending upon the environment, legal authorization may or may not be needed using these methods. Overhearing a conversation in public by simply standing near the suspect would not need authorization to listen, as the conversation is in the public. However, if the suspects were in a hotel room, and listening to the conversation required a bidirectional device to amplify the sounds through a window or wall, legal authority may be needed. Using technology to capture communications is the first indication of a reminder to check for authorization first.

Trap and Trace/Pen Registers/Dialed Number Recorders

Before getting into wiretaps, let us discuss the Trap and Trace/Pen Registers. The most important difference between a Trap and Trace/Pen Register and a wiretap is the type of information obtained. A wiretap captures content. A Trap and Trace/Pen Register captures metadata. That one difference makes all the difference in authorization requirements. There is also a difference between a Trap and Trace and a Pen Register. A Trap and Trace captures incoming call information, whereas a Pen Register captures outgoing call information. These distinctions in content and metadata apply to e-mail as well. With e-mails, the subject and e-mail content is not captured with a Trap and Trace/Pen Register,

Table 8.1 Metadata Versus Content Capture

Pen Register	Metadata: **outgoing** call records, e-mail header information, no content
Trap and Trace	Metadata: **incoming** call records, e-mail header information, no content
Wiretap	Both metadata and content

but most, if not all, of the e-mail headers are captured. A wiretap captures the e-mail content and metadata. Table 8.1 below shows these differences.

The ease of obtaining incoming and outgoing calls is due to the information being collected in the normal course of business, regardless of law enforcement demands. In order to properly bill customers, this information must be collected by the provider. In regard to equipment, providers arrange for equipment, installation, and technical assistance to law enforcement for the devices, or devices can be purchased by agencies.

The value of metadata cannot be stressed enough, and in planning to apply for a wiretap authorization, phone call/toll analysis from Trap and Trace/Pen Registers is generally a default step in the process. Analysis of dialed numbers and incoming calls is instrumental in identifying conspirators as phone numbers are identified. In many cases, Trap and Trace/Pen Registers provide more than enough evidence and intelligence than needed to identify criminals and their co-conspirators. Particularly important is that Trap and Trace/Pen Registers provide real-time data rather than historical billing records which is beneficial to dynamically moving investigations.

Wiretaps

The Electronic Communications Privacy Act (ECPA) was passed in 1986 and includes the Wiretap Act, the Stored Communications Act, and the Pen Register Act. One of the more comprehensive sources of information for review is the Electronic Privacy Information Center at https://epic.org/privacy/ecpa/, and the act can be found at https://epic.org/privacy/ecpa/. As wiretap laws have changed in an attempt to keep up with technology, it is prudent to be up to date with current laws on wiretaps.

The type of communications you seek as well as the storage location of the communications will determine the type of authorization you need. For example, Table 8.2 shows an example of authorizations needed for different locations of e-mail. As you can see with Table 8.2 example, depending on where e-mail is stored, the authorization required is either a search warrant or subpoena.

Wiretapping communication devices provide a wealth of content that can easily overwhelm the "wire room." The wire room monitors, records, and organizes the communications for analysis. When multiple phone lines are being

Table 8.2 Authorization Required for E-mail, https://epic.org/privacy/ecpa/

Type of Communication	Required for Law Enforcement Access	Statute
E-mail in transit	Warrant	18 US Code § 2516
E-mail in storage or home computer	Warrant	4th amendment, US Constitution
E-mail in remote storage, opened	Subpoena	18 US Code § 2703
E-mail in remote storage, unopened, stored for 180 days or less	Warrant	18 US Code § 2703
E-mail in remote storage, unopened, stored for more than 180 days	Subpoena	18 US Code § 2703

intercepted, including text messages, the amount of information can grow quickly, especially when other sources of communication are added, such as social networking accounts, forums, and e-mails. One of the most important case management points to keep in mind is organizing content and metadata according to the respective suspects. Discussion of tying communications to one person is discussed in a later chapter as "Digital Identity."

WHAT ABOUT COOPERATING WITNESSES?
Consent
Depending on the case jurisdiction (federal or a specific state), a cooperating witness may be able to give consent to access, listen, and record communications to which they are a party. One-party consent means that as long as one party allows access, the communications are open for capture. When in doubt, sometimes getting legal authorization is best in case consent is revoked.

Internet
Being able to observe a suspect's Internet traffic, including e-mails, can reveal not only communications with co-conspirators but also implied intentions. For example, a criminal suspect searching the Internet for explosive devices implies an interest in explosives. Combined with other evidence, such as conversations or e-mails discussing criminal acts where explosives will be used, Internet usage gives clear intention of the suspect's intentions specific to the websites visited. Placing a "packet sniffer" on a network allows for Internet traffic to be captured as it happens in real time, although the captured data need to be decoded to be readable.

Wiretapping a suspect's Internet use is not technically as easy as wiretapping a cell phone line. Without having access to the end points of the suspect's Internet traffic, monitoring the traffic is difficult at best. A simpler method is to target specific uses of the Internet, such as a videoconference application or social networking account. By having access to the provider of the application, the provider may be able to capture communications that occur in its application, to include social networking chats and videoconference calls. In this manner, the communication is captured in the middle (between the source and the receiver) at the service provider level.

WIRETAPPING SOCIAL MEDIA
Social media: Good for connecting with friends and wiretapping for evidence

A 2133% spike in wiretap requests have been sent to Facebook during the first half of 2015 as compared to the entire year of 2014. Conversely, the trend in "traditional" wiretaps has decreased (US cops are asking Facebook to wiretap more chats than ever before, 2015). The content in social media is so valuable as evidence that it sometimes overshadows traditional communication means.

Cloud storage is another avenue to monitor in real time; files that suspects store and share using third-party storage providers can result in capturing evidence in real time. Monitoring cloud storage activity can also give investigators leads to IP addresses (which can lead to physical addresses), connected devices, and associated users of shared files.

Practically any server-side application service, such as a social networking or file sharing site, can provide law enforcement access to user content that may be of evidentiary value. If not for the sole purpose of content, the leads generated through IP address connections, device identification, and potential geolocation data can be helpful beyond the actual content.

TECHNICAL BARRIERS

For the most part, equipment technical barriers are solved by the service providers as they not only can provide technical assistance but sometimes full management of devices used in the interceptions. However, there are technical issues that can prevent interpretation of collected data regardless of support given by service providers.

For example, Voice Over Internet Protocol (VOIP) phones are telephones that use the Internet rather than phone lines to transfer (voice) data. If the VOIP calls are encrypted, the content will be unintelligible and only the metadata will be of use. Metadata is still valuable, but when the necessity of the case requires the content, encrypted VOIP calls prevent capturing evidentiary content.

Along the same lines as encrypted VOIP is encrypted e-mail and Internet chats. When suspects employ encryption to protect the contents of their communications, the content is virtually impossible to recover without decryption keys or brute-force/dictionary attacks that may not be effective. A solution to bypassing encryption is for the product developers to incorporate backdoors for law enforcement into their products. However, this would not only defeat the purpose of having encryption in the first place but could also create vulner-abilities that may be exploited by hackers and identity thieves.

Coded communications are not so much a barrier since these types of com-munications can be broken through analysis, guesswork, and informants. For example, suspects in a drug deal conversation may refer to "cocaine" as "tires," such as "I need to buy four tires." Although suspects may believe that not stat-ing the actual drug terms will protect them in the event their calls are inter-cepted, once the coded language is translated the effect is the same as if they spoke plainly.

"LET'S GO TO THE MOVIE THEATER" MEANS...
"They are following me, and I have money with me"

A large-scale drug and money laundering investigation by the US Department of Homeland Secu-rity used wiretaps, Pen Registers, informants, and e-mails for evidence. Members of the orga-nization used a set of codes to communicate. One code used was "Let's go to the beach" which was code for "Make an appointment." Numbers were coded as well, such as 96 coded as 9. One method of distributing the codes was through e-mail (United States of America v. Diego Pineda Sanchez et al., 2015).

More effective than coded communications is using no communications or communications that seem to have no purpose. If an intercepted phone line receives a wrong number call, potentially the call itself may be evidence even if the only words spoken by the suspect is "Sorry, wrong number." This type of communication is typically a preplanned call that is intended to make both caller and receiver appear unrelated. As an example, the caller may ask to speak to a specific person, and regardless of the name, the receiver simply informs the caller of a wrong number, but in reality the name asked ("Is Bob there?") could be a code to either initiate an action or inform that an action has been completed. As long as the caller and receiver have preplanned the wrong names to correspond with the information to pass, and that the caller uses a phone number that is not related to the case, a wrong number may be easily overlooked.

In this type of instance, the Trap and Trace/Pen Register is extremely import-ant. With a call from a "wrong number," it may be pertinent to obtain the subscriber information for the number. Possibly, it may be a misdialed call by an innocent party, but potentially it may be more. A misdialed number most likely will have a history of phone calls, but a number used in the manner to fake a misdial could be a prepaid phone with no history of use. That in itself would be suspicious enough to investigate, especially if the phone was recently activated and subsequently not used again. In this instance, the call did convey some communication, even if the communication cannot be deciphered at the time of the wiretap.

A method to counter-encryption and coded communications is placing an audio transmitter ("bug") in the place where the communications take place, such as an office or residence with a wiretap warrant. Placing such a device requires a high level of planning to reduce the high risk of compromise. However, once in place, the conversations in that specific location between persons in the room, including conversations spoken on phones and Internet video-conferences, can be captured regardless of encryption employed. This method may also be the only method of obtaining computer communications evidence that is encrypted if a covert video is installed to observe a computer monitor and keyboard.

FINDING CELL PHONE NUMBERS

A hurdle to applying for a wiretap is obtaining the targeted cell phone numbers. Since anyone suspect can control multiple cell phones and these phones are typically discarded and replaced constantly, obtaining the numbers is a monumental task but necessary for a wiretap. Without the use of informants, technology is practically the only method to identify cell phone numbers.

Cell phones are convenient to use since they can be carried with a user inside and outside his home. Because a cell phone needs reception to make and receive calls, it is constantly seeking reception by connecting with cell phone towers. Reception is simply the strength of the connection between a cell phone and a cell tower. The connection to cell towers is fluid as the cell phone travels with its user and continues to connect with a series of cell towers, releasing from one to connect to the next strongest cell tower. The next strongest cell tower is not necessarily the closest tower, which can give inaccurate geolocation information to investigators who base location on tower location rather than tower strength. Cell tower connections are seamless to the user and continue whether or not the phone is being used in a call.

VIRTUAL NUMBERS
To add complexity to tracking phone numbers, there are virtual numbers
A virtual number is just a phone number that forwards to another number or can forward to more than one number. Virtual numbers can be set to varying options of forwarding based on time of day or based on the caller's phone number. This adds another third party to consider to obtain subscriber information and lists of forwarding call numbers. Virtual numbers add time and complexity to tracking phone numbers since an unlimited number of forwarding call numbers could have been used. But this can also provide more investigative leads.

Finding the phone carrier leads to a third party, such as any cellular service company. Fig. 8.2 shows an online (free) service to look up phone number providers. This example shows the carrier to be a virtual number provided by

FIGURE 8.2

Free carrier lookup (http://www.freecarrierlookup.com/).

Google Voice (https://www.google.com/voice/b/0). A Google Voice number requires a Google e-mail account, which requires user information and verification by an automated phone call from Google. The amount of investigative data available doubles when a service such as Google Voice is used. The creation of the original required Google e-mail account, the creation of the Google Voice account, and each login is logged by Google by IP address. If a suspect uses a system such as this, giving all false or misleading information, every IP address logged should be checked as only one actual (home or work) IP address may be needed to identify the user. Refer back to Chapter 3 for more information on looking up carriers.

Cell towers collect and log the cell phone's Electronic Serial Number (ESN), Mobile Equipment Identifier (MEID), or the International Mobile Subscriber Identification (IMSI) number. In this manner, geolocation data of any cell phone can be collected and analyzed based on cell tower strength, environmental conditions, and physical obstacles. The cell tower information holds the key to identifying the suspect's cell phone.

One method of identifying a suspect's cell phone is through a "cell tower dump." A cell tower dump is a collection of all connections of all cell phones within a specific period of time for a specific cell tower. If a suspect was seen using a cell phone at 10 am on January 3, 2015 in the vicinity of a specific cell tower, a cell tower dump request for that time would result in a list of every cell phone connected at that time to that cell tower. Unless there was only one cell phone connected to the tower at that time, this is only the beginning of identifying the suspect's number because of the sheer number of concurrent connections.

Requesting a series of cell tower dumps, including cell towers in the area of the suspect's residence, will be the start of a process of elimination. If the same cell numbers (ESN or IMSI collected by the cell towers) appear at each location the suspect travels, it can be assumed that those devices belong to the suspect. This is a time-intensive method of surveillance and analysis of cell tower dump records because of the need for a painstaking process of elimination.

CELL TOWER DUMPS: MORE THAN ONE USE
Tracking a bank robber by cell tower dumps

In 2014, a bank robbery suspect robbed multiple banks, each time carrying a cell phone. He even approached bank tellers with a cell phone held to his ear. The FBI collected cell tower dumps at each of the bank robbery locations, identified the common number between the cell tower dumps, and identified the bank robber through the cell phone subscriber information. Process of elimination = case solved (United States of America v. Wossen Assaye, 2015).

A common method to bolster cell tower dumps is the use of a "cell site simulator." A cell site simulator is a device that acts like a cell tower in order to trick cell phones into connecting with it. Once connected, the cell site simulator has access to the same data as a real cell tower, along with the benefit of not alerting the cell phone user. Cell site simulators, also known as "Stingrays" or "Triggerfish," are used covertly and out of sight of the suspect. Simply being in a vehicle in an area near the suspect is enough to capture the cell phone's ESN/IMSI.

As cell site simulators are basically a computer and antenna, they can be used not only in vehicles but also in planes, drones, and even carried in a backpack, depending upon the method best needed to capture the suspect's cell phone ESN/IMSI without detection. Depending upon the environment, a cell site simulator can be used to target only the suspect while not collecting innocent cell phone users. An example would be using a cell site simulator in a fairly remote location where the suspect is located, and few (if any) other cell phones are in the same area. The process of elimination still stands when using a cell site simulator, but using a simulator allows investigators more options which are more accurate in identifying cell phones by pinpointing the suspect and not a massive collection of cell tower dumps of all cell phones that happened to be caught in the cell tower dump.

STINGRAY DETECTORS
For every move, there is a counter-move, and another counter to the counter

An open source Android mobile application is the Android-IMSI-Catcher Detector – AIMSICD (https://secupwn.github.io/Android-IMSI-Catcher-Detector/). Users of this application can find if the cell tower connections are real or simulated. Although this application would seem to be an anti-law enforcement tool, there are also uses for it as a law enforcement tool to detect illegal cell site simulators. As an investigative note, when using cell site simulators, be aware that a case can be partially compromised if suspects use technologies such as this as a counter-surveillance method.

SUMMARY

Wiretaps, Pen Registers, Trap and Trace, packet sniffers, and cell site simulators are high-tech and intrusive into an individual's privacy. Yet when other methods to obtain covert communications fail, these are sometimes the only methods that may work. Because of the intrusiveness of these techniques, it is imperative that investigators consult with their prosecutors to avoid obtaining evidence that could be inadmissible. Jurisdictions vary in this regard, so accordingly the processes to obtain authorization vary as well.

Historical covert communications, such as that recovered on electronic devices, are valuable to any investigation, but real-time communications have pertinent value in the prevention or interruption of planned crimes, results that may not be possible with archived e-mail conversations. Additionally, relying on the recovery of communications from storage devices cannot be depended upon due to data encryption and corruption, and potential destruction of devices.

REFERENCES
Funderburg, J. A. (2014). *Bootleggers and beer barons of the prohibition era*. Jefferson: McFarland and Company, Inc. Publishers.

James McCord Demonstrates a Wiretap (1973). [Motion picture]. The WPA Film Library.

Landau, W. D. (2007). *Privacy on the line*. Cambridge: The MIT Press.

US cops are asking Facebook to wiretap more chats than ever before. (November 12, 2015). Retrieved from Motherboard http://motherboard.vice.com/read/us-cops-are-asking-facebook-to-wiretap-more-chats-than-ever-before.

United States of America v. Wossen Assaye, 1:15-mj-171 (Eastern District of Virginia March 20, 2015).

United States of America v. Diego Pineda Sanchez et al., (Northern District of Illinois Eastern Division February 9, 2015).

CHAPTER 9

Digital Identity

INTRODUCTION

A suspect's identity is a key factor needed in any investigation in order to bring closure to a case by solving crimes as well as preventing future crimes. Investigations benefit greatly when uncovering secret communications that discuss past and future crimes; however, without knowing the participants of the conversations, an investigation does not move toward resolution and becomes a collection of information rather than an investigation. Basic investigative methods are effective in identifying and locating suspects, yet as technology becomes commonly used, basic methods must evolve alongside technology.

A digital identity, or online persona, is not issued by a government similar to a license, nor is it based on any physical characteristics. A digital identity is created over a period of time by users of technology such as e-mail, text messaging, social media, and other electronic communication tools. The longer period of time a suspect uses technology to communicate, the greater the likelihood of a unique digital identity being created.

Other than attempting to identify physically a suspect through a digital identity, the purpose to find the digital identity is to tie both the physical person to the electronic person. Tying a physical identity to a digital identity is more than placing the suspect behind the keyboard (or mobile device). Tying both identities together gives a complete picture of the suspect's beliefs, intentions, and motivations which can be used to corroborate evidence in an investigation. This chapter intends to show methods to tie physical identity to digital identity.

IDENTITY

Identity isolates a person by unique traits so specific that a person is not confused with or wrongly identified as someone else. One of the requirements for any case closure is identifying the suspect. A case cannot be closed without knowing the identity of "who did it." In cyber-related investigations, identifying the suspect takes an entirely different approach as the trace evidence of identity is electronic, not physical. Additionally, cybercriminals can commit crimes in one or more locations at the same time while never having to be physically present at any of them.

Cybercriminals communicating by means of technology are especially difficult to identify for the same reasons applicable to physical location issues, but cybercriminals have additional effective methods of protecting electronic conversations as compared to meeting face to face. Regardless of the protections used to protect electronic communications (such as encrypted chats), identifying the suspects and associations with co-conspirators may be just as important as the conversation content.

Biometric Identity

Biometric identity is the cornerstone of a person's physical identification. Biometrics generally cannot be changed without either a medical procedure or injury. Biometrics also cannot be copied exactly. Biometrics is intrinsic to the person, down to the DNA, with very few exceptions.

Biometrics is such an effective method of identification that governments use biometrics when issuing licenses, identifying corpses, prosecuting criminals, and as security measures to access protected areas or computer systems. Different types of biometrics have higher rates of identifying specific individuals than others; however, when used in combination the risk of misidentification is very low. The success rate of positive identification with biometrics cannot be practically proven, since in order to know the actual rate of success, every person alive would need to be sampled for comparison against the person in question.

However, the identification rate with even a biometric method with a low identification success rate is greatly improved when coupled with multiple biometric systems. For example, using both a fingerprint comparison and retina scan for identification will be vastly more accurate in identification than just a fingerprint comparison alone.

The reason for discussing biometrics in this chapter is to show how an individual is identified through the physical body, and then how to compare the digital identity to the physical (personal) identity. Obviously, any identifier created electronically is chosen by the computer user and can be changed, contain disinformation, or be an accurate representation of the person. In the context of this book, identifying suspects is a primary goal when intercepting or recovering covert communications, with the identification being both personal and digital.

Table 9.1 shows a variety of biometric features used or being researched today as unique identifiers. Some have been in use for a century while others have been only recently discovered to be useful as security measures.

Table 9.1 Biometric Identifiers

	Biometric	Description
	Retina	Pattern of the retina blood vessels in the back of the eye.
	Iris	Pattern of the irides (colored portion of the eyes) to determine the unique pattern.
	Fingerprint	Pattern of the friction ridges and valleys on fingertips; however, fingerprints can be unreadable when the skin is damaged/injured.
	DNA	Genetic code, unique to the person; however, identical twins will have the same DNA.
	Voice	The sound, pattern, and rhythm of an individual's voice is known as a voice print, unique to the person.
	Ear	Based on ear symmetry and shape.
	Gait	Based upon an analysis of the way a person walks; however, injuries can affect the identification.
	Keystroke dynamics	Analysis of the dwell time (duration of keystroke) and flight time (duration between keystrokes); however, the rhythm of keystroke dynamics can be affected by hand/arm injuries.
	Signature	Based on pen pressure and duration, spatial coordinates, azimuth, and inclination and direction of writing.
	Odor	Based upon the person's body odor as a unique and identifiable pattern of odor.
	Hand/finger geometry	Based upon the shape of the person's hands and fingers.
	Facial recognition	Analysis of the spatial geometry of distinguishing features of a face; is affected by aging of the person.

Digital Identity

A person's digital identity is not like the personal identity. For example, a personal identity is based on physical features, whereas a digital identity is based on self-descriptive information created by a person in which the accuracy ranges from factual to fictional. Additionally, a digital identity can change at the user's whim and needs. Usernames and profiles are only those which a user inputs and depend upon how the user wants others to see him; profiles and usernames can be created to bolster a perception desired by the user.

A digital identity, unlike a personal identity, represents only a snapshot in time because the digital information can change by simple virtue of the suspect changing it to suit a specific purpose. However, just because a digital identity can evolve or change does not mean it is useless. The most important aspect of a digital identity is tying it to a physical person, regardless whether the digital identity accurately describes the person.

More problematic than a dynamically changing digital identity is a shared digital identity. Since the information that creates a digital identity is controlled by a user, it can be shared with another person or persons. One social media account could potentially be used by several persons in which that one persona is actually more than one person. However, it is possible to gather enough information online about a single digital identity to effectively identify a person or particular information about a person, which can then potentially be tied to a physical person.

One identifier of major importance is the username of a suspect. A username is required for online service accounts, such as social media user accounts and forum user accounts. Because a username is chosen by a user, the word or numbers in the username may be descriptive of the suspect. A user with the username of "seattledrugdealer" gives the impression that the user is a drug dealer in Seattle. Whether the user is actually a drug dealer in Seattle is irrelevant inasmuch as the user intentionally gives that impression. When a username is accurate, it may be helpful to tie it to the physical person.

Another important aspect in identifying a username is the broad use of usernames across multiple platforms. A suspect may have the same username on several social media sites, blogs, and forums. If the suspect uses the same username with different accounts, finding the accounts will be much quicker. As with any online persona, more than one person can choose (unintentionally) the same username; therefore, the mere virtue of being the same username does not necessarily mean that it is the same person using each of the accounts.

E-mail addresses are also chosen by the user and sometimes may be self-descriptive. A user who wants to have a specific username but finds that it is unavailable with one e-mail provider can easily look for other e-mail providers in order to use the desired username. As an example, if person wants to use "skyman" as a username, but it has been taken already by someone else with Gmail, the user can try to use "skyman" with Yahoo, Hotmail, or other providers. Or he may try a close variant, such as "skyman1."

A user profile is a mini-biography created by the user that is either required or recommended by social media services such as Twitter and Facebook. The contents of the profile may or may not be as important as the account itself. Many times, the information in a profile can be corroborated by investigative research, such as verifying employment stated in a profile being checked independently of the profile. Fig. 9.1 is an example of a Twitter profile that gives an abundant amount of information including a photo, location, and link to a website.

User-controlled blogs and websites are highly valued in establishing digital identity since the user controls the content. Blogs are easily and freely created,

Brett Shavers
@Brett_Shavers

Digital forensic analyst, author, university instructor, former Corporal of Marines, past life as undercover officer. Not necessarily in order or at same time.

Seattle, WA

brettshavers.cc

FIGURE 9.1
Twitter bio.

requiring nothing more than an Internet connection and user account. Google Blogger (http://www.blogger.com/) is one example of many services that freely provide a platform to create and post content online in a blog format. When identifying a user's digital footprint, the content of a blog includes a description or interests of the user. A blog created by a user with content about scuba diving would suggest that the user is not only interested in scuba diving, but may also engage in it as well. The digital identity is the blog, the username, and the content. Although an interest can change, the descriptive nature of an interest can lead to clues about the user to help build the digital identity.

Membership in online groups and forums contribute to a digital identity in terms of usernames, content, interests, and conversations. Additionally, the content posted to forums and as blog comments can help build the digital identity.

Social network sites have been a boon to investigations, in that confessions to crimes, planning of crimes, and bragging about crimes continue to be found after being posted by witnesses and suspects. When a user controls multiple social network accounts, such as having a Twitter, Facebook, and other accounts, the digital identity becomes more solidified as each account may corroborate the other with similar content and associates.

Content, which includes not only photos but also the words typed by users, is important, but so are grammar and language usage. Grammar and usage, whether proper or informal, give an indication of various aspects of the user, such as education level, socioeconomic status, and ethnicity. Spelling or grammar errors may be intentional, but if used consistently will build upon the digital identity's specific word usage that may reflect the personal identity.

With communication devices, at least, there are objective-identifying markers, such as, for example, a cellular telephone number, which contribute to the digital identity. Before the mass acceptance of cellular phones, telephones were considered as part of a fixed address, such as a home telephone number for a phone that could not leave the home. Private phone numbers are now commonly associated with individual persons and not to a physical address, since cellular phones usually travel with people 24/7. Phone numbers are not indicative of anything specific to a person since generally only the area code of a cellular number can be chosen by a user. Of course, the area code can be an important geo-location marker of where the user resides or wants others to believe he resides.

PHONE NUMBER SPOOFING
This is not the phone number you are looking for ...

Phone numbers can be spoofed; that is, a caller can change the number displayed on the Caller ID of the receiver. Spoofing is practically simple, and many online services provide free and paid call spoofing as a novelty. "Swatting" is an unintended consequence of spoofed calls, where pranksters spoof their number with someone else's and make a 911 emergency call that results in a police response to a victim's home. In these cases, the phone number that was spoofed is not part of the digital identity, but it can be a clue to the suspect based on relationships known to the victim of the Swatting.

Shopping club card accounts and credit card purchases, although not available through public Internet searches, also contribute to a digital identity, even if the accounts are in a false name and controlled by the suspect. Given legal access to purchases through court order, the items purchased are helpful in profiling the suspect by his interests and provide leads to communication devices. If cell phones or other devices are purchased and have not been identified, investigators can have an idea of what types of devices need to be discovered.

The digital identity of Internet users is a valuable commodity for commercial businesses to determine purchasing trends. By placing cookies on a user's computer, an advertiser can gain digital identity information through Internet surfing habits and identifying the types of websites visited. This commercial application applies to any investigation for the same purpose: identifying online activities that give insight to the person in order to predict future behavior.

Collecting online information about a suspect's digital identity includes a side benefit of geolocation data. Every visit to a website, post on a forum or blog, online purchase or e-mail sent can provide a specific date/time/location for the suspect. On its face, this information can be incredibly valuable to track movements, place the suspect at a location with other suspects or activity, and corroborate investigative information from other sources. Like any other evidence or information, online evidence must be corroborated and validated. Suspects can use a variety of means to hide IP addresses or other means to alter online information that may be collected.

Some examples of specific evidence of a digital identity are shown in Table 9.2. One person can have dozens of identifiers spread out over many e-mails and social networking sites in both true name and anonymous usernames. When a user uses the Internet for both good and bad purposes, users may mistakenly confuse the "good" identity with the "bad." For example, a suspect could mistakenly communicate with a co-conspirator in a chat room using their "good" account which contains his true name, and refer to the "bad" account inadvertently. Once that happens, the good account has been linked to the bad account and contaminated.

Unlike a physical identity, the identifiers in a digital identity can be used as leads to each other. With the physical identity, knowing the retina pattern of a suspect does not give you the suspect's fingerprints but with the digital identity,

Table 9.2 Digital Identifiers

Identifier	Description (IP Addresses, Logins, and Account Information May Be Obtainable in Many of These)
Social networking accounts	Any number of social networking accounts can be used by a single person. One person can also control several different accounts (different usernames) from the same social networking site.
User-controlled blogs, websites, forums	A suspect can control or own any number of blogs, websites, forums, or e-mail lists.
Moderator of blogs, websites, forums	A suspect can have limited control over any number of blogs, websites, forums, or e-mail lists.
E-mail	Suspects will generally have multiple e-mail accounts from the same provider as well as other e-mail providers.
Online comments	Suspects posting comments onto blogs or websites can also communicate to others through the comments.
Retail accounts	Purchasing products online generally require creating an account, which typically requires an e-mail, username, and personal information.
Telephone	Any number of phone numbers can be controlled, either by true name or fake name.
Online storage	Identifying online storage accounts provide more sources of potentially identifiable information as well as potential sources of communications via file and folder sharing.
Usernames	Identifying as many usernames as possible increases the odds of tying one or more usernames to a real person. Once a real person has been identified, the odds of identifying others in communication with the suspect increase.
Public and private keys	Encryption keys (public and private) are tied to a user, and almost always the private key is never shared. If a suspect's private key is recovered, entire threads of communications with co-conspirators may be recovered.
Uploaded photos	Uploaded photos add to a digital identity regardless of the content. Metadata may be recovered, such as date, time, and location of the photo, which can place the suspect at a location. Metadata can also identify the camera used to take the photo.

knowing one username can lead to an e-mail address or blog comments which can lead to a real name or phone number. The elements of a digital identity are often interconnected and can be used to leapfrog from one identifier to another to build a complete digital identity.

FINDING THE DIGITAL IDENTITY

Searching for a digital identity is not that different from searching for information about a person on the Internet. The methods used are the same; therefore, consider that searching for the digital identity means searching for suspects as well. The most important thing about searching for someone online is that it is more than just "Googling it." Without a broader process and strategies as described above, random Internet searches will usually lead the best of investigators down a rabbit hole of never-ending, overwhelming, and useless information.

First Things First

Information on the Internet typically is dynamic and ephemeral. Not only can information online spread like wildfire through numerous websites and social media, but it can also disappear instantly. For example, finding a blog comment submitted by a suspect may be an important part of an investigation, but only if you can find and capture it. Finding any information online should give rise to immediately capturing it before continuing the search. Capturing the information is more than simply bookmarking the page, but doing something that can be archived. Whether it is creating a PDF or screen capture of the web page, or downloading the entire website to a local storage, every relevant item should be captured at the time it is found. Potentially, evidence may have been captured or cached by websites such as The Wayback Machine (https://archive.org/) or CachedView (http://cachedview.com/). Every user account found, every blog comment, every social media post, and every access to a website potentially locks a suspect to an exact location by date and time, and to a specific device as well. Even if a suspect is well versed in anonymous Internet use through proxies or simply uses the Tor browser, the suspect must do this 100% of the time without making a single mistake. Good investigators know everything won't be found, but they also know that it is the errors made by suspects that often provide breaks in cases.

Google is not the only Internet search engine. Although Google is one of the most popular search engines, it is just one of over 100 search engines. Additionally, new Internet search engines are developed just as fast as others are discontinued. Each search engine performs a basic search by the user's entering a search term or terms and clicking the search button. Some search engines like Google allow for advanced searching through specific targets. Search engines can be grouped in categories based on the type of information they are developed to search. For example, Blog Search Engine (http://www.blogsearchengine.org/) searches blog content, whereas Knowem (http://www.knowem.com) searches the Internet for accounts used by a specific username.

It should be noted that different Internet search engines will likely give different results for the same search term. Additionally, when searching the Internet, the results are not in real time because the searches are made in the database of the selected search engine. For example, search engines crawl the Internet and create a database of the words from the crawled web servers around the world. When using a search engine, the database is searched, not the Internet, and the hits shown as results simply links from the database to websites of interest. Since every search engine will crawl and index data differently and at different intervals, the search results will be different. This is important to know because if the information is not found using one search engine, try another. Also, if a result is not found one day, it may be found on another day when a search engine updates it database by adding newly crawled data.

An effective Internet search strategy is to be methodical and stay on an investigative track. If a wrong lead has been chased on the Internet, hours of work will have been wasted, or worse, the investigation can be taken in the wrong direction. If the goal is to gather information about a digital identity, start with the known information and use the appropriate search engines to find targeted information and corroborate everything. The username is the next most important thing to the suspect's actual name. Either of these two items is a good start, but if not available, other identifiable information is useful, such as a phone number. The order of searches and order of search engines are dependent upon the information on hand. For example, if you have a first and last name, use those names to search for a username, and subsequently search for any information posted online with the newly discovered username(s). Conversely, if a username is known, a search for information posted online may lead to the suspect's true name.

Google makes Internet searching easy. With its basic search (http://www.google.com), search terms are simply entered into a search box without needing any qualifiers which results in Google presenting a list of URLs that it believes contains hits. A search for a general term or name may result in tens of thousands or millions of hits that are irrelevant to what was intended to be searched.

The following Google searching tips can be considered "Google hacking." Not that Google is actually hacked, but with the aid of a combination of operators and symbols, the Google database can be searched for results not typically produced with the basic or advanced search options. Vulnerabilities, passwords, usernames, and other sensitive information can be found using Google hacking search strings; however, the searches are run across the entire Google database and focus on a specific web server or person. In the context of an investigation, only those search strings effective for finding digital identity information should be used to target specific suspects.

Before getting into Google hacking techniques, an option to reduce the number of search hits with the basic search Google interface is to use the advanced search function of Google. Any investigator regularly using Google should consider only using the advanced search (https://www.google.com/advanced_search) as the time saved by eliminating irrelevant search hits is well worth the effort. The advanced search is an easy-to-use Google option that uses search operators and symbols behind the scenes after the user has entered plain text information for the search.

For example, when the search terms are placed in the "this exact word or phrase" of the Google Advanced Search, only search hits that have exactly the word *John* followed by the word *Smith* will be displayed.

This same search can be made in the Google Basic Search by typing *"John Smith"*. The double quotation symbols force the search engine to find only hits that have *John* followed by *Smith*. This one search technique (Google hacking) can effectively eliminate tens of thousands of irrelevant hits in name searches.

CASE DOESN'T MATTER
The Google search engine doesn't discriminate!
Search terms can be uppercase or lowercase as the results will be the same. Google does not give different results for *jOHn SmItH* or *john smith*. This makes it much easier to search without worrying about capitalizing names.

Another example of a Google Advanced Search option is the "none of these words." For example, searching for *john smith* in the Google Advanced Search box of "this exact word or phrase" while also typing *computer* in the "none of these words" results in hits that only have *john* followed by *smith* but not having the term *computer* anywhere in the hit. Using the Google Basic Search to get the same kind of result, use the Google search operator "-" symbol placed before the word not to be included in the search hits. In this example, the Google basic search string would appear as: *"John Smith" – computer*.

If there is a specific search needed, Google and other search engines usually are able to provide a narrowing scope for a search. An example would be searching for a suspect's phone number. Databases exist online, such as http://www.whitepages.com that maintain published phone numbers. However, this database not only does not contain prepaid cell phones with the owner's information, but the information can also be spoofed if the suspect creates an account and changes the contact information.

Using Google to find an unlisted number requires a simple combination of symbols. If we know the suspect's name is John Smith and we know that he lives in Seattle, we can search Google with a chance that John posted his number somewhere. A search string such as *John Smith "my cell is 206"* would result in hits where *john smith* and *my cell is 206* would be on the page — and also showing the full cell phone number. Potentially, a comment on a social networking site or comment would state, "My cell number is 206-555-1234" posted by John. Like any search and any search result, false hits are certain to occur, positive hits may be uncertain as well, and search strings will need tweaking; but if there is a chance to find an unlisted, unpublished, and secret prepaid cellular number online, this is the way to go.

Using Google operators and symbols not only reduces the number of hits received, but it also helps to eliminate false hits which may result from following up the unrelated results and wasting time on the Internet. For common search terms, more qualifiers can be entered to narrow the results to a manageable number. Unique search terms or names may not need much more than double quotations to find relevant hits.

Google has been known to create new operators and symbols as well as phase out the use of others. To find the current Google operators, look through Google's help pages: http://support.google.com/websearch/answer/2466433?hl=en.

"WHICH SEARCH ENGINE IS THE BEST?"
It depends...
Internet search engines are unique in design by the way information on the Internet is crawled, searched, and displayed. Some search engines, like http://www.hotbot.com search through multiple search engines at the same time. Some search engines focus on blog content or usernames. Depending on what you are searching for, pick the search engine that best fits the needs of the investigation.

Once the username has been discovered, finding relevant content online is both easier and cumbersome depending upon the commonality of the username. For example, usernames can be chosen by as many people that want to use the username within an individual service. John Smith can choose johnsmith@gmail.com as long as no one else created it before he did, and of course, he can use johnsmith on a different service if his first choice is not available.

Usernames can be used across blog sites to post comments. John Smith can post a comment to an online newspaper as johnsmith and use the same username to post to a forum. The importance of finding John Smith's usernames is to find more easily where he is posting comments online. Finding John Smith's online comments serve several purposes. First, the content may be important. Second, the date/time/location available may be important. Every comment, whether to an online newspaper or social media networking site, creates a date/time/location (IP address) stamp which places John Smith somewhere at a specific time.

Let us take an example of searching a username using one online search engine (http://knowem.com/). Knowem.com searches across hundreds of social networking sites for any username. If the username is not being used, the social networking listing shows it to be available. This is a quick method of searching usernames across the majority of social networking sites to find where a specific username is being used. As mentioned, many different and unrelated people can be using the same username (but not same e-mail), and any social networking site using that username needs corroboration that the same person is using the username in question.

One of the benefits of finding many uses of a username across social media sites is to take advantage of mistakes made by the suspect. A suspect may take extra precautions to post on one forum but may be open on another. This can happen where a suspect may make an anonymous threat on one forum and use the same username on another forum and inadvertently give identifying information since he is not trying to be anonymous. Suspects communicating in forums or chat rooms make errors in the content by either bragging or making statements to prove a point, and could provide some identifying information.

"YOU CAN TRUST ME; I USED TO WORK THERE"
Trust… the one thing on the Internet that doesn't exist

Matthew Keys was a former employee of the Tribune Company. Matthew joined an online chat, identified himself as a former employee of the Tribune Company and used the username AESCracked. Keys gave Tribune login credentials in the chat room and asked for damage to be done (which it was). Stating he was a former employee of the company narrowed the list of suspects… (United States of America v. Matthew Keys, 2014).

Usernames are typically tied to e-mail addresses which are hugely beneficial to identify suspects. Once a username has been identified, the e-mail address can be identified through court orders. The information behind that e-mail address includes the IP address when created, IP addresses upon login, and any personal information required to create the e-mail. To keep an e-mail completely anonymous, a suspect has to take steps to protect the IP address at every login and use of the e-mail. Investigators need only to find one mistake that identifies a chain of communications and identities.

If the physical identity of a suspect is unknown, and only the suspect username name is known, it is possible to identify associations of the suspect, identify an associate, then track back and identify the suspect. The security break rests with associates in this type of instance since regardless of the steps a suspect takes to protect his identity, his associates may not be as secure.

One case example of this type of method was used with hacker Higinio Ochoa. Ochoa, username "w0rmer", hacked into several government databases. Ochoa's girlfriend posed for a photo with a sign pinned to her skirt bragging about Ochoa's hacks. The photo was taken from the neck down and face not shown and was posted online. Most likely, Ochoa's girlfriend did not realize that the metadata in the photo contained GPS coordinates where the photo was taken which led to the girlfriend's identity and location. Identifying the girlfriend subsequently led to identifying Ochoa through associations on social media sites (United States of America v. Higino O. Ochoa, 2012).

In the Ochoa case, his username was searched across social media sites, forums, chat rooms, and online comments to find any communications with others. In this particular case, his identity was discovered and his true identity established (along with his nonsecret usernames). Another error made by Ochoa was logging into his Twitter account without hiding his IP address. Other IP addresses used to login to the Twitter account were found to be obscured and originated in foreign countries, but the one unprotected login originated from Houston, Texas. This one mistake tied all activity to his real IP address, regardless of how secure he had been logging in prior and afterward.

Ochoa provided an immense amount of digital identity information in both the open (unhidden information between him and his girlfriend on social media) and secret (anonymous use with hidden IP address) Internet. Once his physical identity was discovered, it was immediately tied to his digital identity, consisting of both his open and formerly secret online communications. More importantly, the Ochoa case provided information on even more hackers through his online associations and communications that were directly attributed to Ochoa.

"WHUPS!"
Darn usernames and e-mails

The creator of the Silk Road, Ross Ulbricht, made a huge error with his username. Silk Road was an online illegal drug market on the dark web that facilitated mail order drug sales, among other illegal sales. Ulbricht collected a commission on the sales in bitcoin.

One of Ulbricht's usernames was "Altoid" which he used on the dark web to encourage business on his Silk Road drug market. Unfortunately for Ulbricht, he used the same username on an IT forum on the open Internet and even listed his e-mail address as a contact. To make his error even more dramatic, the e-mail address he listed on the open Internet was....rossulbricht@gmail.com (Hume, 2015).

Dark Web

The dark web, that is, the Internet that is not indexed by search engines, contains communications between criminals which is very difficult not only to track but even to find. Mere access to the dark web requires the use of the Tor browser which by default hides the true IP address of the user. But as seen in the Ross Ulbricht case, information from either the dark web or open Internet can be tied together when errors are made by suspects.

Using the Ulbricht case for another example, Ulbricht's co-conspirator was unidentified until Ulbricht's laptop was examined. Once examined, not only was his co-conspirator identified by an image of his passport on the laptop, but Ulbricht had also maintained an extensive record of chat logs that were thousands of pages long between himself and co-conspirator Roger Clark. Although the chats were most likely impossible to intercept through the dark web, analysis after the fact recovered enough covert communications to help in placing Ulbricht in prison for life (United States of America v. Roger Thomas Clark, 2015).

Third-Party Providers

Identifying online service providers, such as a chat room, blog, listserv, or other site where Internet users interact can be an important consideration in an investigation. When suspects use a third-party provider to communicate, they are trusting the third party to provide the communication channel. This can be a forum or social networking site. Third-party services give investigators one level of security to prevent compromising investigations when search warrants or subpoenas are issued to the third party. A search warrant to Facebook for a user's account and activity is an example where the suspect should not be alerted by Facebook if required in the search warrant.

Conversely, if a suspect controls the service, such as hosting a forum, the suspect holds all information and access to the forum. Serving a search warrant for the suspect to turn over evidence on his own service would be counter-productive before the investigation is complete. One method of bypassing both a third-party service and a suspect-controlled service is to create a honeypot website or forum to draw the suspect(s) into. If a suspect has been identified by a username and seems to be interested in classic sports cars, a website for sports cars can be created with the intention of the suspect accessing or creating an account on the site to leave comments.

To draw the suspect into the honeypot website, undercover conversations may have to be conducted on his current third-party sites to entice him to visit the honeypot site. Lots of work goes into setting up this kind of legitimate-appearing website, and its success may depend on luck. But if successful, IP addresses can be captured without warrants and a direct line of communication is possible with the suspect.

Any third-party website may contain a link to a suspect. Even a product review on Amazon.com by a suspect can identify a purchase and IP address of the post, delivery address of purchase, method of purchase, e-mail address, and telephone number. If a suspect is using a unique username that may even be personal to the suspect, the same username could be used in legitimate areas of the Internet, such as Amazon, but also in criminal areas. Although the same username can have different e-mail addresses, if a suspect likes the username enough, he may use it with several e-mail providers and keep some for open use, others for covert use.

SUMMARY

As the digital identity is recovered through an Internet investigation, keep in mind that the goal is to tie the digital identity to a real person (the physical identity). The digital identity can also be used for more than establishing an identity; it can expose the user's Internet activity; connections to associates;

user intentions; confessions, and admissions. By starting with the known, which can be either a username or true name, the unknown may be found through Internet searches which can lead to connections between associates, Internet activity of suspects, and chat content containing evidence of crimes.

Investigators should keep in mind that finding plaintext Internet chats containing evidence of crimes is important, but it will most likely be the non-evidence chats and communications that will lead to identifying the extent and nature of evidence communications. Just as the case examples have shown, an innocent comment on one forum can identify the suspect in another which may reveal the evidence needed when mistakes are made by the suspect.

REFERENCES

Hume, T. (December 13, 2015). *How FBI caught Ross Ulbricht, alleged creator of criminal marketplace Silk Road.* Retrieved from CNN: http://www.cnn.com/2013/10/04/world/americas/silk-road-ross-ulbricht/.

United States of America v. Higino O. Ochoa, 1:12 M 163 (Western District of Texas March 15, 2012).

United States of America v. Matthew Keys, 2:13-CR-00082 KJM (Eastern District of California December 4, 2014).

United States of America v. Roger Thomas Clark (Southern District of New York April 21, 2015).

CHAPTER 10

Putting It All Together

INTRODUCTION

The goal of initiating an investigation is to complete successfully the case with a positive outcome which can be prosecuting criminals, remedying a civil matter, or simply reducing the risk of an incident from reoccurring. To put all relevant communication information together to paint a picture requires collecting communications from as many sources as possible. Most likely, capturing every conversation is improbable, but enough can be captured to serve a purpose in an investigation. Putting together communication evidence requires attempts to obtain all of it while realizing that limits exist that prevent or restrict the amount possible to obtain. The intention of this chapter is to show examples and give guidance on case management, development, and presentation as well as review investigative techniques discussed in this book.

COLLECTING REAL-TIME COMMUNICATIONS

Capturing real-time communications benefits an active case as it is useful in gaining information on past crimes through admissions and, more importantly, preventing and identifying future crimes. Real-time communications also show new associations between suspects as they are taking place. In most instances, historical communications are needed for analysis before electronic intercepts are approved through court orders.

Online Communications

Communications that occur on the open Internet are the easiest to collect and monitor since the only legal authority needed is that of being able to access the Internet to view that which is publicly viewable without bypassing logins. On the face of how easy it is to find communications online, such as those seen in public chat rooms, forums, and website comments, it would be a fair assumption to believe no one will publicly communicate criminal intent openly. However, this is far from reality as criminals and terrorists regularly post and communicate openly as if expecting no one else will read the communications.

COMMUNICATING OPENLY ON SOCIAL MEDIA...
...as if no one will find it...
Mohamed Elshinawy communicated with terrorists using cell phones, e-mail, and social media. Although some communications were unable to be captured or even found, the communications posted on social media were freely available for anyone to see, including the open Internet evidence captured by the FBI which led to his arrest for attempting to provide material support to ISIL (United States of America v. Mohamed Elshinawy, 2015).

Once an online communication channel is discovered, leads to other communications can be discovered if a suspect refers to other channels, such as mobile devices. It would be an investigative error to assume that communications of great evidentiary value cannot be found on the open Internet where the value can be a simple reference to a phone number to communicate.

Electronic Intercepts
Intrusion of personal privacy is the greatest with electronic intercepts of a person's e-mails and phone calls, or through audio/video surveillance in their homes. When warranted, electronic intercepts provide some of the best evidence available simply because suspects are more comfortable communicating in secret when they believe their conversations are private. The information gained from electronic intercepts can be more than the content of the conversations, and also the intentions of suspects can be revealed through their planning of criminal or terrorist operations.

SEND ME AN E-MAIL...
...because no one else can read my e-mails...
By use of electronic intercepts, the FBI captured cell phone and e-mail communications between Jamshid Muhtorov and terrorists. During one phone conversation, the topic was to be careful about speaking on the phone because of potential wiretaps...they then continued to use the phone to talk about planning a terror attack knowing someone could be listening. They were right, the FBI was listening (United States v. Jamshid Muhtorov, 2012).

Similarly, many people believing no one is reading their public conversations posted on the open Internet, criminals under active surveillance through an electronic intercept may also believe their conversations are secret and not being monitored. Even when they suspect their devices are compromised, they still continue to use the communication channels as if their criminal plans are still secret. This continues to happen because communications must occur to plan and carry out plans, even at the risk of compromise.

COLLECTING HISTORICAL COMMUNICATIONS

Historical communications encompass any system, device, platform, or item capable of storing communications such as text messages on a smartphone. Historical communications provide for analyzing trends, identifying associates, and uncovering criminal or terrorist plots that have been documented in some fashion.

Online Historical Information

Social networking sites are designed to make it easy to create accounts, find other accounts, and communicate via open posts or direct chats and messages. Suspects using social networking sites to communicate or express their intentions to others may not even be aware that their communications are on the open Internet, especially if they do not understand or correctly use privacy settings on their accounts. If a social medium account, such as Facebook, is set for open viewing by the public, anything posted is available for use as historical information. That which has not been set for public view is typically available only by court order.

Social networking sites are also designed to build relationships between people specifically. Several software applications, such as X1 Social Discovery (http://www.x1.com/), ingest social networking accounts into a database for analysis. For example, when a suspect under investigation is known to have multiple social media accounts, X1 Social Discovery can download all publicly accessible information (posts, contacts, and so on), into a searchable database.

The historical information of social networking sites includes: location data, posts and comments, status updates, connections, photos, and more. Once a social networking account is identified, it is possible to obtain years of geolocation data and conversations that can corroborate other investigative information.

Other online historical communications typically exist in blogs, forums, and public comments on websites and blogs. Although connections are not easily determined in forums since they appear on a social networking site as "friends" or "followers," both the content and user account information is valuable. Considering that geolocation has several uses in an investigation, every post and comment that has an IP address can provide historical geolocation data over a long period of time.

Government Access Resources

Government databases generally contain only historical data (with some exceptions). Driving records, warrants, criminal histories, and past cases are all historical information which can contain relevant communications between suspects. Depending upon the jurisdiction and agency, some databases are searchable across cities, counties, and states. By researching past cases of suspects, the potential to find communications and statements made by a suspect and others is good if the prior case captured communications. These can range from dialed number recorders (DNR/Pen Registers), recorded conversations, or other electronic communications. Statements made in a past investigation that were initially believed to be pertinent to an investigation may actually provide some value to current or future investigations. For example, a previously recorded conservation between two suspects in an older and unrelated investigation may refer to a third suspect in a current investigation.

From Seized Electronic Devices

Seizures and discoveries of electronic storage devices in an investigation typically occur toward the end of an investigation. Occasionally, storage devices and phones can be recovered in trash runs (searching a suspect's discarded garbage) or seized with the authority of a search warrant surreptitiously in order to avoid compromising the investigation, such as a sneak-and-peek warrant where the suspect is not informed of the search.

Devices under the control of suspects may have a great deal of historical information depending upon the length of use, sharing the particular device, and type of device. A drug dealing organization, for example, may use cheap prepaid cell phones called "burners" because they are discarded after a short period of time. Many of these types of phones are not smart phones and have no internal GPS or applications that create user data other than stored phone numbers. However, cell tower information may provide geolocation data, and calls/texts provide metadata of communications which can be just as useful as the content of the conversations.

Fig. 10.1 is an example of call records (State of Florida v. Casey Marie Anthony, 2011) showing metadata of calls. Geolocation data is also available through cell tower information that, when combined with other cell towers' information, track the location of a cell phone as it travels.

TURNING INFORMATION INTO INTELLIGENCE

Investigations involving electronic communications and the Internet quickly create more information than initially appears to be possible for analysis, yet the information must be carefully analyzed in order to create intelligence. When the information seems overwhelming, technology is a solution to turn a mountain of information into manageable bits of intelligence.

Link and Social Networking Analysis

Link analysis and social networking analysis are methods of visualizing massive amounts of data to find specific types of information, such as key persons,

CASEY ANTHONY TELEPHONE TOLLS
JUNE 15-20, 2008

CASEY ANTHONY TOLLS JUNE 15-20, 2008

TARGET NAME	TARGET NUMBER	DATE	TIME	DURATION	RECORD TYPE	DIRECTION	NUMBER DIALED	SUBSCRIBER
CASEY ANTHONY	(407) 619-9286	6/15/2008	0:13:00	0:12:00	Unknown	INCOMING	(631) 902-5443	ANTHONY LAZZARO
CASEY ANTHONY	(407) 619-9286	6/15/2008	6:33:00	0:01:00	Unknown	OUTGOING	(407) 619-9286	CASEY ANTHONY
CASEY ANTHONY	(407) 619-9286	6/15/2008	8:56:00	0:01:00	Unknown	OUTGOING	(954) 328-9214	AMY HUIZENGA
CASEY ANTHONY	(407) 619-9286	9/15/2008	9:15:00	0:01:00	Unknown	OUTGOING	(631) 902-5443	ANTHONY LAZZARO
CASEY ANTHONY	(407) 619-9286	6/15/2008	12:51:00	0:10:00	Unknown	OUTGOING	(954) 328-9214	AMY HUIZENGA
CASEY ANTHONY	(407) 619-9286	6/15/2008	13:01:00	0:01:00	Unknown	OUTGOING	(407) 619-9286	CASEY ANTHONY
CASEY ANTHONY	(407) 619-9286	6/15/2008	14:44:00	0:01:00	Unknown	OUTGOING	(407) 619-9286	CASEY ANTHONY
CASEY ANTHONY	(407) 619-9286	6/15/2008	17:05:00	0:04:00	Unknown	OUTGOING	(407) 275-4909	CYNTHIA ANTHONY
CASEY ANTHONY	(407) 619-9286	6/15/2008	19:10:00	0:01:00	Unknown	OUTGOING	(407) 275-4909	CYNTHIA ANTHONY
CASEY ANTHONY	(407) 619-9286	6/15/2008	20:38:00	0:00:00	Text Message	OUTGOING	(631) 902-5443	ANTHONY LAZZARO
CASEY ANTHONY	(407) 619-9286	6/15/2008	20:48:00	0:01:00	Unknown	OUTGOING	(407) 619-9286	CASEY ANTHONY
CASEY ANTHONY	(407) 619-9286	6/15/2008	21:08:00	0:00:00	Text Message	OUTGOING	(631) 902-5443	ANTHONY LAZZARO
CASEY ANTHONY	(407) 619-9286	6/15/2008	22:06:00	0:11:00	Unknown	OUTGOING	(631) 902-5443	ANTHONY LAZZARO
CASEY ANTHONY	(407) 619-9286	6/15/2008	22:08:00	0:00:00	Text Message	OUTGOING	(631) 902-5443	ANTHONY LAZZARO
CASEY ANTHONY	(407) 619-9286	6/15/2008	22:38:00	0:05:00	Unknown	OUTGOING	(631) 902-5443	ANTHONY LAZZARO
CASEY ANTHONY	(407) 619-9286	6/15/2008	22:45:00	0:04:00	Unknown	INCOMING	(631) 902-5443	ANTHONY LAZZARO
CASEY ANTHONY	(407) 619-9286	6/15/2008	23:44:00	1:21:00	Unknown	OUTGOING	(631) 902-5443	ANTHONY LAZZARO
CASEY ANTHONY	(407) 619-9286	6/15/2008	23:50:00	0:00:00	Text Message	OUTGOING	(631) 902-5443	ANTHONY LAZZARO
CASEY ANTHONY	(407) 619-9286	6/16/2008	2:18:00	0:00:00	Text Message	OUTGOING	(631) 902-5443	ANTHONY LAZZARO
CASEY ANTHONY	(407) 619-9286	6/16/2008	3:07:00	0:15:00	Unknown	INCOMING	(631) 902-5443	ANTHONY LAZZARO

FIGURE 10.1
Call record details, Casey Marie Anthony case.

phone numbers, patterns, and events. Link analysis can be done manually with spreadsheets or with software designed specifically to organize data into something meaningful and easy to understand. One of the more full featured analysis tools is IBM's i2 Analyst's Notebook (http://www-03.ibm.com/software/products/en/analysts-notebook). The i2 Analyst Notebook is a data visualization software application designed to display massive amounts of data using link analysis charts, graphs, and varying displays.

An open source option to the i2 Analyst Notebook for visualization is NodeXL (http://www.nodexlgraphgallery.org/y). NodeXL is used for graphing network data in Microsoft Excel with built-in connections to several social networks including Twitter, Flickr, and others. Fig. 10.2 shows one example of a graphed Twitter network (world heritage) using NodeXL.

Regardless of the tool used, the goal of identifying connections, conversations, events, and patterns are the same. In many instances, graphing data into a visual requires separating the data into individual displays. Social networking accounts and phone calls can quickly turn a graph into an incomprehensible display of lines and numbers. The connections can also be drastically different between the communications methods used to make a combined visual useless. It is better to create visuals that more easily represent a specific mode of communication (for example) or display of associations. Metadata of communications is the preferred primary dataset in these types of visualizations over content since key points of contacts are sometimes easier to determine through

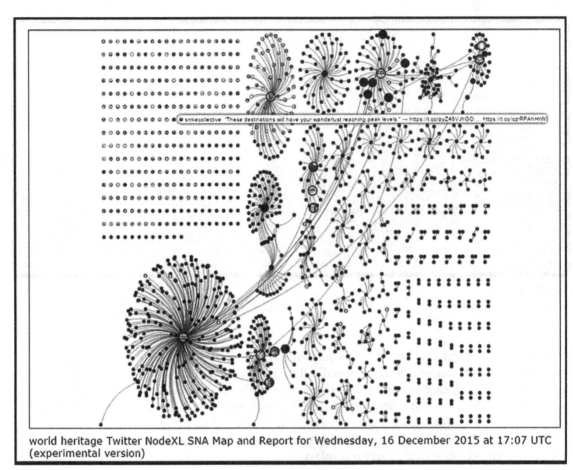

world heritage Twitter NodeXL SNA Map and Report for Wednesday, 16 December 2015 at 17:07 UTC (experimental version)

FIGURE 10.2

NodeXL (https://nodexl.codeplex.com/).

metadata when the datasets are large. The main concept of a visualization of communications is to determine "who contacts whom, how often, when and for how long."

When multiple communication methods are uncovered, it is reasonable to assume that each device and mode is being used to communicate, and also that every conversation on any one device or method is not a complete conversation. For example, Fig. 10.3 shows Alice with three e-mail accounts, one phone, and one chat account. Bob is shown with one chat account, one group chat, and three cell phones. Of these, communications have been discovered through two chat accounts, two e-mail accounts, and two cell phones. Potentially, a cell phone conversation can be continued later in a chat or e-mail. A

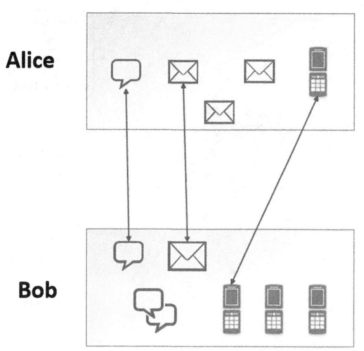

FIGURE 10.3
Electronic modes of communication.

conversation can also be continued face-to-face or through other unidentified means. It is the collection of as many communication devices and channels that helps bridge entire conversations.

Although Fig. 10.3 is a simple representation, it shows that a single person can have several different types of electronic communication with other suspects in an easy-to-describe manner. Simple visualizations also convey information in a way that is easier to decipher. When comparing Fig. 10.2 with Fig. 10.3, Fig. 10.2 visual display shows a massive amount of information that can create visual clutter or information overload where Fig. 10.3 takes one pertinent item from many items and produces an easier to understand visual. With multiple key items (phone calls, e-mails, and so on), many individual visuals of each key item will be helpful to see the big picture as well as the smaller yet just as important key items.

Creating a visual of specific incoming and outgoing phone calls is seen in Fig. 10.4. In this example, John Q is the focused suspect in the visual but may or may not be the primary suspect. However, the total number of incoming and outgoing calls by number can be easily seen in the visual. When multiple phones are

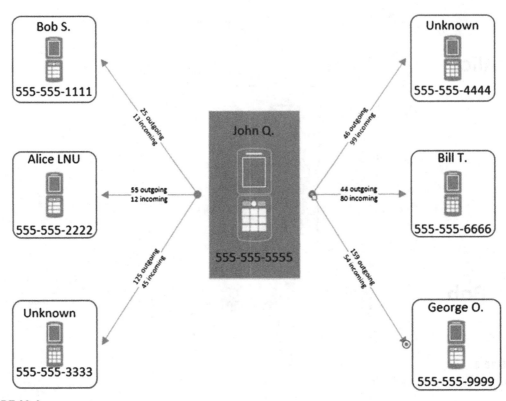

FIGURE 10.4
Phone analysis visual.

used by multiple suspects, this type of visual requires a separate chart for each phone for each person, which will quickly overwhelm the intended effect of using a visual aid.

Keep in mind that some types of communication, such as cell phones, are discarded and frequently replaced with new devices, each contacting different suspects in order to compartmentalize communications. Some content may also be encrypted and unavailable, but the metadata (dates, times, length, and so on) will be available through call detail records, billing history, and analysis of the physical devices. When suspects frequently change cell phones, an effective visual is combining all cell phones of all suspects to show the total number of calls between persons without having to show each specific phone number used. Fig. 10.5 shows an example of illustrating the phone calls between a key suspect based on the person rather than the device used. This type of visual eliminates the confusion seen in Fig. 10.4 when multiple phones are being used by multiple persons.

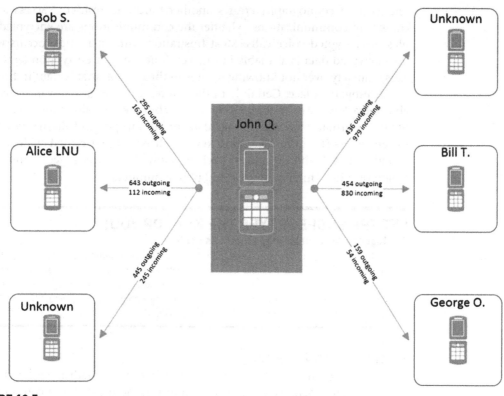

FIGURE 10.5
Phone analysis visual.

THE (VIRTUALLY) IMPOSSIBLE

A level of frustration is easy to develop when an investigator wants to capture all communications from all devices from all suspects. In an ideal investigation, all content is readily available and in real time. In reality, this is rarely true. The best advice to avoid frustration is to accept the fact that some communications will never be found and others, if found, will have content that is unavailable. This is a fact of life in investigating digital devices in complex cases.

Cryptography and Steganography

Some things are possible today but may not be possible tomorrow. Communications hidden with steganography often remain unknown because as a practical matter they do not exist except to those who know where to look. Software detection of data hidden with steganography methods could be much better, but as of today steganography is an effective means of hiding communications because it is impossible to know what you cannot find.

The issue of cryptography creates another hurdle to restricted access to the content of communications, whether the communications are encrypted text files or encrypted voice calls. Most frustration with encryption occurs when the encrypted data is available but inaccessible without decryption keys; that causes anxiety over not knowing what is in the content that is right in front of the investigator's face. Certainly in the future, technological advances will be able to crack some of yesterday's encryption, but the only alternative today is to use the information available (metadata for instance) or find alternative means to gain access (find the decryption keys). At least with encrypted evidence, the metadata is valuable in and of itself to show dates, times, geolocation, the length of calls, e-mail addresses, and phone numbers.

LET THE SUSPECT TYPE THE KEY FOR YOU!
Key loggers work when other methods don't

Nicodemo Scarfo was under investigation by the FBI for illegal gambling. Scarfo used PGP for encryption, and the FBI could not access evidence without the private key. With a search warrant, agents secretly installed a key logger onto Scarfo's computer which captured all his keystrokes, including his private key. Scarfo basically gave up the key without even knowing it (United States of America v. Nicodemo S. Scarfo and Frank Paolerio, 2001).

Software Applications

Software programming skills, particularly where high math is required such as encryption programs, are not needed to use the most secure communication systems. Given the rise in awareness and demand for privacy in general public use of technology, the odds that secure communications will be used in criminal or terrorist acts are certain. Additionally, providers of technology that promise personal privacy take great steps to avoid maintaining user data.

The application WhatsApp (http://www.whatsapp.com) is an example of secure communications that is freely available, just one example of several that make uncovering content practically impossible. WhatsApp is an SMS (short message service) replacement on mobile devices that uses the Internet to send messages and also make calls. The content of any message is not stored on WhatsApp servers after messages are received. Messages sent but not yet received can remain on the WhatsApp servers for up to 30 days before being deleted. WhatsApp retains as little information as possible, and messages enjoy end-to-end encryption for privacy. Hence, although content may not be available in either real-time or as historical use, metadata of use exists that can show communications did occur between suspects with WhatsApp.

The number of privacy desktop and mobile communication applications grows regularly, including simple webmail services. One recent addition to the many freely available webmail services is ProtonMail (http://www.protonmail.com). ProtonMail is a web-based e-mail service that provides users with encrypted e-mail while also keeping user data out of government reach by being physically located in Switzerland. In the case of ProtonMail, not only are the contents of e-mail encrypted, but metadata may be inaccessible due to the privacy laws of Switzerland preventing law enforcement from obtaining user records.

Regardless of the encryption employed, security apps used, or methods of use, it is possible to obtain access to the content if access is gained by controlling the decryption keys. If the device has been seized, the potential to access the data regardless of the encryption exists. Much like the best safe in the world is useless if the combination is written down on a piece of paper, the best encryption is useless if the key is found.

Tor and Anonymous Chat

Tor works and is expected only to get better as an easily accessible, anonymous Internet browsing network. However, the mistakes of criminals are constant and the odds of discovery increase the longer they use any system of communication. Investigations involving Tor do not necessary result in the absence of useful evidence being obtained when an error by a suspect can unlock a trove of evidence.

An example of Tor misuse is not understanding how a personal e-mail can still be traced back to the sender even when sent through the Tor network if the sender errs. If a personal e-mail account is created on the open Internet, that is, not using Tor, the e-mail provider captures the date, time and IP address of the e-mail creation. Regardless of any future use of that particular e-mail, the originating records point to the true IP address of creation. So, even if Tor is used to send e-mails in this example account, obtaining the account creation records via court order will trace back to the actual IP address, which may be related to the suspect's using the account. Although the e-mails will not have the actual IP addresses when sent, the account will have the true IP address when created and every time it is accessed outside of Tor. Thus, for the investigator this simply means requesting the subscriber information of every e-mail account under investigation in hopes of finding a true IP address created outside of Tor.

Devices

Computing has become more than inexpensive; it has become almost free. Prepaid cell phones can be purchased for less than $10. Used laptops can be found for less than $50. Free and open WiFi exists throughout the world in cafes, restaurants, libraries, and even provided by governments throughout an entire city. The means to communicate electronically make it so that any and probably every criminal organization uses technology to some degree for communications.

Because of low cost and easy purchase, devices are often purchased for a specific act and quickly discarded. Inexpensive devices such as the $10 prepaid phone generally have little user data stored compared to the current models of smartphones. However, cell phone records and cell tower records do provide information needed to find connections to locations and co-conspirators. On one hand, this may seem overwhelming to investigate, but on the positive side, every device is a potential point of failure in a criminal or terrorist organization. The more devices used the more points of failure possible.

NON-TECH COMMUNICATIONS

Geolocation has been mentioned throughout this book as an important aspect of communications. Whether the geolocation is obtained through surveillance video, security cameras, stored photos, cell tower records, or GPS coordinates from tracking devices, geolocation can help pinpoint conversations occurring outside of technology in face-to-face communications.

Where two suspects communicate with each other using multiple devices, it is fair to assume that some communications also occur in person. Without full-time surveillance, finding these occurrences may be impossible. Yet, given historical geolocation data, the locations of both suspects can be plotted on a map to find common locations. If the cell phones of both suspects prove to be in the same location at the same time, most likely the suspects are speaking with each other or exchanging evidence. If this can be found to happen in a public area that could be indicative of the possibility that the contact is of greater importance than if it occurred in a residence. Further, security cameras in nearby businesses may have recorded the suspects together.

Another covert non-technical communication method is dead-drops. A dead-drop is a specific location where one person leaves information for another that is to be retrieved at a later time. By having the receiver pick up the communication (letter, electronic storage device, and so on) at a later time, neither suspect is observed together. A counter to the security of a dead-drop is using geolocation data. Using cell tower data as an example, two suspects can be tracked with historical data or in real time. The suspects may never meet at the same location at the same time, but if a location converges where one suspect arrives and leaves before the second suspect arrives, there is a possibility that this was a dead-drop location. If this location is often used, verified through real-time geolocation tracking, it may be possible to observe with active surveillance the second suspect arriving after the first leaves.

The contents of a dead-drop communication may be unavailable unless the materials are physically intercepted, but when observed under surveillance it does most likely show a means of communication and ties the suspects together.

Related to a dead-drop is a signal site where a visual signal is left by one person to inform the other of a message, such as, "There is a package to pick up at the dead-drop." The visual signal can be as seemingly insignificant as a chalk mark on a mailbox or a photo placed in a window. This kind of strategy is important to know, since not only will both suspects not meet at this location, but there is no communication that will be found at the signal location. With geolocation that shows both suspects intersecting at a location yet nothing is left or picked up, it is potentially a signal site informing of a dead-drop.

BUSY AT THE DEAD-DROPS!
But I don't want to walk too far

In addition to phone conversations, there were 12 diskettes, tens of thousands of dollars, and 6000 pages of paper exchanged at least 55 times using dead-drops in the Robert Hanssen spy case. The dead-drop was walking distance from his residence...(United States of America v. Robert Phillip Hanssen, 2001).

A twist on the traditional dead-drop is an electronic dead-drop, where information is accessed electronically from a previously placed WiFi or Bluetooth device. In this scenario, one suspect can broadcast a WiFi connection for a short distance and at a predetermined time. A second suspect, using nearly any device can connect to the broadcast, download the information and depart the area without ever coming near the first suspect. This type of dead-drop can be done by simply leaving a device hidden in the area by one suspect with the second suspect arriving after the first suspect leaves. Again, the suspects do not meet although they can have a meaningful exchange of information. Geolocation data can however show both suspects to be near or at the same location, albeit at different times, creating the inference that some type of communication occurred.

The only counters to geolocation that suspects can take are: not to carry any electronic devices that are trackable, avoid security cameras, and not to make any purchases with credit or debit cards. Even driving can create geolocation data with traffic light cameras, license plate readers, and traffic and parking citations. Since these countermeasures are not practical for most criminal organizations, some geolocation data regarding their activities are bound to be found.

Another variation of a dead-drop for covert communications is an online dead-drop. One example is the Vuvuzela messaging system (http://github.com/davidlazar/vuvuzela). Vuvuzela encrypts the metadata of communications as well as confuses any eavesdropper seeking to intercept or access other persons' data and those persons associated with the data. Fig. 10.6 shows how users can drop data into an anonymous network and receivers can access the data afterward; however, it is unclear to observers which data has been dropped and by whom, as well as which user is accessing data. The originator of data sends an

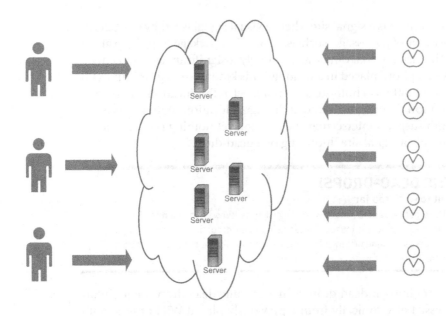

Users "drop" encrypted data on hidden servers for receiver to access at a different time. Observing any activity only shows that a user accesses the server at one time and another user accesses the server at another time, with all content encrypted and no direct relation between any two persons.

FIGURE 10.6

Overview of Vuvuzela's conversation protocol (https://davidlazar.org/papers/vuvuzela.pdf).

encrypted message to the intended receiver. The receiver then connects directly to the data (not to the originator) to retrieve it. There is no direct connection to the originator and receiver while collecting the data, and it is impossible to determine which data was dropped and accessed. As with Tor, more users equate to more privacy since if only two users are using any communication service, identifying the users is easy.

PUTTING THE CASE TOGETHER

Devoting a single section here on putting a complex investigation together does little justice to this broad subject; but it should nevertheless not be overlooked. All information, intelligence and evidence collected need to be integrated into a story, with each item being an integral part of the story. It is not enough to simply state that a piece of evidence is evidence. Every item of evidence needs to be described in a manner to explain why it is evidence, how it was discovered, and the role it played in the investigation.

To perform this task properly requires having not only an intimate knowledge of the investigation but also an ability to see the entire investigation from a

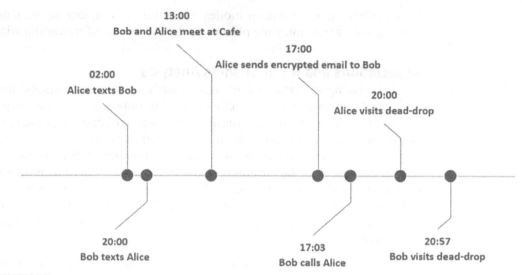

FIGURE 10.7
Sample communication timeline.

broad perspective. You need to see the forest and the trees in order to put the case together in a manner that anyone will be able to understand it. In regards to evidence of communication, every known and suspected mode of communication helps build the story of the investigation of how crimes were planned through as many modes of communication as can be found.

One of the best visuals in a forensic analysis is that of a timeline to show the flow and relationships among the events. Timelines are easy to understand since events occur in chronological order, like scenes in a movie, and they are easy to visualize and understand. Digital forensic timelines and communication timelines are similar in design but use different data. A digital forensic timeline will show activity that occurred on a computer system, such as a login, program executions, file creations, and so forth. A timeline of communications shows the when, where, and how communications occurred between any numbers of people. As discussed earlier in this book, the content of some communications may not be available, but the metadata, for example, the mere fact that communication occurred, is evidence in and of itself.

A simple example of a communication timeline is seen in Fig. 10.7. In this example, two suspects are shown communicating with each other with different methods, including a face-to-face meet. Even without the content or context of the communications, the fact of association through these communication methods does imply an association with intention to communicate secretly with encryption and dead-drops. A real-life example would most likely include many more modes of communication, such as social networking comments, multiple phones, and other means of communication.

Associations and Relationships Analysis

When analyzing the relationships based solely on communications, there are several factors to consider before assigning importance to one suspect over another. Some organized criminal or terrorist groups have well-defined protocols for contacts and communications. Some groups may not communicate at all until an operation or act is being planned, and even then the communications may be purposely sparse to reduce the risk of compromise. In this type of situation, the mere lack of communication does not give any indication as to the scale of operation being planned, nor may it determine a hierarchy of suspects. However, at a minimum it does show associations and metadata.

In most organizations, a small number of persons are relevant as bridges or brokers between groups. These persons oversee one-to-many contacts, where one person communicates with a large number of persons from two or more groups as the only contact between the groups. In this type of scenario, the "middleman" or "broker" may not be part of any formal organization but is instrumental in bridging communications between organizations. In a drug-trafficking organization, this kind of liaison is the middleman between drug sellers and drug buyers. In a terrorist investigation, the broker may be the middleman between arms dealers and terrorist buyers. The types and count of communication methods of the broker will typically far outweigh those in the associated groups. Fig. 10.8 shows a visual of how one person can interact with separate groups as the bridge of communication.

Although the middleman is extremely important in an investigation as the conduit between groups and the middleman's communications (phone calls, texts, e-mails, chats, and so on) may consist of thousands of contacts, this does not diminish the importance of those with fewer phone calls or connections. A supplier of weapons may use one phone to connect to a middleman and by a mere lack of calls could seem unimportant. Any connection to a middleman is generally going to be important on some end of a crime or incident. Identifying the middleman can lead to the identification of several organizations through an analysis of the communications between them.

When looking for a mode of communication, a helpful investigative tip is to use the known to find the unknown. If the content of the communication is available, the suspects may give away other modes of communication with one suspect telling the other to use a different mode of communication. It may not

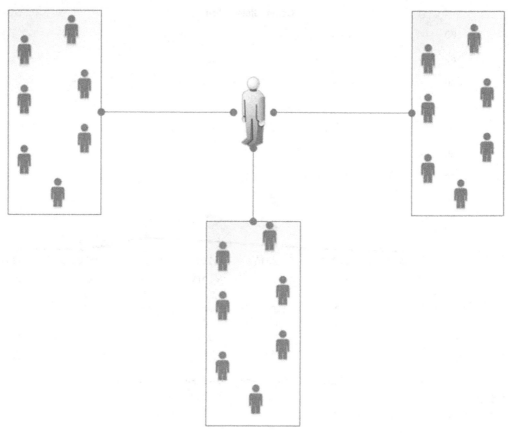

FIGURE 10.8
The middle man.

be possible to find the additional modes of communications, but the content does give leads as to how the suspects are communicating outside the known modes of communication.

An illustrative case involved a US citizen, Jalil Ibn Ameer Aziz, who maintained dozens of Twitter accounts and publicly posted comments on Twitter to initiate contacts with terrorists. Once a terrorist was contacted through Twitter, Aziz advised the terrorist to download and use an encryption program to communicate outside of Twitter. Aziz was arrested for conspiring and attempting to provide material support and resources to a foreign terrorist organization, identified through open postings on Twitter by his IP address (United States of America v. Jalil Ibn Ameer Aziz, 2015).

Visualization of key communicative data may also be able to predict events, or show where an important historical event may have occurred. Fig. 10.9 shows

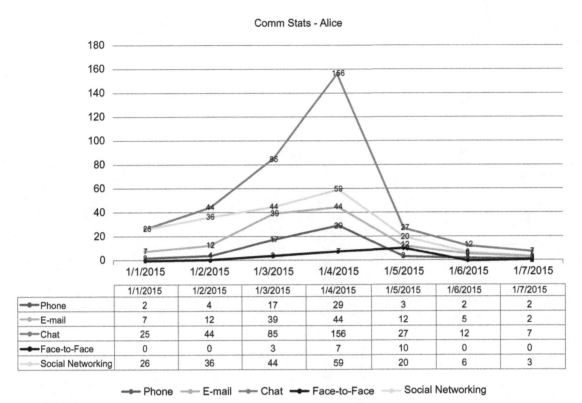

Comm Stats - Alice

	1/1/2015	1/2/2015	1/3/2015	1/4/2015	1/5/2015	1/6/2015	1/7/2015
Phone	2	4	17	29	3	2	2
E-mail	7	12	39	44	12	5	2
Chat	25	44	85	156	27	12	7
Face-to-Face	0	0	3	7	10	0	0
Social Networking	26	36	44	59	20	6	3

Phone   E-mail   Chat   Face-to-Face   Social Networking

FIGURE 10.9

Visual depicting an event based on communications.

a chart of combined communicative methods and contacts made with Alice as the primary suspect. An inference can be made that on or around January 4, an event may have occurred due to the buildup of communications before January 4 and the subsequent lack of communications afterward. If all communications ended after January 4, it is possible that all communications were solely for the event or perhaps all communications were exchanged if the suspects felt their communications to be compromised. Either way, the date shows that something affected communications and this information can be used to determine events or case compromise.

SUMMARY

Accept that finding every communication method is unlikely. Also, accept that being able to access the content of every communication is unlikely. But remember that the metadata of communications can be just as important and usually provides more intelligence than content will provide. Unless a crime or terror operation is conducted by a single person who never communicates with another to plan or brag about the incident, there is always some communication occurring with respect to unlawful acts. Some communications may be covert or hidden while others are in plain view on social networking sites or forums. By using known information, such as a username, leads can be generated with advanced Internet searches to find online communications and even face-to-face occurrences.

As with all case work, stay organized and be prepared to tell a story about how the suspects communicated, and took steps to secure their communications with encryption or dead-drops. The more complicated the communications, the more effort is needed to simplify the description. With dozens of "burner" cell phones, temporary e-mail accounts, dead-drops, face-to-face meetings, and social networking communications, entire conversations can be pieced together in a timeline with content and metadata. The goal of putting it all together is for your audience to understand what happened, just as if they were watching a good movie.

REFERENCES

State of Florida v. Casey Marie Anthony, 48-2008-CF-15606 O (Circuit Court for the Ninth Judicial Court in and for Orange County, Florida July 25, 2011).

United States of America v. Jalil Ibn Ameer Aziz, 1:15-MJ-81 (Middle District of Pennsylvania December 15, 2015).

United States of America v. Mohamed Elshinawy, 15–2716TJS (District of Maryland February 11, 2015).

United States of America v. Nicodemo S. Scarfo and Frank Paolercio, 00–404 (District of New Jersey October 4, 2001).

United States of America v. Robert Phillip Hassenn, 01-188-A (Eastern District of Virginia June 14, 2001).

United States v. Jamshid Muhtorov, 12-MJ-01011-CBS (District of Colorado January 19, 2012).

CHAPTER 11

Closing Thoughts

INTRODUCTION

Less than two generations ago, researching information about a person usually required hiring a private investigator or personally visiting court houses to search for any public records that might exist. Less than three generations ago, communicating with a person meant either sending a letter, making a phone call, or meeting personally face to face. Today, these can be (and are being) done at a computer or using a smartphone to communicate globally and instantly.

Technology has made individual privacy a shrinking luxury of the past and at the same time, technology is making connecting with others not only easy, but instantaneous. To communicate with anyone is not a question of "if," but rather, "by which of a dozen methods" from which to choose. The benefit of technology is that it has made it easier to investigate criminals. Conversely, technology has made it more difficult to investigate communication methods used by criminals due to the number of varying methods to uncover.

PRIVACY EXPECTATIONS

Anyone born into the Internet age cannot be expected to have a high level of privacy expectations or even realize how much privacy has been lost in the past few decades. Social networking, personal blogs, chat rooms, and easy access to public information allows anyone with access to the Internet the ability to search and find more personal information than ever before. Children born today are virtually born online. Photos of every life event (and nonevents) in their lives are posted, e-mailed, shared, and micro-blogged by their family from birth until the point they themselves contribute to adding their own personal information using their own social media accounts.

Where personal information was primarily maintained by government entities, such as birth records and court records, individuals openly post personal information as if privacy was not a concern. However, none of this precludes

Constitutional protections of the home and personal effects of a person. It just makes it easier to investigate suspects when they contribute to the loss of their privacy through electronic communications in the open. This is a major aspect of criminal investigations.

The content of encrypted communications may be practically impossible to access, but when suspects openly communicate, encryption is not an issue. Even when suspects plan to use encryption for communications, when "meeting online" for the first time, encryption is not possible until both ends of the communication arrange to communicate using encryption on future contacts.

FACEBOOK
Also useful for connecting criminals directly to the police
A complainant received a Facebook friend request from a Facebook user "Almalk Benitez," who was unknown to the complainant. Almalk Benitez tried to recruit the complainant to join the Islamic State of Iraq and the Levant (ISIL). The complainant reported the friend request to the FBI, who after looking at the extremist rhetoric, obtained the Facebook records, associated e-mail account, and multiple Facebook login IP addresses leading to identifying Benitiz as Harlem Suarez. Suarez then communicated via text messages and met with the complainant during undercover FBI operations and discussed bomb making. Suarez was arrested for Attempt to use a Weapon of Mass Destruction (United States of America v. Harlem Suarez, 2015).

Investigators cannot assume that every criminal using the Internet to communicate is aware of the information created on their devices or third-party servers. Even when a criminal or terrorist is aware of the potential risk of open Internet postings being captured by law enforcement, some will still take the risk to meet others online to further their criminal or terror acts for any number of reasons.

LEGAL AND TECHNICAL CONSIDERATIONS

Court rulings attempt to keep up with technology at the same time technology attempts to keep up with investigative needs. Investigators must constantly be aware of both aspects of law and technology to (1) know what they can do legally and (2) know what they can do technically. To be unaware of what is technically possible or legally permissible hinders any investigation and by the same token, to exceed what can be done legally compromises both the investigation and investigator.

Legal Considerations
If suspects are openly posting evidence (admissions, confessions, threats, and so on) on the open Internet where anyone can see it, investigators can as easily capture it as evidence just as anyone on the Internet could. To do more than

this, such as intercepting and reading the contents of an e-mail, requires both a degree of authority and approval. Law enforcement generally has the authority to wiretap a phone but certainly needs the approval to do so first.

Legal considerations arise when technology outpaces individual protections, or the technical specifics must be interpreted case by case to make a determination of what is allowed and what is not. One area where courts may continue to rule differently based on the specific case is that of defendants being required to disclose their passwords. Where one court may demand the defendant to provide login credentials, another court may rule otherwise based on interpretation or case specifics. With any investigation, it may be best to not assume a suspect will be ordered to provide login credentials, and even then, trusting a suspect to provide the correct credentials may not be a good idea since login credentials can be forgotten even a misdirection such as providing credentials to one volume but not to a hidden volume of a computer hard drive.

Technical Considerations

A cybercrime investigator does not necessarily need to be a technical expert, know computer programming, or be able to decipher cryptography. Much of the work investigating a cybercrime involves traditional investigative methods. Consider that an investigation is basically a research project. Using any resource to find information about a suspect constitutes investigating a suspect. There is no magic other than being a good researcher of information and following leads to more information.

GOOGLE
Google is more than searching for recipes

IRS Special Agent Gary Alford's preferred investigative tool was Google's advanced search features. With a Google search, Alford found a chat room post made before the Silk Road market went live on the dark web, posted by a username of "Altoid." The post asked, "Has anyone seen Silk Road yet? It's kind of like an anonymous Amazon.com."

Then, using "Altoid" as a Google search term, Alford found a message that linked the username "Altoid" to an e-mail address of rossulbricht@gmail.com. That e-mail address plainly gave away the name of the Silk Road creator, Ross Ulbricht (Popper, 2015).

Using the Internet as an investigative tool should be one of the most important and most (always) used investigative methods. Nearly any case can benefit by searching the Internet for more information about suspects, their associates, and their crimes. A simple admission of guilt made innocently in an open forum, chat, or social networking site may give just enough evidence for probable cause or further investigative leads.

Electronic evidence that is inaccessible, such as encrypted messages, frustrates investigations. The mere fact of having access to evidence but not being able to read the content can give an impression of being useless. However, that is not completely true. Remember that metadata gives plenty of useful information. Geolocation, dates and times, length of calls, and phone numbers called are evidence in and of itself. To hope that any and all encryption will be accessible through legal processes or technology is unrealistic; therefore, do what you can with what you have.

Secure messaging applications generally live up to their marketing hype in most aspects. One example is Wickr (http://www.wickr.com). Messages sent and received using Wickr are AES256 bit encrypted, bound to only the sender and receiver devices, encryption keys deleted after the message has been decrypted, and all user content is forensically wiped from the devices. On the face of this information, Wickr appears to be an unbeatable, secure messaging service. However, Wickr does store useful information about the users and messages, such as the dates accounts were created, type of devices used with the accounts, dates of last use, total number of messages sent/received, and associated e-mail addresses. Message content might be unavailable, but the metadata and account information is useful in identifying not only the account holder, but also recipients of messages.

ENCRYPTED MESSAGES
The most certain method to access content of encrypted messages!
A confidential informant (CI), under direction of law enforcement, assumed an online dark web identity that was previously used by a trafficker in illicit materials. An unknown person on the dark web wanted to purchase ricin from the CI and conversed about the deadly effects and usage with the CI. All communications between the CI and suspect were encrypted and conducted through the Tor network, which hid the suspect's true IP address.

But since the CI worked under the direction of law enforcement, every communication was accessible. Encryption works, but not when someone gives away the access. And although the suspect communicated through the Tor network, at the point of where the Internet world connects with the physical world, he was identified when he provided a physical mailing address for the CI to mail ricin to him. At that point, traditional investigative methods positively identified Cheng Le as the suspect attempting to purchase ricin on the dark web (United States of America v. Cheng Le, 2014).

The Internet Does Connect to the Physical World
At some point, cybercrime committed in cyberspace connects to the physical world. Some cybercrime incidents directly connect to the physical world, such as when a physical item is mailed from one person to another. Indirectly, a cybercrime connects to the physical world by using information stolen from someone online and used in the physical world, such as applying for credit cards in a victim's name that was stolen online. Investigating any communications between suspects or between suspects and victims also has a real world connection at some point. To have value, stolen data must be useful to

a criminal. Usefulness is usually described as having a financial value, which requires one or more transactions to occur. An identity theft example would be stealing the required information from a victim, applying for a credit card in the victim's name, and physically receiving a credit card. The fraudulent card must be used for financial gain, which requires making purchases (online or in a store) to physically receive goods. Much of this type of investigation is traditional even though the underlying crime is virtual (online).

TAKING ORDERS
No matter how much you hide your IP address, it doesn't help at the post office!

Two top Silk Road drug traffickers, Steven Sadler and his partner Jenna White used the dark web and bitcoin to sell various types of illegal drugs through the US Mail. The US Post Office interdicted several packages of drugs and through surveillance and traditional investigative means, Sadler and White were identified.

Sadler was found to have opened multiple post office boxes in different post offices. Undercover (online) purchases of drugs were made from Sadler and eventually, both Sadler and White were arrested. The Tor network protected their IP addresses but even the Silk Road required them to operate in the physical world. Traditional investigative methods broke Tor in this case (United States of America v. Steven Sadler and Jenna White, 2013).

Technology Makes Crimes Easier to Commit and Easier to Get Caught

Growing up in today's generation means being connected online, practically from birth. The ease of growing up constantly connected to information and ease of communication creates a wealth of information available on the life of any person who regularly maintains a social networking presence. The longer any social networking account is maintained and updated, the longer historical information is made available for criminal investigations, such as long term geolocation data based on posted comments, IP address logins, metadata in photos, and more.

Historical communications between suspects come into play long before the suspects may have even been under the investigative radar. Historical communications include e-mails, texts, and other methods where suspects communicate without concern that anyone will read their messages. Many times, it is the historical message content that can not only solve one crime, but solve a string of crimes.

I KNOW WHAT YOU DID LAST SUMMER
Text messages are better than a diary!

Jason Glenn Pierce and his girlfriend were arrested for one burglary in Alabama in 2011. After examining their cell phones, detectives found that the girlfriend's cell phone had text messages with Pierce that showed conversations of multiple burglaries, potentially responsible for 40–50 burglaries. In the words of Jefferson County Chief Deputy Randy Christian, the text messages were "Like a thief keeping a diary" (Christian, 2011).

SUMMARY

The day should not arrive where any and every communication can be intercepted at the will of any person or government. Some communications must be secure for the sake of the security of a nation, operation of a business, or protection of a personal reputation. However, given probable cause of a crime or security of a nation, some of these communications need to be captured with full content or metadata. Given legal authority to capture communications, you have to think like a detective, where there is no limit to the creativity in gaining access to illicit communications. Whether it be through subterfuge with informants or undercover officers, electronic intercepts, or through brute-force password attacks, keep trying to find the one weakness of the communication method. Just as pulling a single thread can unravel a sweater, finding one key to break a communication opens up entire threaded conversations and can make your case.

REFERENCES

Christian, R. (August 8, 2011). *SCU arrest of suspect leads to clearing as many as 40 to 50 burglaries.* Retrieved from Jefferson County Sheriff's Office http://www.jeffcosheriff.net/pr_pdf.php?id=779.

Popper, N. (December 25, 2015). *The Tax Sleuth who took down a drug Lord.* Retrieved from The New York Times http://www.nytimes.com/2015/12/27/business/dealbook/the-unsung-tax-agent-who-put-a-face-on-the-silk-road.html?partner=msft_msn.

United States of America v. Cheng Le, 14 MAG 2881 (Southern District of New York December 24, 2014).

United States of America v. Harlem Suarez, 15-5016-SNOW (Southern District of Florida July 27, 2015).

United States of America v. Steven Sadler and Jenna White, MJ13–487 (Western District of Washington at Seattle October 2, 2013).

Index

Note: Page numbers followed by "f" indicate figures, "t" indicate tables and "b" indicate boxes.

Printed in the United States
By Bookmasters